"You've never met an investment advisor like Don Simmons! *The Steward Investor* will challenge you to live as God's fiduciary and invest in Kingdom Businesses in the world's hardest frontier markets. The book weaves together biblical truth, beautiful stories of life change, and practical counsel on how you can start today."

—Matthew Rohrs, CEO, Sinapis, Kenya

"This small book packs a huge punch! It is a potential game changer for thousands of Christ followers who are serious about loving the world in the name of Jesus and who perceive that the financial resources placed in their care by God are not theirs but His and, furthermore, can be actually invested in business enterprises to advance the kingdom of God here on earth. Having known and worked for over a decade with Don, I can attest to how he walks the talk and to his passion for a world of justice, kindness, and humility in our walk with God."

—Peter Shaukat, Co-Founder of a UK-based global economic development fund

"This book is dynamite. It will cause explosions in many peoples' lives, and so it should come with a health (comfort) warning. It gets to the heart of God's design for the money that He entrusts us with like nothing that I have read before. It is also very timely and will play a big part reshaping my own investment portfolio and in catalyzing the necessary shifts in the global tectonic plates that are happening now in finance."

—Malcolm Johnston, Partner, Angello, Belfast City, Northern Ireland

"*The Steward Investor: Investing God's Resources for Eternal Impact* is the most comprehensive book I have read that encourages Christians to invest differently than our secular counterparts. Drawing on Don's experience as a lifelong wealth advisor and his in-depth knowledge of scripture, the reader is presented with practical ways to be faithful stewards of the resources God has entrusted to each of us. Don masterfully explains why all Christians should invest with kingdom returns in mind, not just financial returns."

—Greg Lernihan, Faith-Driven Investor, Co-Founder of Convergint Technologies

"*The Steward Investor* is one of the only resources I have ever seen that discusses how to steward investments so that they are aligned with God's Great Commission objectives. It is a call for each of us to partner with God and deploy the investments entrusted to us in a way which advances His kingdom. For too long our investment portfolios have looked all too normal. I pray this book challenges your mind and heart to rearrange your investment portfolio so that it includes distinctly missional businesses across the globe."

—Ryan Crozier, Founder, Good Bureau, Bucharest, Romania

"In *The Steward Investor: Investing God's Resources for Eternal Impact*, Don Simmons presents the quintessential model for how a disciple should properly steward the financial resources with which God has blessed them. His charge is rightfully challenging in calling God's people not to conform to the pattern of the world in the area of finances but to use wealth to join God's kingdom work of reconciling the world to Himself. Don's vulnerability in providing personal examples is encouraging. This is a must-read for any Christ follower who wants to heed the imperative to build one's treasure in heaven."

—Dodd Roberts, Director, Halbert Center for Missions and Global Service, Abilene Christian University

"*The Steward Investor: Investing God's Resources for Eternal Impact* is an insightful and challenging call to action for every Christian to release back to God what He has allowed them to accumulate. The time has come for us to awaken to the reality that wealth is a powerful tool in the Lord's hands and a dread to us when held back from Him."

—Garry McDowall, COO, SuperGreen Solutions, and Kingdom Entrepreneur

"In *The Steward Investor: Investing God's Resources for Eternal Impact*, Don Simmons has blazed a bold and exciting new trail. Followers of Jesus know we are stewards, not owners, of everything we have. Still, until now, there hasn't been such a compelling articulation of how investing in redemptive businesses allows us to be ambassadors for Christ. Don weaves in his decades of wealth management experience serving clients with his personal journey as a faithful steward investor to challenge us to invest/steward differently. 'The mandate of the Lord's fiduciary is to deploy resources to fulfill His purposes as laid out in the Great Commission and Great Commandment.' For me, accepting this challenge looks like a better route to one day hearing, 'well done, good and faithful servant.'"

—David Simms, Founder and Managing Partner, Talanton Fund

"This book provides a framework that has the power to help transform our minds from the patterns of the world to those of God's kingdom economy. Through decades of experience advising hundreds of clients in wealth management, Don brings unique insight into the powerful patterns that animate personal financial decisions, even among the most generous Christ followers, especially as it pertains to investments, a practice few consider a spiritual pursuit. Don seeks to change that. He addresses and redresses each point with a combination of biblical scholarship, intellectual rigor, and personal testimony that can only come from one who has personally grappled with the issues and been willing to play a fool for God on the path of discovering and faithfully executing His principles for investing. I look forward to seeing the ripple effect of wealth deployed by those made newly aware of the powerful force for good they wield when making strategic kingdom investments in real enterprises going about their Father's business in some of the toughest environments around the world."

—Rose Nelson, Executive Director, Freedom Business Alliance

"There are many books on stewardship as it relates to giving to donor-based ministries like churches and mission agencies. But, until now, I've not seen a book about stewardship as it relates to investing. Don Simmons opens our eyes to seeing the big picture and what it means to be God's fiduciary in literally all aspects of our finances. Don comes at this question from decades as a successful financial planner, investor, and passionate follower of Jesus. Seeing the responsibility of having a kingdom focus for my portfolio as well as my bank account through Don's writing has been challenging, encouraging, and convicting."

—Mike Baer, CEO, Third Path Initiative

"Don Simmons' book is engaging on a topic extremely relevant for all followers of Christ: how do we thoughtfully steward everything we have so God is delighted and people's lives are transformed due to our obedience? It is an insightful blend of biblical understanding, personal stories, and the use of relevant case studies. Written in such a personal way that couples could study it together, families could discuss its implications, and small groups could use it for a deep dive on maximizing their impact for God."

—Randy Dirks, PhD, Senior Stewardship Advisor at Bethany International

"I want to die broke! I'm in tears, Don. . . . God is using your words to wreck me!"

—Anonymous Reader

"In *The Steward Investor: Investing God's Resources for Eternal Impact*, Don Simmons does a terrific job of illustrating the impact kingdom investing can have on the world. His ability to integrate the impact of real-life stories, coupled with applicable biblical references, will make every reader think twice about their own investment strategy. Not only does Don challenge the reader but he also makes it very clear that he is not asking others to do something that he's not willing to do himself. Throughout the book, Don illustrates without question that he truly 'walks the talk' with his own finances. His transparency regarding this subject is refreshing, and I am confident the book will impact every reader in a positive way . . . both personally and for the kingdom as well."

—Robert Bush, Managing Director, IBEC Ventures

"Don's work is timely and poignant. Young people are hungry to understand solid biblical financial wisdom. They understand investing and want to do so more responsibly. There is a call amongst this generation to be stewards of our resources and to make financial decisions that align with people and planet, along with profit. *The Steward Investor* will challenge your thinking and impact your investment goals and decisions. We need this biblical call to see all our investment decisions as a chance to build the kingdom of God. This book will encourage God's people to help the poor, pursue justice, seek solutions, and create a better world ('Thy kingdom come, Thy will be done on earth as it is in heaven'). I can't wait to integrate this book into my teaching on personal finance."

**—Professor Ervin Starr, PhD, Chair of Undergraduate Business,
Roberts Wesleyan College, Rochester, NY**

"As a Christian who has worked in the technology sector for over twenty years, I've long wrestled with how to use the talents and prosperity God has given me to be a blessing to others. In *The Steward Investor*, financial advisor Don Simmons develops the idea of stewardship and shows what it means to invest in the kingdom of God . . . thoughtfully, deliberately, and holistically for both local and global impact. Great book with fantastic examples."

—Anthony K, CTO of a technology incubator in Silicon Valley

"Rather than relying on existing options, this challenge to invest in Kingdom Businesses should drive us all to create, enable, and support profitable companies that holistically transform the world. For me, this challenge to dream big, to seek out, to lead and enable missional enterprises has become a life calling. As an obedient Christian, Don highlights how we work to ensure our income is virtuously earned, but our retirement, the surplus of that income, is often left to increase by and enable evil. If we miss the connection between 'what' and 'who' we support with our investment and savings, we miss the opportunity to play it large with our short lives. We say all 'our money is His,' so invest like it's His and build companies that let others do the same."

—Matt Hangen, President and CEO, Water4.org

"This book about stewardship is on a completely different level than we are used to hearing as Christians. Simmons invites us to see ourselves as '*oikonomos*' or steward investors. Many of us who consider ourselves 'ordinary Christians' may not think ourselves wealthy, let alone put ourselves in the category of 'investor' and may mistakenly feel this book is directed at someone else. But the truth is, we are investors if we've got money in the bank, and this book has much to say to us. Simmons issues a timely challenge for those who want to follow Christ wholeheartedly and use our resources to align with His kingdom purposes. His compelling stories bring to life how God is already using Christ-led companies and investors to have a tremendous impact for God's kingdom around the world today. However, Simmons doesn't leave us hanging; he also gives a framework for action and practical advice to help us respond to the vision he casts."

—Jo Plummer, Co-Chair, Business as Mission Global, Thailand

THE STEWARD INVESTOR

INVESTING GOD'S RESOURCES FOR ETERNAL IMPACT

DONALD E. SIMMONS, CFP®

innovo
PUBLISHING

Published by Innovo Publishing, LLC
www.innovopublishing.com
1-888-546-2111

Providing Full-Service Publishing Services for Christian Authors, Artists & Ministries: Books, eBooks, Audiobooks, Music, Screenplays, Film & Curricula

THE STEWARD INVESTOR
Investing God's Resources for Eternal Impact

thestewardinvestor.com

ISBN: 978-1-61314-845-7

Cover Design & Interior Layout: Innovo Publishing, LLC

Printed in the United States of America
U.S. Printing History
First Edition: 2022

As followers of Christ, we recognize that investment success is measured by multiple bottom lines and not only a financial one. It is necessary, however, to print disclosures and disclaimers at the beginning of this book which are required by the securities industry:

DISCLOSURE

THE COMPANIES REPRESENTED IN THIS BOOK HAVE NOT BEEN REGISTERED UNDER THE SECURITIES ACT OF 1933, AS AMENDED. ANY SECURITIES ADMINISTRATOR UNDER ANY STATE SECURITIES LAWS OR ANY OTHER GOVERNMENTAL OR SELF-REGULATORY AUTHORITY. THE COMPANIES HAVE BEEN CITED AS EXAMPLES AND NOT WITH A VIEW TO, OR IN CONNECTION WITH, THE SALE OR DISTRIBUTION THEREOF. NO GOVERNMENTAL AUTHORITY HAS PASSED ON THE MERITS OR ADEQUACY OF THE INFORMATION CONTAINED IN THIS BOOK. ANY REPRESENTATION TO THE CONTRARY IS UNLAWFUL.

DISCLAIMER

This book discusses numerous companies and investing techniques. The author is not either directly or indirectly engaging in any general solicitation with respect to the examples discussed. The stories have not been independently verified and the author does not make any representation or warranty, express or implied, as to the accuracy or completeness of the information contained in this book, or otherwise made available, nor as to the reasonableness of any assumption contained herein or therein, and any liability therefor (including in respect of direct, indirect, consequential loss or damage) is expressly disclaimed and no liability is assumed by any such persons for any information, opinions, errors or omissions in this presentation. Nothing contained herein or therein is, or shall be relied upon as, a promise or representation, whether as to the past or the future and no reliance, in whole or in part, should be placed on the fairness, accuracy, completeness or correctness of the information contained herein or therein. Further, nothing in this presentation should be construed as constituting legal, business, tax or financial advice. The author expressly disclaims any intention or obligation, to amend, correct or update this presentation or to provide the reader with access to any additional information that may arise in connection with it. All information presented or contained in this presentation is subject to verification, correction, completion and change without notice. This presentation contains information which has come from third party sources. Third party publications, studies and surveys generally state that the data contained therein have been obtained from sources believed to be reliable, but that there is no guarantee of the accuracy or completeness of such data. While the author believes that each of these resources have been prepared by reputable sources, the author has not independently verified the data contained therein. Accordingly, undue reliance should not be placed on any of the company, industry, market, or other data contained in this book.

Forward-looking Statements

This book (including information incorporated by reference in this book), and oral statements made regarding the example companies contain information which are, or may be deemed to be, "forward-looking statements." By their nature, forward-looking statements involve risk and uncertainty because they relate to events and depend on circumstances that will occur in the future and are beyond the control of any company and their management. There are a number of factors that could cause actual results and developments to differ materially from those expressed or implied by such forward-looking statements. These factors include, among others, risks relating to: investing in and/or lending to Christian-led companies; local and global political and economic conditions; foreign currency and exchange risks; restrictions on repatriation of capital and profits; general economic conditions; taxation; lack of investment diversification; speculative investment; no certainty of distributions; dependence on the services of management; tax audit; the various companies' economic model and liquidity; their brand, reputation and trust; the environment; safety and technology; changes in or enforcement of national and local government legislation, taxation, controls or regulations and/or changes in the administration of laws, policies and practices, expropriation or nationalization of property and political or economic developments in the United States and other jurisdictions in which the companies carry on business or in which the companies may carry on business in the future; lack of certainty with respect to foreign legal systems, corruption and other factors that are inconsistent with the rule of law; legal or regulatory developments and changes; the outcome of any litigation, arbitration or other dispute proceeding; competition and market; pricing pressures; acts of war, terrorism, sabotage and civil disturbances; and business continuity and crisis management. Other unknown or unpredictable factors could cause actual results to differ materially from those in the forward-looking statements. Such forward-looking statements should therefore be construed in the light of such factors. Neither the company nor its shareholders, directors, officers or advisers, provide any representation, assurance or guarantee that the occurrence of the events expressed or implied in any forward-looking statements in this presentation will actually occur. You are cautioned not to place undue reliance on these forward-looking statements.

Except where required by law, the author is not under any obligation, and the author expressly disclaims any intention or obligation, to update or revise any forward-looking statements, whether as a result of new information, future events or otherwise.

Accredited and Sophisticated Investors

Private investment such as those described in this book should be made by accredited investors as defined in Rule 501(a) of Regulation D promulgated under the Securities Act. Such investors understand and acknowledge that investing in securities of companies in the development stage carry substantial risk and further acknowledge that they are able to fend for themselves bearing the economic risk of such investments and has such knowledge and experience in financial or business matters that he/she is capable of evaluating the merits and risks of such investments.

To Jesus Christ, my Savior and Lord,
and
to Amy—my cheerleader, friend, and true love.

CONTENTS

Acknowledgments xv
Foreword by Mats Tunehag xix
Introduction 21

Chapter 1: ***God's Oikonomos*** **29**
Chapter 2: ***Investment and Charity*** **43**
Chapter 3: ***A Dog's Bone*** **59**
Chapter 4: ***Righteous Business*** **69**
Chapter 5: ***What Is Missional Business?*** **83**
Chapter 6: ***Planting Trees*** **97**
Chapter 7: ***A Dangerous Prayer*** **113**
Chapter 8: ***The Parable of the Talents*** **123**
Chapter 9: ***Proactive Values Investing Basics*** **133**
Chapter 10: ***Risk and Return for the Steward Investor*** **149**
Chapter 11: ***In Search of the Optimized QBL Portfolio*** **163**
Chapter 12: ***Mammon's Influence on Capital and Investment*** **173**
Chapter 13: ***Six Qualities of Kingdom Capital and Investment*** **185**
Chapter 14: ***Retirement Planning*** **201**
Chapter 15: ***Give Us This Day Our Daily Bread*** **215**
Chapter 16: ***Die Broke: Rich Fools, Faith, and Poor Heroes*** **225**

Next Steps 239
Appendix A: Investor Attestation Regarding Missional Investments 249
Appendix B: The Entrepreneur's Pledge 253
Appendix C: Sample Kingdom Impact Plan 257
Appendix D: Additional Resources 263

ACKNOWLEDGMENTS

It would be impossible for me to acknowledge everyone who has influenced the writing of this book. The thoughts and conclusions that I make regarding steward investing are drawn from innumerable interactions since 1987 when I first began my career as a financial planner who wanted to integrate my vocation with faithfully following Jesus and the Word of God. Whether you are a family member or friend, client or colleague, seminar attendee or curious conversationalist, you have likely affected my thinking and opinions on the topic of how Christians should invest.

I can easily estimate forty to fifty thousand client meetings or phone calls over the course of my career where I discussed portfolio construction, risk and return, and economic outlooks, as well as the personal emotions, attitudes, and behaviors that accompany financial planning meetings. I have observed people's reactions to investment gains and losses, and I have made mental notes of how Christians and non-Christians think and behave regarding investments. I became an expert on the psychology of investing through decades of observation and interaction with investors. If you are a client who has ever met with me, had a phone call with me, or exchanged an email with me, thank you; your interaction helped to shape my thinking regarding investor behavior and investor psychology.

I can think of personal interactions with family members and friends discussing matters of faith and finance and the implications when these two spheres converge. Sometimes it was over breakfast at Panera, the diner, or Lakeside Farms, or over lunch at "the pub" down the street from my office or another restaurant. Conversations occurred at all hours of the day and sometimes late into the night over a glass of wine or scrumptious dessert. Some conversation took place around the dinner table at our home, your home, on the porch of an eleventh-floor apartment in the middle east, watching the sun set over the city skyline, or on a dock at Long Lake in the Adirondack Mountains. I can think of deep conversations around campfires in Kyrgyzstan and other unique places, frequently in countries where I did not know the language and where most people would not choose to vacation. Long car rides and international flights hosted banter about missions and investing and the sacredness of work and how business can be used to bring the Gospel to unreached parts of the world. Conversations occurred on Skype and Zoom long before they were household tools used for video communication. If you recall having such a conversation with me, then I am in debt to you for the way that we sharpened each other and the way that our conversation honed my understanding and ability to articulate the ideas of becoming a steward investor. You helped me understand the eternal nature of investments and to look beyond temporal outcomes. Our conversations strengthened my call to be a catalyst for helping to move capital from where it is in abundance to where it is in short supply, so that the kingdom of God can be established on earth as it is in heaven. Thank you.

It is nearly impossible to try to estimate the number of emails, conversations (agreeable or disagreeable) that I have had over the past fifteen years within the Business as Mission, Business 4 Transformation, and Faith Driven Investor communities about how Christians think and behave regarding investment selection and portfolio design. Some conversations involved people who think similarly to me regarding our role as investors of the Lord's resources, often ending in prayer for guidance on how best to steward investments for the True Owner, God, and on occasion resulted in an agreement to make substantial investments into missional enterprises. Other exchanges were with people seeking to better understand God's precepts about investing, concluding with gratitude as minds opened to new ways of thinking about the powerful impact investing can have to bring about justice, mercy, and shalom in places with great hurt, pain, corruption, and brokenness. Some exchanges revealed conflicts with people who disagreed with my conclusions regarding stewardship and how Christians should invest. We discussed and debated issues such as eternal or temporal risk, concessionary or market-like returns, clear and short-term exit strategies compared to long-term patient capital strategies, prioritization of stakeholders, and how to effectively measure holistic impact. Sometimes these discussions popped up organically following a seminar or in the hallway at a conference. Whether the interaction was agreeable or contentious is irrelevant; both helped to refine my understanding of what it means to be God's *oikonomos*. Thank you.

Thank you to everyone who read and commented on this manuscript before it went to the publisher. You know who you are because you read a PDF or paper copy of the manuscript. Thank you for your advice, polishing, corrections, and suggestions and for helping me bring this project to completion. This is truly a collaborative effort from all of us. I am honored to speak on your behalf.

Finally, thank you to Bobi for creating the study questions at the end of each chapter, and to Becky, who worked tirelessly typing, retyping, editing, formatting, spell checking, and researching. I would have printed a few hundred copies on my LaserJet, sent them to people who I thought should read the ideas, and then thrown in the towel regarding publishing if it weren't for you. Thank you.

FOREWORD

BY MATS TUNEHAG

I've read thousands of books, and very few have the potential to become game changers. But this book could very well become one.

In *The Steward Investor: Investing God's Resources for Eternal Impact,* Don Simmons invites us to profoundly rethink money, stewardship, wealth, pensions, generosity, savings, and investments. These are all familiar words, but too often we define them using a secular worldview, adding, perhaps, a superficial Christian veneer.

In contrast, this book defines these terms using a biblical worldview with a focus on doing business as justice, especially in areas with dire spiritual, economic, social, and environmental needs. We can honor God and make a kingdom difference for people and societies by providing affordable, patient, catalytical, and serving capital where these needs exist.

Don's book is a great disruption to Christian jargon and challenges traditional views of stewardship, charitable giving, and faith-inspired investments. He helps us align our thinking and behavior with God's principles for wealth and investment. *Alignment* is a key word! He uses real examples to contrast the stark difference between secular and biblical worldviews of business and investing. He helps us see the short-sightedness of a business-as-usual approach to money and investments and the very real, present-day, and eternal benefits of becoming missional investors. When Christians invest, they must be diligent to support businesses that match their values and seek to achieve God's priorities. As Don says, "Aligned with His [God's] purposes, we are called to fearlessly deploy resources to fulfill His Great Commission mandate and energetically pursue opportunities that accomplish His goals."

While it is often easy to say "Hallelujah!" to a great idea, it is another thing to put the idea to work. Don addresses this issue by providing practical, thoughtful, and actionable "next steps" that guide the reader step-by-step into their missional-investing journey.

In short, Don's book is rooted in Scripture, underpinned by professional experience, connected to global realities, and guided by Business as Mission (BAM) principles. Don fills the pages with demonstrations of his and his wife's own commitments and offers a practical path forward.

There are many groups and initiatives for Christian engagement in the marketplace, but they are not all the same, just like all Italian restaurants are not the same. Check the menu, the chef, the service, and the reviews! Not all burgers are the same, and not all apple pies are equal. Check the ingredients and the mix!

Thus, the issue is not labels but content. A Christian-sounding name on a business or investment program does not necessarily mean they carry a biblical flavor or have authentic Christian ingredients. Don sources good ingredients and bakes an authentic BAM cake, as it were.

We must embrace the concepts and seek relevant applications with a global mindset. But remember: Business as Mission and missional investing are not techniques but an internalized worldview and a daily lifestyle.

This book is an important invitation to an ongoing conversation and an exciting journey. Read it, do it, share it with others, and allow yourself to be challenged to rethink and reorient. Go with God and join other missional investors! My prayer is that missional investing "shall be more widely known, more deeply understood, and more penetrating in its effects."[1]

—Mats Tunehag
Chairman, BAM Global
MatsTunehag.com
BAMglobal.org
BusinessAsMission.com

1. I am borrowing these words from Pope St. John XXIII's opening address at the 2nd Vatican Council.

INTRODUCTION

Elisha the prophet lived during the 9th century BC in a time when Israel was divided into the northern kingdom of Israel and the southern kingdom of Judah. Many people at that time were worshiping the false god Baal. It was not a good time in Israel's history, but out of that time comes the story of a man willing to say yes to God, following Him wholeheartedly in a new direction.

What's interesting about Elisha is that he was not interesting. When we first meet him, he is an ordinary guy, living at home with his parents, working on the family farm, plowing with twelve teams of oxen. He isn't a spiritual giant, the son of a priest, a great warrior like Samson or Gideon, or even a notable leader. He didn't live in Jerusalem with the kings; there was nothing special about him. He was like you and me—ordinary.

And then God called him to do something incredible.

Elijah, the famous prophet, arrives at the farm, goes to the back of the line of oxen where Elisha was working, and tosses his coat across Elisha's shoulders.

Elisha knows exactly what this action means: God was calling him to become Elijah's successor. Even though he didn't know exactly what this call would mean, his response shows full acceptance. First, he requests to say good-bye to his parents, showing them respect. Next, he takes his yoke of oxen—the animals that provided his livelihood—and slaughters them, then burns the plow, his most important piece of equipment. With his animals and tools now gone forever, Elisha knows he cannot return to the fields. Having burned "plan B," he shows full commitment to God's call, no turning back! In not holding on to what he had, he made himself available for God to do much through him.[2]

TOTAL COMMITMENT TO GOD AS HIS STEWARD INVESTOR

Those who follow Christ halfheartedly don't follow Him very far. Elisha showed that he was willing to follow God's call on his life with abandon, and the same should be true of our calling to

2. 1 Kings 19:15-21

be stewards of God's resources, especially as investors. Have you given God your finances with the same commitment as Elisha? You don't have to fully understand at the beginning what total obedience will entail, but I'd like to lead you to a better understanding of the broad responsibilities of your call to be a steward of God's portfolio. Over time, as you begin obeying more completely, you will see the implications of being a steward investor.

WHY I WROTE THIS BOOK

The biblical principles I present are pertinent to the global body of Christ, especially those who live in developed economies. Although the examples provided are of American financial mechanisms, the principles apply to wealthy Christians worldwide. Depending on where you live, you will need to consider what mechanisms exist within your own national financial structures and laws. This book is written for every Christian who owns a stock, a bond, or a mutual fund; a USA IRA or 401(k), a Canadian RRSP, a UK Pension Scheme, or an Australian SuperAnnuation account; or a savings plan in any other country and who wants to obediently follow God's call to be a steward of His resources. If you have a job and a retirement account and are serious about responding to God's call, this book applies to you. The Bible teaches us many things about our role as God's stewards, and there are many warnings for those who are entrusted to manage investments. Investments are a form of ownership, and when you invest in any of the accounts listed above, you become a business owner, and God has plenty to say about how business owners should conduct business. The warnings in scripture should make most Christian investors uneasy regarding the modern and generally accepted teaching about stewardship, wealth accumulation, and investing.

Are you hoarding wealth? Is it possible that the companies you invest in have unfair labor practices? Are you living a life of self-indulgence? Have your investments exploited the innocent? These are hard questions that scripture directly addresses.

This is not a book about generosity or giving money away after it is made, although generosity is one component of stewardship. This book is about our calling and responsibility to *inves*t money so that God's purposes are achieved, because the investments we select are an equally important component of stewardship. Donations are not sacred, and investments are not secular, although many behave as though this is the case. We pray for God's kingdom to come on earth as it is in heaven, but do we invest to achieve that goal? What does a portfolio that seeks to advance God's kingdom look like? Are we investing just to increase our personal net worth?

Donations are not sacred, and investments are not secular, although many behave as though this is the case.

Many stewardship writers and advisors start by teaching sound money management principles and how they operate within the world's economic system. Then they apply biblical principles as an add-in. However, as we seek godly wisdom in how to steward His investments, I believe it's crucial to *begin* with biblical principles and mandates as our foundation then apply these in a way that influences our behavior in the world's economic system. It is not trivial to urge this distinction. The difference between these two approaches could not be more basic or far reaching. The order we use produces immensely different results in the decisions we ultimately make.

It is incumbent upon us as stewards of God's resources to invest in ways that accomplish His eternal purposes. Since the beginning, God has had a plan to be in relationship with men and women. After the Fall, He planned to restore the resulting broken relationships, and we are privileged to participate in this plan. He entrusts resources to us, but we often don't see them that way—instead we squander or invest them poorly relative to achieving spiritual objectives.

This book is designed to help break us out of this worldly investment approach and open the floodgates of our resources to build God's kingdom.

STEWARDSHIP'S INSUFFICIENT DEFINITION

I have studied finance most of my life, and I have lost count of the books I have read on stewardship. Although I have never been a person who reads for pleasure, I have always read daily for research purposes. I remember devouring Randy Alcorn's book *Money, Possessions, and Eternity* in the early 2000s and deepening my already-established convictions about stewardship, namely an acknowledgement that God owns everything, and I am His steward.

Most stewardship books and resources provide important teachings on financial competencies such as getting out of debt, living on a budget, saving for the future, getting market-like returns, avoiding high expenses while investing, and the importance of charitable giving. Some books provide details of lives that have been transformed, usually after achieving great wealth, and then go on to describe how those individuals start to experience great joy and fulfillment in being exceedingly generous. Some books even provide deep challenges to the reader about our need to be generous givers because it is part of our role as stewards of God's resources, showing verses like Malachi 3:10 and teaching that the Lord asks us to "test Him" in our giving. But a steward investor is committed to tithing first and *deploying the remaining ninety percent to further God's purposes.*

Other books go further, promoting a new line of thinking for Christian investors by challenging them to adhere to Biblically Responsible Investing (BRI) principles. BRI is an investment discipline which suggests that Christians should screen their portfolios for companies that do not align with their Christian values. Christians can and should act on BRI principles and avoid participation in the negatives of the investment world. BRI alone is insufficient for a steward investor. We need to go beyond filtering out what we don't like or are opposed to and instead deliberately seek investments that promote the good things that Christians believe and which align with the loving God we serve. We ought to learn how to proactively invest in ways that advance God's kingdom, not simply avoid investments that are in opposition to His values.

Teachings are scarce regarding the biblical principles that should be applied during the "making of the money."

With the plethora of stewardship books and materials available, I have not found any that provide an in-depth view of our role as Christian *investors.* The role and responsibilities of a steward investor are foreign to most Christians because our teachers and pastors rarely have a robust understanding about the financial services industry or the investment world. Similarly, many financial advisors are unaware of the investment opportunities available that achieve both financial *and* spiritual outcomes. Books and sermons discuss what a good steward should do *after* they have made money through work or investing, but teachings are scarce regarding the biblical principles that should be applied *during* the "making of the money." Twenty-first century Christians, especially those living in the West, are among the wealthiest in all human history, but most lack an understanding of the dangers when wealth is mishandled.

A steward investor needs to address these concerns: What does an optimized kingdom-impact portfolio look like? Can I accomplish good in the world through investments and not just charity? Might I be guilty of living a life in pursuit of pleasure, luxury, and self-gratification to the detriment of those who are vulnerable, exploited, or impoverished?

OVERVIEW

This book will walk us through a more robust summary of our role as God's stewards, better understood as His *oikonomos* (explained in chapter one), with real-life examples that illustrate how we can invest in ways that bring salt and light and the Gospel to unreached locations. After covering basic investment terms and concepts and the differing roles charity and investment play in missions and economic development, we will define righteous business and missional enterprise and discuss why it is so hard for Christian investors to fulfill their role as fiduciaries of the Lord's resources. We will discuss what a quadruple bottom line (QBL) investment is and how to design a QBL portfolio, as well as the difference between the personality of capital when influenced by the spirit of mammon and how capital might be personified in the kingdom of heaven. Building on a better understanding of stewardship, we will discuss how to invest after-tax, pre-tax, and charitable capital to fulfill the Great Commission and the Great Commandment. We will challenge some of the current thinking regarding modern portfolio theory, private equity, and venture capital, and will suggest how to use these concepts in better ways to advance the kingdom of heaven here on earth. Finally, we will test modern financial planning concepts such as financial independence, the 4% Rule, capital retention, and traditional estate planning techniques as we seek a biblical model for investing, retirement, and wealth transfer.

The pages of this book contain many concrete examples of these practices and principles from my family's personal journey of investing as God's steward. Although I manage portfolios for clients who invest similarly, my confidential relationship as their fiduciary prevents me from sharing their personal investment stories. The apostle Paul warns the believers in Philippi to "do nothing out of selfish ambition or vain conceit" (Phil. 2:3), so I sought counsel from my closest friends and advisors concerning my transparency in sharing personal financial decisions that are generally held in secret. *Would these personal stories be helpful or misinterpreted as boasting?* I asked. My advisors agreed that providing personal, concrete examples for readers to emulate would be the most helpful way to communicate the abstract and mostly unfamiliar concepts presented. So, I opened the curtain to share our private investment stories for two reasons. First, a picture is worth a thousand words. Practical, real-life examples demonstrate how any person can successfully use the financial resources entrusted to them to deliberately and proactively invest in missional enterprises. What I present is not theory; it can actually be done. Second, I hope that a reader who accompanies me on my personal journey will join with me and the others who are making similar sacrificial investment decisions. The more of us who deploy our investments for God's purposes, the greater the spiritual, economic, social, and environmental transformations that can happen in cultures enriched by missional businesses.

If you are willing to accept God's call to be His steward investor in the same way that Elisha obediently and fully accepted God's call to be His prophet, then let's get started.

QUESTIONS FOR STUDY

1. Having had a brief introduction to the concept of a steward investor, how does this author's definition compare to or contrast with your previous understanding of stewardship?

2. What have been the primary objectives of your previous investments in savings and the market? What has influenced your personal philosophy of what your goals ought to be? Are your investment goals any different than your coworkers', neighbors', or friends' goals? Are their investment goals shaped by a biblical worldview? Are yours?

3. To date, have you pursued investments with monies in your savings, retirement, or brokerage accounts in businesses that intentionally seek to accomplish God's purposes? Do you know anyone who has?

4. Reflect on the biblical account of God's call to Elisha. Recount any occasion that comes to mind in your life that is similar. Has there been a time that you didn't hold on to what you had but unconditionally, without fully grasping what would be required of you, made yourself available to God to do His will?

   How has that experience impacted your faith?

5. The author suggests that God wants total commitment from you in investing. Do you believe that is true? What do you think that might look like?

6. You have committed areas of your financial life to God. Have you ever considered a commitment to follow God's lead as to how, where, and why you save and invest? Have you considered that God might wish to see the resources He has entrusted to you to be deployed differently? How does this idea make you feel?

7. How willing are you today to submit yourself to God as His steward investor, with abandon, and with the total commitment demonstrated by Elisha?

Chapter 1

GOD'S OIKONOMOS

Now listen, you rich people, weep and wail because of the misery that is coming on you. Your wealth has rotted, and moths have eaten your clothes. Your gold and silver are corroded. Their corrosion will testify against you and eat your flesh like fire. You have hoarded wealth in the last days. Look! The wages you failed to pay the workers who mowed your fields are crying out against you. The cries of the harvesters have reached the ears of the Lord Almighty. You have lived on earth in luxury and self-indulgence. You have fattened yourselves in the day of slaughter. You have condemned and murdered the innocent one, who was not opposing you. (James 5:1-6)

Three taboos in casual conversation are politics, religion, and money. Families rarely share the naked truth of family finances at the dinner table, let alone in friendly chats with friends. Sure, we love to talk about the economy, the stock market, or the latest trends in a particular stock or crypto currency, but we seldom talk about our salary, share our tax return, or leave our open checkbook or investment statements lying on the kitchen counter when we have dinner guests. Why is it that our financial affairs are off-limits for discussion or evaluation by family or friends?

My vocation, for nearly thirty-five years, has required that I ask questions about personal finances and spending habits. I am not bashful about getting to the core of how people behave with their money. To have a successful financial planning outcome, I require all clients to provide three years of tax returns; a monthly budget; checkbook summaries; and copies of all investment, bank, and insurance statements. By the time I prepare my analysis of a family's financial health, I typically know more about their financial affairs than they do. I know the nitty-gritty of their tax situation—whether they cheat or if I can save them money. I know how much their home and cars are worth and how big their mortgage and car payments are. I know exactly how much they spend on vacations, hobbies, indulgences, shopping trips, and Amazon purchases. I know whether they are generous or stingy, and I know their religious affiliation. If they are Christians, I can easily determine if they tithe or if they, like most Americans, give only two percent of their income.[3] Most importantly, I know exactly what is in their portfolio and the underlying performance of each investment.

During my analysis and recommendations, I always ask why they selected the investments they own. Most of the time, investors have no explanation for why they select their portfolio holdings other than the occasional, "My advisor recommended it," "I read an article about the company," or "for diversification" responses. Rarely do people include any moral or ethical objectives in their investment choices.

For Christians, it is important to understand what is in their portfolio and why. But it is equally important to remember that *every* financial resource that God entrusts to us, not just tithes and donations, should be used to serve Him and to accomplish His purposes. God's mission in the world is to reconcile all that was broken during the Fall and to restore our personal relationship with Him, one person at a time. Christ died "that those who live might no longer live for themselves but for him who died for them and was raised again" (2 Cor. 5:15).

DISASTER IN SOLDOTNA, ALASKA: A FAILURE TO USE AVAILABLE RESOURCES

The following real-life story will help illustrate how critical it is to use every resource, including our investments, to complete God's mission.

3. "Church Giving Statistics" (December 31, 2021): https://balancingeverything.com/church-giving-statistics/.

Flight service specialist Stan Gerlitz was on duty on a Friday afternoon when the pilot of airplane N6908D, a single-engine Piper PA-22, reported having engine trouble. The despairing pilot was crossing the notoriously difficult and frigid waters of the Cook Inlet near Kenai, Alaska, with passengers on board who were returning from Bible Camp at Port Alsworth on Lake Clark, just one hundred twenty miles away. Under normal conditions this was a routine flight of just over one hour. However, on this day, strong headwinds and insufficient fuel proved deadly.

Gerlitz, upon hearing the plane's tail number, recognized the plane and pilot and knew immediately that his daughter was one of the passengers aboard the four-seat aircraft. Gerlitz was unable to talk to either his daughter or the pilot because the pilot, in his panic, kept his microphone keyed, preventing him from receiving any incoming communication from either the Federal Aviation Administration (FAA) or other pilots. But Gerlitz was able to hear the pilot tell his passengers they would be going down—the plane ran out of fuel and crashed into the icy waters. To make matters worse, the aircraft had been traveling without cold water survival gear.

Cook Inlet is beautiful with high, snow-covered mountains surrounding it, but it is considered one of the most dangerous bodies of water in the world. Glacial currents keep the average water temperature below fifty degrees even in mid-June, leaving the pilot and three passengers with even less chance of surviving the plane crash. Cook Inlet had already claimed countless lives, and on June 16, 2009, it claimed four more.

State trooper Tom Sumey confirmed that the plane ran out of gas, the third documented instance for this pilot. Sumey added that like some other bush pilots, the pilot habitually took off on a short flight from a remote location with a minimum amount of fuel, planning to fill up at a larger airport.[4]

Maybe arrogance, self-confidence, or boredom that can accompany a routine flight were in play. We don't know the exact reason that the pilot failed to use all the resources at his disposal. We are not even sure whether he checked the winds aloft forecast, a factor critical for any pilot to determine the amount of fuel needed for a trip. We do know that he did not have lifesaving survival

4. Jeff Berliner, "Pilot Radios FAA Official that Daughter's Plane Going Down" (June 19, 1989): https://www.upi.com/Archives/1989/06/19/Pilot-radios-FAA-official-that-daughters-plane-going-down/8672614232000/.

equipment and that he did not fill up his fuel tank. He abjectly failed to employ every resource that was available, and in this instance, the ramifications were fatal.

My family and I were in Soldotna, Alaska, in 2017 working at a children's camp for the summer when I came across that true story. It poignantly illustrates my point about failing to use resources properly. It resonated with me because I am a trained private pilot myself. I know how important it is to always use every resource available to avoid a tragic accident. Similarly, we are to use every resource available to help those in need avoid a tragic outcome.

I wonder how many other people have died needlessly because someone did not effectively manage or use the resources they had at their disposal. I also wonder how many have died without Jesus, spiritually speaking, because we have been poor stewards of the resources God has placed in our care. The stewardship of resources is a serious business, and God expects us to give it serious attention.

The stewardship of resources is a serious business, and God expects us to give it serious attention.

I wonder how many Christians, just like the negligent pilot, fail to manage the resources God provides and entrusts to them in ways that bring prosperity, justice, mercy, and redemption to the world. Donating is important, but we are also managers of God's resources when we select investments long before we give the earnings away. Christian investors can learn to employ investment techniques (in addition to their charitable giving) that bring salt and light to a broken world.

In the chapters ahead, we will see examples of investing in ways that bring transformation to communities that also make Jesus familiar in locations where His name is mostly hidden. We may begin to realize that financial competency and generosity are insufficient as we take a deeper look at the meaning of the word *steward*. When we deliberately invest with a proper stewardship mindset, we can accomplish far more for God's kingdom than we ever thought possible.

WHAT IS A STEWARD?

The word *steward* is rooted in the Greek word *oikonomos* (pronounced "oy-ko-NO-mos"). The *oikos* was the household in

Greek society and the *oikonomos* the manager of the household.[5] Our English word *economics* derives from *oikonomia,* which means household management. As we will see, the very root of our "economic system" is connected to management of someone else's resources. A steward in ancient Greek culture was not the owner of the house but the appointed manager of the house and all household affairs. He was responsible for making sure the home was clean and ready for the owner's use. He was also responsible for managing the finances and servants in the household as well as children not yet of age. A steward managed everything on behalf of the owner, including the care of receipts and expenditures.[6] The *oikonomos* would similarly be responsible for management of vineyards, farms, and other business or investment affairs as the owner delegated authority.

In the ancient Greek context, stewardship was about utilizing and managing *all* resources entrusted to, but not owned by, the steward in order to fulfill the true owner's purposes. In the same way, our stewardship role requires that we use *all* resources entrusted to us to bring God, the True Owner, glory and achieve His purposes. In both cases, financial competence is a given: competence is a prerequisite and necessitates that a steward keeps expenses below income, spends within a budget, and does not allow excessive debt. Generosity, which reflects one of God's primary attributes, is also a basic characteristic for a steward of God's resources. A steward knows the character of his master and manages resources accordingly. Providing adequate finances for our family is also one of our responsibilities, but stewardship must include purposes beyond competent household budgeting and saving. The central essence of biblical stewardship is managing *everything* God brings into the

The central essence of biblical stewardship is managing everything God brings into the believer's life, including—and especially—investments in a manner that honors God and fulfills His purposes.

5. Lin Foxhall, "*household*, Greek," in *Oxford Research Encyclopedia of Classics* (March 7, 2016): https://oxfordre.com/classics/view/10.1093/acrefore/9780199381135.001.0001/acrefore-9780199381135-e-3168.

6. https://www.biblestudytools.com/lexicons/greek/kjv/oikonomos.html

believer's life, including—and especially—investments in a manner that honors God and fulfills His purposes.

The ideas of "steward" and "stewardship" are overused and misunderstood in contemporary circles. When we define stewardship as mere competent money management, achieving good financial returns, providing for our family, and giving a portion back to God, we minimize the scope and responsibilities of this important role. I prefer to use the word *fiduciary* to define our role as God's stewards based on a more complete understanding of what the role entails.

WHAT IS A FIDUCIARY?

Although the word *fiduciary* is a legal term and not frequently used by the typical investor, I believe it provides us with a more complete description of what it means to be a biblical steward. For this reason, throughout the remainder of the book, I will use the words *fiduciary* and *oikonomos* to describe our role as Christian stewards. My hope is that these words in particular will serve as a reminder of the important and comprehensive responsibilities of this role.

Advisors in the financial services industry define a fiduciary as a person or organization that acts on behalf of another person or persons, putting their clients' interests ahead of their own, with a duty to preserve good faith and trust. Being a fiduciary thus requires being bound both legally and ethically to act in the other's best interests.

Perhaps one of the best modern-day embodiments of an ancient Greek *oikonomos* (a biblical steward) and modern-day fiduciary is the fictional Alfred Pennyworth. Alfred was far more than just the butler to Thomas and Martha Wayne, Bruce Wayne's (Batman's) deceased parents. The Waynes trusted Alfred so much that upon their death, he became Bruce Wayne's legal guardian and fiduciary of the entire Wayne estate. Alfred was a surrogate father to Bruce and the legal custodian of everything he would inherit. Alfred was not only the caretaker of the mansion and the overseer of the land, but he was also the successful fiduciary of the multinational business and coordinator of all the other advisors regarding legal matters and financial management of Bruce's trust fund. Bruce's parents were generous philanthropists, and one of Alfred's duties was to continue their benevolence, but his fiduciary duties extended far beyond making generous donations.

Similarly, our job as God's fiduciaries requires us to do far more than make generous donations to churches or other worthy causes. We must manage all our affairs in a manner worthy of being God's *oikonomos*. We must seek to fulfill His purposes and not just our own.

I have been a fiduciary of other people's money for almost thirty-five years. As their fiduciary they expect me to be competent. More importantly, I am legally bound to put my clients' best interests ahead of my own. My responsibilities and duties are both ethical and legal. Acting as fiduciary, I am required, first and foremost, to accomplish the objectives that the actual owner has for their assets.

Strict care must be taken to ensure no conflict of interest arises. A fiduciary is compensated for their time and expertise, but no profit is to be made from the relationship or the successful accomplishment of the stated goals. The fiduciary does not own anything that they manage. They can be sued and imprisoned for failing their fiduciary duty by operating as though their assets were their own. I have noticed that many Christians consider both the investments they hold and the growth on the investments to be their own, but a fiduciary realizes that the investments and earnings are owned by the Master.

The apostle Luke reminds us that "you also, when you have done everything you were told to do, should say, 'We are unworthy servants; we have only done our duty'" (Luke 17:10). What would you say to God if you sat and spoke together about the investments He trusted you to manage on His behalf? Would you consider changing the way you invest—both what you invest in and how you envision the earnings on those investments being used?

A diminished understanding of what it means to be God's fiduciary will result in inappropriate management of investments. Christians may mistakenly think that we are managing resources for our own benefit and interest when in fact our job is to accomplish the True Owner's goals. The apostle Paul tells us that even our bodies are not our own, that we have been purchased for a price (1 Cor. 6:19-20). If even my body is not my own, then surely the other things that I call "mine" are also not my own. This includes "my" investment portfolio, "my" nest egg, "my" retirement account, "my" home and everything in it. Since God trusts me to be His fiduciary, then He must want me to realize that stewardship is far more than competent money management and generous giving, and He must want me to invest in ways that bring Him glory.

INVESTING 101: THE BASICS

I have met with thousands of investors who had difficulty describing what investments they owned and why. Let me explain some basic financial principles and definitions so that we have a good foundation to build upon. We must understand the basic building blocks of an investment portfolio so we can apply these principles in our role as God's fiduciary.

Four Cornerstones of Investing

There are four key areas of a sound investment plan. First, cash reserves are monies we have on hand for an emergency or for short-term cash flow needs. They are very safe and easy to access, but they earn a very low rate of return. Examples include savings and checking accounts, money markets, and credit union accounts. The second area is adequate protection. These are investment strategies such as insurance products used to protect you in the event of a tragedy. Insurance products can alleviate the financial burden of a severe disability, long-term nursing care, or premature death. The third and fourth areas are fixed investments and variable investments, respectively. Fixed investments earn a fixed rate of return and are generally used to produce income. Examples include Certificates of Deposit (CDs), bonds, fixed annuities, and mutual funds that hold bonds or loans. Variable investments, on the other hand, are used to grow our money for the future. They grow at varying rates depending on the economy, and an investor is never sure, in the short term, whether their value will increase or decrease. But, over time, they tend to provide excellent long-term returns. Variable investments include stocks, mutual funds that own stocks, or any other business interest.

While past performance is no guarantee of future returns, a balance of fixed and variable investments can help an investor increase their net worth through reduced risk and increased returns.

INVESTING 201: STOCKS, BONDS, BANK INSTRUMENTS, OR ALTERNATIVES

Since all investments fall into one of four categories—bank instruments, bonds, stocks, or alternatives—it is critical that we understand the differences. As fiduciaries for God, we will see that these four different asset classes can be used either to achieve God's purposes or to bring damage to the cause of Christ.

Most people can explain how *bank instruments* work: an investor deposits money at a bank, and the bank promises to pay a fixed interest rate. The bank, in turn, assumes the risk by lending our money to other people for mortgages, credit cards, or other loans, and charges a higher interest to the borrower than they pay to the depositor. But if you are like many American investors that I have talked with over my career, you may still be unclear on the difference between a stock and a bond.

A bond is a loan. When you invest in a bond, you are making a loan to the bond issuer which could be the government or a company. The bond issuer promises to pay you back interest as a stream of income over a set period. At the end of the time (maturity), the bond issuer will repay the loan. Assuming the bond issuer does not go out of business, you will receive a steady stream of income plus your principal back at maturity. It is for these reasons that bonds are considered conservative investments and are frequently used by income-oriented investors.

A stock represents ownership in a company. Investors can make money in two ways with stocks. If the company is profitable, the company can take the profits and use them to grow the company by building new stores, creating new products, manufacturing more efficiently, selling more products, and so on. Generally speaking, when the company grows its business, the value of the company will increase. As a result, the value of the stock, which represents a partial ownership in the company, will also increase. This is called a capital gain. The second way that investors can make money in a stock is if the company decides to pay out the profits to the stockholders (owners), which is called a dividend.

> ***In either case we have a responsibility to know whether the companies dishonor God in practice or expand His kingdom on earth.***

Alternative investments include real estate, commodities, or crypto currencies. For most Americans, their investments fall into the first three categories: bank accounts, bonds, or stocks. Even the mutual funds that most Americans own are simply a pool of stocks or bonds.

Most of us do not think of ourselves as business owners unless we have a family business. However, when we invest, we become either owners of businesses or lenders to businesses. In either case we have a responsibility to know whether the companies dishonor God in practice or expand His kingdom on earth. Investors are business owners, and the Bible has a lot to say about what business owners should and shouldn't do, like pay fair, timely wages and provide a form of social security through gleaning and margins (some of these social support systems required the vulnerable to work, other systems did not require labor). The Bible also cautions about things that employers should not do. For example, exploit widows, orphans, and foreigners, or use unjust scales. The ancient world did not have the construct of our current economic system with shared ownership through stocks and stock markets to conduct trading of companies, but today, if you own stocks or mutual funds, you are, in fact, an owner of the business. The scriptures that are directed to business owners therefore apply to us as investors as well. James tells us,

> You have hoarded wealth in the last days. Look! The wages you failed to pay the workers who mowed your fields are crying out against you. The cries of the harvesters have reached the ears of the Lord Almighty. You have lived on earth in luxury and self-indulgence. (James 5:3-5)

As an investor, you must ask yourself how James's words apply to you because of your ownership in companies held in your portfolio. James is not the only apostle who warns investors about how to use their wealth. The apostle John writes, "But whoever has this world's goods, and sees his brother in need, and shuts up his heart from him, how does the love of God abide in him?"(1 John 3:17, NKJV). Thinking of doing good things but failing to do them is not the same as being rich in good works. Jesus is not impressed by our bank statement but by whether we use His things to bring blessing and further His kingdom (Matt. 25:31-46).

MOVING BEYOND BASIC FINANCIAL COMPETENCE

Why bother with these definitions in a book about stewardship? Because to be God's fiduciary you must be, at a minimum, competent in financial matters. The idea that God would expect a manager of His money to be competent is very much like our expectation that those we hire are fit for the task. We expect the mechanic who services our car to be competent in automobile diagnostics and repairs.

We expect the electrician who wires our house to be competent, otherwise his poor work could result in a fire. We expect those who teach our young children to competently assemble the best resources for teaching so that our children learn how to read, write, and do arithmetic. God expects you to have basic financial competencies like those I have outlined above to serve as His *oikonomos*.

This book assumes financial competence. If your family carries excessive debt, cannot live on less than what you earn, is not saving for the future, and is not practicing generous giving, then you do not yet have the financial competence to completely fulfill your role as God's steward. I suggest that you read one of Randy Alcorn's books, either *The Treasure Principle* or *Managing God's Money,* or John M. Templeton Jr.'s short book, *Thrift and Generosity,* as a foundation for being God's *oikonomos*. These books will teach you basic financial competencies before you explore the more advanced role of being God's fiduciary as His portfolio manager.

If you are already competently managing financial affairs—if you do not carry excessive debt, if you have accumulated wealth, and if you are faithfully generous with the resources entrusted to you—then let's explore how wealth can be used to build the kingdom of God on earth. Let's consider what a missional enterprise is and how to invest to achieve God's goals. Is it possible that even in your financial competence, the harsh warning from the apostle James might apply to you? Could you be condemned for not investing the way God, the True Owner, would like you to invest, though you are a competent money manager? Could you be charged with living in luxury, being self-indulgent, or being a hoarder, whose investment portfolio has cheated workers, exploited the vulnerable, and profited from others' weakness or vulnerability? Are you ready to build God's kingdom by investing as God's fiduciary?

Are you ready to build God's kingdom by investing as God's fiduciary?

QUESTIONS FOR STUDY

1. Read James 5:1-6. When are the "last days" James is referencing? Is Christian community talking about the "last days" being upon us? What do you think?

   Have you ever watched the TV series *Hoarders*? How would you define hoarding? Does a hoarder possess stuff or does stuff possess the hoarder?

2. How would you define wealth?

3. Our financial affairs are off-limits for discussion or evaluation by family or friends. Why do you think this is?

4. How much understanding do you have regarding the moral or ethical objectives of the companies held in your investment accounts? Have you requested that kind of detail from your advisor? If so, how did your advisor's response impact your decision regarding those holdings?

5. Compare and contrast your previous understanding of *stewardship* with the author's definition of *fiduciary*. The story of Joseph in Genesis is frequently cited as a great example of stewardship as defined by financial competence, sound financial management, and long-term planning. How does Joseph's management of Potiphar's house and Pharoah's kingdom help you better understand that stewardship is being a fiduciary of someone else's resources? What was the ultimate result of Joseph's actions? What should the ultimate outcome from your role as God's fiduciary be?

6. What biblical accounts come to mind that instruct that stewardship of resources is serious business or that God is deeply concerned with how money is handled?

7. Christ died "that those who live should no longer live for themselves but for him who died for them and was raised again" (2 Cor. 5:15). How might God desire that you use the financial resources stored in your cash and investment accounts to serve Him and to accomplish His purposes?

8. How has this chapter impacted your personal understanding of the breadth and depth of your responsibility as God's fiduciary?

Chapter 2

INVESTMENT AND CHARITY

"Do you know the best way to help an impoverished child who is starving and illiterate?"

For many in extreme poverty, even the first rung on the ladder of development is out of reach. Structures may be in place to assist, but without outside help in the form of capital or other investments, the poorest in our community have little hope of achieving economic mobility.

I have a friend who frequently asks his listeners if they know the best way to help an impoverished, starving, illiterate child. After asking, he waits for a while then finally answers his own question: "Give the parents a job by investing in a sustainable business in their community."

Most Christians are concerned about the poor and are genuinely motivated to alleviate suffering associated with poverty. Typically, Christians turn to charitable giving and respond to direct pleas for help from relief agencies, support fundraisers for short-term mission trips, or provide monthly support for agencies serving the poor. As a result, countless Christians are generous donors to thousands of charities.

However, donations alone are insufficient and can be damaging. Donations may not be the most successful means for addressing global issues such as poverty. Andrew Carnegie notes that charity can even hide more effective solutions especially when it masks systemic and root causes. It may be necessary to completely rethink which economic relationships can be most effective in achieving significant improvement in people's conditions.[7]

Leveraging the power of investments provides more robust and effective help.

The word *investment*, when speaking of charitable giving, is confusing because professional fundraisers and development officers frequently use the term to describe the donations they seek to raise. Although donations can have a compounding impact like an investment, professional fundraisers are technically soliciting donations and not raising investment capital because a donation does not expect any return of principal. It is a gift which is never expected to be returned to the giver.

On the other hand, an investment, by nature, expects a return of principal. Depending on the goals of the investor, the financial return above and beyond the return of principal may range from zero to high, but the investor does not expect a complete loss of their capital. Sometimes loss occurs when we invest—even a complete loss—but an investor does not presume at the outset that they will lose their investment. Therefore, few grants or donations should be categorized as investments.

In reality, both donations and investments are necessary, but when God's fiduciaries choose donations only and not investments, we hinder the completion of His goals. So we need to be wise in determining which method is most appropriate and most effective for resolving a particular problem. Donations are the most frequent solution for evangelism, church needs, and other concerns. Sometimes they are necessary, but so often the body of Christ uses charity because it is the easiest but not the best solution.

Let's explore the roles that charity and investment play as we seek to achieve God's objectives and why investment is absolutely necessary.

---

7. Ben Davis, "How Does Carnegie View Inequality?" (May 7, 2021): https://www.mvorganizing.org/how-does-carnegie-view-inequality/.

CHARITY IN THE FORM OF RELIEF

When communities experience catastrophic events, donations, grants, and philanthropy are generally the most effective solutions for relieving the immediate pain and stress these tragedies cause. This form of giving is considered *relief*: the urgent provision of resources to reduce suffering resulting from a natural or man-made disaster. Relief is both modeled and taught in scripture. Jesus explains relief to us in Matthew 25:35-36:

> "For I was hungry, and you gave me something to eat, I was thirsty and you gave me something to drink, I was a stranger and you invited me in, I needed clothes and you clothed me, I was sick and you looked after me, I was in prison and you came to visit me."

Relief: The urgent provision of resources to reduce suffering resulting from natural or man-made disaster. Development: The process which enables a community to provide for its own needs, beyond former levels, with dignity and justice.

Similarly, the psalmist writes, "Defend the weak and the fatherless; uphold the cause of the poor and the oppressed. Rescue the weak and the needy; deliver them from the hand of the wicked" (Ps. 82:3-4).

However, relief alone has limitations for providing rescue, defense, and deliverance. Relief that extends too long has been shown to cause dependency and can exacerbate the very problems it is trying to solve. For example, a January 13, 2010, headline read, "Emergency Drinking Water Relief for Haiti: Nestle Waters North America Pledges $1 Million in Bottled Water for Quake-Stricken Haiti."[8] The article showed the Port-au-Prince airport tarmac strewn with thousands of boxes of clothes and cases of bottled water stacked so high they looked like hundreds of towers of Pisa. The clothes and water were necessary relief to provide emergency safe water to the more than two million people in Port-au-Prince and surrounding areas without potable water following an earthquake.

8. Nestle Waters North America, "Emergency Drinking Water Relief for Haiti" (January 13, 2010): https://www.prnewswire.com/news-releases/emergency-drinking-water-relief-for-haiti--nestle-waters-north-america-pledges-1-million-in-bottled-water-for-quake-stricken-haiti-81385267.html.

But, when the free resources of water and clothing continued beyond what was needed for relief, the excessive donations damaged the livelihood of local water purification and bottling companies and crippled local clothing manufacturers.

FROM RELIEF AND REHABILITATION TO DEVELOPMENT

Charitable and philanthropic donations are necessary during severe crises but are best suited when *rehabilitation* is the end goal. Rehabilitation is restoring a community to pre-disaster conditions and rectifying any conditions that brought about the disaster.

Once rehabilitation is achieved, it is generally accepted that *economic development* should begin. Economic development is the process which enables a community to provide for its own needs, beyond former levels, with dignity and justice. It is a process of ongoing change that moves all the people involved, both those helping and those receiving help, "closer to being in a right relationship with God, self, others, and the rest of creation."[9] "Development must be indigenous, comprehensive, long-term, and aimed for improved self-reliance,"[10] says Robert Munson. Art Beals, in his book *Beyond Hunger: A Biblical Mandate for Social Responsibility*, further explains economic development in the eye of a Christian as a process that provides people with an ability to make life choices different from their current situation, choices that match what God in His goodness intends for His creation. Component parts of the process of development include self-determination in meeting the needs of the individual and their community; movement toward just distribution of material, economic, and personal resources; and increasing access for each person to participate in their country's economic and political life. These and other experiences are part of God's intentions for His humanity.[11]

9. Steve Corbett, Brian Fikkert, and Katie Casselberry, *Helping Without Hurting in Church Benevolence: A Practical Guide to Walking with Low-Income People* (Chicago, IL: Moody Publishers, 2015), 26.

10. Robert H. Munson, "Challenges in Church-Initiated Community Development" (September 2007): https://www.slideshare.net/bmunson3/challenges-in-doing-churchinitiated-christian-development-in-the-philippines, slide # "introduction." Used with permission.

11. Dr. Art Beals, *Beyond Hunger: A Biblical Mandate for Social Responsibility* (Portland, OR: Multnomah Press, 1985), 87.

Development requires Christians to go beyond charity and begin investing to create sustainable solutions that bring human flourishing.

Water4Ever: Development in Sierra Leone

In contrast to the overwhelming flood of bottled water that devastated local bottling companies in Port-au-Prince, the company Water4Ever is a catalyst and partner that invests in people, enterprises, and places that are "thirsty for change" by providing safe water solutions to communities in Sierra Leone. Water4Ever is one of nineteen local, missional businesses supported by Water4, an Oklahoma-City-based non-profit which supports many safe water projects across Africa. (Water4 uses the word *safe* water in place of *clean* water because although water may appear clean to the eye, it can still be unsafe and have harmful substances within it that could cause disease to those who drink it.) A recent investment was made through Water4 to support expansion of Water4Ever's service area. The new water infrastructure alleviates systemic poor water conditions in a new customer service area while helping prove the sustainability of the business model.

Sierra Leone has high disease mortality rates from people drinking and using unsafe water. It is a country with many coastal regions where groundwater is contaminated by flooding and pollution. Sewage spilling from inadequate treatment infrastructure along with refuse and garbage fermenting in the hot sun further contaminates water sources.

The poorest residents are forced to retrieve water from the foul and rancid ponds, puddles, and mostly dry riverbeds. Waterborne illnesses linked to unsafe water include cholera and diarrhea. In 2019 the child mortality rate for Sierra Leone was 109.2 deaths per one thousand live births, one of the highest in the world.[12] Local people don't understand the link between health problems they experience and their unsafe drinking water because education about health and hygiene means are absent.

Unfortunately, many of the community wells that have been established over the years no longer function because the communities were unable to maintain them—a common occurrence for many charitable relief projects that are designed to meet a short-term need

12. "Sierra Leone - Under-Five Mortality Rate, 1960–2020": https://knoema.com/atlas/Sierra-Leone/Child-mortality-rate.

but are not well-thought-out for long-term sustainability. Many philanthropic organizations tug at peoples' hearts by asking them to donate to well drilling projects because wells fitted with hand pumps can be relatively inexpensive to get started. But, in the absence of training local people to take care of the hand pump and charging for water so that there is money available to pay for maintenance, water projects are doomed to fail.

Sierra Leone is predominantly Muslim, but because of the region's history, most people also practice traditional animism, devil worship, and other ancient African religions. The key to reaching these people with the light of the Gospel is showing them God's love in tangible ways and sharing the good news of Jesus. One tangible way to serve the communities in this way is providing access to safe water.

Water4Ever uses a Business as Mission (BAM)[13] approach to provide safe water in Sierra Leone while also bringing residents the message of the Gospel. Working together with community leaders, Water4Ever establishes water points, a central water station with a borehole, and a filtration and pumping system. Water is sold from these locations at an affordable rate. Sometimes smaller substations containing a storage tank and metering capabilities are needed to bring water closer to residents who don't live near one of the main water point stations. Alternatively, those who can afford it may wish to pay to have the water pumped to home connections so they can have water piped directly to their homes. (For more about Water4's goal of empowering people to be the solution to the global water crisis, see the Appendix for information about CEO Matt Hangen's 2021 TEDx talk.)

Steve Corbett and Brian Fikkert, in their book *When Helping Hurts,* state that "[m]aterial poverty alleviation is working to reconcile the four foundational relationships so that people can fulfill their callings of glorifying God by working and supporting themselves and their families with the fruit of that work."[14] Water4Ever's community

---

13. Water4 is building missional businesses that are designed, at their very core, to scale. Water4 invests in business leaders who are making disciples both in the company and in the communities they serve. They start with finding a market that will work with the business model, then building discipleship activities into the business. Business as Mission will be further explained in chapter five.

14. Steve Corbett and Brian Fikkert, *When Helping Hurts: How to Alleviate Poverty Without Hurting the Poor . . . and Yourself* (Chicago, IL: Moody Publishers, 2014), 74. Used with permission.

development accomplishes four-fold transformation across economic, social, environmental, and spiritual lines.

Economic Impact: The Water4 approach brings economic stability. By installing and managing NUMA (from the Greek word for Spirit) branded water points that generate revenue from water sales, small businesses can provide ongoing operations and maintenance of the infrastructure. For most residents, the cost is well below three percent of their income and is ultimately a far lower expense than lost days of work or illness caused by unsafe water. To bring this kind of sustainable change, patient investment capital from like-minded Christian donors and investors is required to "prime the pump" for such business enterprises that provide employment and prosperity for many local residents.

Social Impact: Water4Ever leadership has a positive influence in the community. Their current staff of eighteen is expanding, and more safe water is anticipated to reach an additional one hundred thirty thousand local residents in the next two years. Water4Ever staff provide WASH (water access, sanitation, and hygiene) training to local residents and educate participants about the value of safe water.

Environmental Impact: The majority of Water4's systems run on solar power, which in Sierra Leone reduces the tons of carbon that would otherwise be emitted through gasoline-fueled generators and pumps. Moreover, water is dispensed and sold in reusable jerry cans rather than small plastic bags and bottles which cause pollution.

Spiritual Impact: NUMA water points, whether a hand pump or a kiosk where people fetch water, are also the center for social interaction. These locations are ideal for Water4Ever staff to share the Gospel message with customers as both customers and water staff continually work and live together in the same communities. Water4Ever has a pastor on staff who oversees the company's spiritual impact. Local leaders hear the Gospel, become believers, and are discipled. They then begin discipling others in the community using Water4's disciple-making program called Multiply. The good news spreads to their families and, by God's grace, throughout the communities where they live and work.

Water4Ever illustrates the transformative process of an economic development plan that enables a community to meet its own physical, spiritual, emotional, psychological, social, economic, and political needs. Creating sustainable businesses in locations that have been fractured by catastrophic events is difficult and risky, and

> ***Christians must be willing to participate in not only economic relief via traditional charitable donations but also in the generous deployment of God's investable resources into viable businesses that can bring economic, social, environmental, and spiritual transformation.***

long-term, patient, and generous capital investment is required to accomplish such lofty goals. But creating sustainable businesses is a critical step in accomplishing true economic community development. As we serve God in our role as fiduciaries, Christians must be willing to participate in not only economic relief via traditional charitable donations but also in the generous deployment of God's investable resources into viable businesses that can bring economic, social, environmental, and spiritual transformation.

ECONOMIC DEVELOPMENT SUSTAINED BY WEALTH CREATION

When we ably deploy God's resources through business, we participate in creating wealth for communities like those in Sierra Leone. While some believe there is only a fixed amount of wealth in the global economy, visionary businesspeople are increasing and adding to wealth in communities around the world.

Paul Stevens says,

> Wealth creation is the process by which needs and wants are satisfied. It is not a zero-sum game that makes one person's gain another's loss, although that might have been the case before the Industrial Revolution, when supply was limited, and one person's meal was at another's expense. Wealth creation is part of bringing shalom to people and the world.[15]

A comprehensive understanding of how deploying investments can accomplish sustainable economic solutions beyond charitable

15. Paul Stevens, *Doing God's Business: Meaning and Motivation for the Marketplace* (Grand Rapids, MI: Eerdmans, 2006), 30. (Also: https://www.bamglobal.org/wp-content/uploads/2017/10/Wealth-Creation-Biblical-Views-October-2017.pdf.) Used with permission.

mechanisms requires us to acknowledge some biblical foundations for wealth creation itself. Mats Tunehag, chairman of BAM Global and the former senior associate on Business as Mission for the Lausanne Movement,[16] notes,

> Wealth creation in and through business is beyond corporate philanthropy. Businesses do not exist to simply give away profit. They primarily exist to create different kinds of wealth for people and societies. It is not only about financial wealth, but also social, cultural, intellectual, and spiritual wealth.[17]

Additionally, the Lausanne Movement's Wealth Creation Manifesto states,

> We believe that creating real wealth is what God desires from us: wealth that blesses families, communities, and countries. That blessing includes sharing faith and love, providing jobs that are meaningful and reflect the creativeness of our God. Building business for the long haul: sustainable and scalable. . . .We trust that these examples will spark the church and business community to consider how they might affirm, align and release wealth creators to the ministry of the gospel.
>
> Wealth creation is rooted in God the Creator, who created a world that flourishes with abundance and diversity. We are created in God's image, to co-create with Him and for Him, to create products and services for the common good. Wealth creation is a holy calling, and a God-given gift, which is commended in the Bible.
>
> Wealth creation through business has proven power to lift people and nations out of poverty.[18]

16. The Lausanne Movement is an agency connecting influencers and ideas for global mission.

17. Mats Tunehag, "Wealth Creation for Holistic Transformation" (March 14, 2017): https://businessasmission.com/wealth-creation-for-holistic-transformation/.

18. "Wealth Creators' Contribution to Holistic Transformation" (March 2017): https://lausanne.org/content/wealth-creators-contribution-holistic-transformation. Used with permission.

Development and Wealth Creation in the Philippines

Dignity Coconuts, a business that produces coconut oil in the Philippines, provides another example of using God's financial resources, both donations and investments together, to create wealth and alleviate poverty.

Coconut slavery, known as "copra slavery," is a real economic issue in many impoverished regions. To reduce production costs, large coconut processing and distribution companies primarily contract with big plantations, leaving owners of small coconut farms at the mercy of middlemen who consolidate these smaller harvests into a larger supply then sell to large manufacturers while making a large profit for themselves. Furthermore, these middlemen take advantage of the small producers by offering loans at their time of need. On the outside, these middlemen look like kind friends since they are providing money to compensate for a low harvest and for medical expenses, schooling fees, and other urgent needs. However, these loans come at a high price, often with interest rates of twenty-five to two hundred percent.

Predatory lending such as this makes it nearly impossible for borrowers to repay loans before another emergency arises, leaving the farmer in a perpetual cycle of enslavement to the debt. Payment terms are rarely written down or explained, so these farmers never realize their "friend" is the very person keeping them in poverty.

Dignity started with a few people and a dream. After years of helping people out of poverty and modern-day slavery through charity-based programs, Dignity's founders knew the task ahead was too big for small, individual efforts. They knew that while non-profits and micro-enterprises were doing good things, global poverty and worker exploitation continued to increase. The UN says that ten percent of the world's population are living on less than $1.90 per day.[19] Because of this extreme poverty, they must make impossible decisions every day. This kind of poverty denies them the dignity of providing for basic needs such as food, health, housing, education, and safety.

Dignity Coconuts was founded with the vision to break the chains of poverty and modern-day slavery. Dignity founders talked to local farmers in the Philippines, asking what they needed most

19. "Goal 1: End Poverty in All Its Forms Everywhere": https://www.un.org/sustainabledevelopment/poverty/.

and what skills or resources they had to contribute. The locals explained that coconuts are abundant and have many benefits for consumers. It was decided that, in partnership with the community and local growers, Dignity would build a business that provides jobs, fair trade, education, life skills training, and an opportunity for local coconut farmers to participate. Dignity located the factory based on the needs of the community, which is rural and hard to access, with unsafe drinking water and high unemployment. "Few businesses would choose to locate here," says one of their founders, "but that's exactly why we are here." Dignity is bringing education, safe water, jobs, and, most importantly, hope. Look at the breadth and depth of Dignity's impact:

Economic Impact: Dignity is connecting local farmers directly to the global economy and giving farmers an opportunity to get fair prices for their coconuts and to be treated with respect by recognizing their innate dignity[20] following years of oppression and copra slavery.

Social Impact: Life in the village has improved and unemployment has dropped dramatically. Prior to Dignity Coconuts, the village was a six-hour jeep ride from the nearest city across muddy, rutted roads; it had poor electricity, no bank, and no medical facility. Dignity required a paved road and stable electricity be supplied to the village to support a processing plant the size needed to process thousands of coconuts per day. After repeatedly visiting, encouraging, and cajoling national federal and provincial officials, a thirty-five-mile paved road now makes the region accessible by car in an hour from the nearest city. A closer bank branch was established to cash workers' checks, stable electricity is available (most of the time), and five times a day buses ply the new route bringing access to city goods and services.

Environmental Impact: Organic agriculture is good for the environment and a healthy option for consumers. Dignity provides training to help coconut farmers properly care for their trees so that they can be organically certified. Following devastating typhoons in 2019 and 2020, Dignity was instrumental in replacing thousands of damaged and lost trees. As an extension of Dignity's training in family, health, and finance, it conducts courses on its land providing hands-on education about growing healthy vegetables.

---

20. For more on the dignity of work, see Mats Tunehag, "Work Is about Human Dignity" (February 21, 2021): https://www.youtube.com/watch?v=YNNqeq8IJPI&ab_channel=MatsTunehag.

Spiritual Impact: In 2017 I visited the Dignity "Community Transformation Plant," as their production facility is fondly called, and I was amazed at the spiritual impact. The local leaders have a genuine love and care for their workers, farmers, and the greater community that has resulted in hundreds deciding to follow Jesus. Many weekends were filled with baptism celebrations in the ocean in partnership with local churches. I listened to many stories of Jesus giving them the power over selfishness, addictions, corruption, fear, and many other struggles through discipleship groups. Medical personnel from the United States have visited to provide free medical clinics to hundreds of people in the community, and lives are transformed physically and spiritually through these events.

Coconut products are doing more than providing a quality, healthy product on grocery store shelves—they're transforming thousands of lives. Dignity is not stopping at the transformation of communities and lives in the Philippines. They have structured their plan to make it reproducible to other industries and products. Once the concept is proven and markets are opened, Dignity will build more plants all over the world. The business model isn't even limited to coconuts. Dignity will go to communities and ask them what resources they have, then build businesses based on the values and culture of Dignity Coconuts while utilizing local abundant resources.

Dignity's founders and investors have a big dream for the future and have confidence that their success in one hard place will encourage other Christian businesses that they too can effect change. Business was the solution. Not just any business, but a new way to do business. The exchange of wealth around the world is vast, but unfortunately, the unequal distribution of wealth leads to extreme poverty. Dignity, using business as a vehicle for change, created a business that would transform the future for the poor.

A project on the scale of Dignity Coconuts does not happen by chance or through donations. Christian investors who agree with the holistic goals and planned outcomes have been willing to invest in the project. Over five million dollars of equity ownership was invested to capitalize the project. By 2021 the project employed 135 workers and supported an additional 156 coconut farming families. Dignity Coconuts' products have found their way to the shelves of more than thirteen hundred grocery stores in the United States.

Rescue, Relief, and Rebuilding for Dignity in 2020–2021

Sometimes catastrophic events occur which devastate even the best plans. At the end of 2019 and in early 2020, the Dignity production facility was at the center of five large typhoons. The devastation, combined with COVID-19 restrictions for work and movement of products, wreaked havoc on the business and community. Complete or partial loss of nearly half of its 89,000 organic-certified coconut trees meant grave financial loss for farmers, lost wages for processing workers, and loss of homes in the community. These catastrophic events required a different answer than more investment dollars. It was necessary to implement some relief measures to stabilize the community and to make sure that families had rice to eat. Dignity, through its network of investors and friends, was able to raise approximately $215,000 in donations through five separate relief and repair events. These donations were used to distribute nearly a quarter million pounds of rice to 5,985 families, to rebuild or repair 336 houses, to replant five thousand coconut trees, and much more. Charity and investment worked hand in hand to accomplish God's purposes of caring for the vulnerable and bringing long-term solutions.

CONCLUSION

While we pray for the kingdom of God to come "on earth as it is in heaven," we must harness every resource that God entrusts to our care, employing them to reconcile brokenness and enable His kingdom to flourish. This imperative holds for every aspect of our lives, including our investable assets, our portfolio holdings, our nest egg, and all that is included in our calculable net worth.

We must harness every resource that God entrusts to our care, employing them to reconcile brokenness and enable His kingdom to flourish

Both charity and investment are necessary components for healing the world's problems. Each has its place in doing good and bringing reconciliation to broken systems. Christians are taught that generous giving is a primary component of their fiduciary responsibility, but when it comes to economic development and healing in a hurting world and bringing hope and a future in desperate circumstances, charity alone is insufficient. Charity can cause dependency and damage a community, culture, and human spirit if extended too long. We need to advance beyond a "charity is sacred" and "investment is secular" mentality. In fact, for the disciple, there should be no sacred/secular divide in any area of our lives.

Perhaps you already give generously to causes that are important to God. Have you considered your duty to invest (not just donate) resources in ways that accomplish God's purposes? There are many opportunities to be generous, but few of them are sustainable investments with multiple bottom-line impact. To achieve long-term flourishing, thoughtful investment is needed.

QUESTIONS FOR STUDY

1. Prior to reading this chapter, have you heard of Business as Mission (BAM) or Kingdom Businesses? Are you familiar with any such enterprises? If so, share how the business seeks to minister the hope of the Gospel through their business.

2. Reflect on the impact Water4Ever and Dignity Coconuts has had in accomplishing God's purposes to bring justice, mercy, prosperity, the good news of Jesus, and transformational change to communities in Sierra Leone and the Philippines.

3. Contrast the impact of relief and charitable endeavors in Haiti to address safe water needs with the impact of Water4Ever, a missional business model.

4. Consider Dignity Coconuts' presence in the Philippines during major typhoons and the coronavirus pandemic. How was God able to use this missional business to bring relief and good news to the surrounding communities devastated by these natural disasters?

5. Discuss the idea that charity is "sacred" and investment is "secular." What is your perception of the truth of this thinking?

6. Perhaps you are already a generous giver toward causes that are important to God. Have you considered your duty to invest (not donate) resources in ways that accomplish God's purposes? Share any opportunities that you might know of where a sustainable investment with economic, spiritual, and social impact bottom lines is being pursued.

Chapter 3

A DOG'S BONE

It is easier to pry a steak bone from a hungry pit bull's mouth than it is to persuade a wealthy Christian to invest resources for God's purposes. (Modern adaptation of an ancient proverb)

While most Christians have been well-schooled in donating a portion of their income to God's causes, relatively few have ever considered investing their long-term savings, investment portfolio, or nest egg into businesses (like Dignity Coconuts) that have social, environmental, and spiritual impact in addition to financial return.

When I ask the question, *What is stewardship?*—nine out of ten people respond with an answer mirroring the popular Wikipedia definition which states, "Stewardship is an ethic that embodies the responsible planning and management of resources."[21] When we automatically accept this definition, we mistakenly define stewardship only in terms of competent financial management and charitable giving while failing to recognize *whose* resources the steward manages. As previously discussed, a proper definition of stewardship must be rooted in understanding ownership and realizing that a steward is a fiduciary of someone else's resources. Failure to recognize that the steward does not own anything they manage is dangerous. A fiduciary

21. https://en.wikipedia.org/wiki/Stewardship

who uses resources for their own purposes and not for the purposes of the actual owner is legally condemned for embezzlement.

When I ask people to state their primary goals in making investments, the answers are always the same: maximize rate of return, minimize risk, and minimize taxes. These three goals are usually followed by their reasons, which often include retiring with financial independence or sending kids to college. Now, if I ask the same people what God's goals are for the world and people, the answers are similarly consistent and include the Great Commission (making disciples); the Great Commandment (loving God and your neighbor); worshiping and glorifying God; and bringing justice, mercy, and *shalom* to humanity by reconciling all that was broken at the Fall.

Now consider this: if we are fiduciaries of God's resources, why don't our investment objectives match His purposes for those resources?

Why don't our financial goals align with God's purposes?	
Our Goals	**His Purposes**
◆ Maximize return ◆ Minimize risk ◆ Avoid taxes ◆ Achieve financial independence (retirement) ◆ Provide for children's education	◆ Reconcile brokenness from the Fall ◆ Make disciples ◆ Love and worship God ◆ Love our neighbors ◆ Do justice and love mercy

Fig. 1: Our goals, his purposes[22]

Why are we quick to give lip service to the idea that "God owns it all" while we are, in fact, managing His resources for our own pleasure or according to our own wisdom?

Matthew gives us a window into Jesus' thoughts on wealth. Following a conversation between Jesus and a wealthy young man, during which Jesus tells the man, "[I]f you want to be perfect, go,

22. All figures except Figure 2 were created by the author.

sell your possessions and give to the poor," Jesus says to the reader, *"I tell you, it is easier for a camel to go through the eye of a needle than for someone who is rich to enter the kingdom of God"* (Matt. 19:21, 24, emphasis mine). Since most of us have never seen a camel, it is hard to relate this metaphor to our lives. For this reason, I have started to explain this hard teaching in terms of hungry dogs with bones.

We tend to dismiss Jesus' instructions and assume they apply only to the man in Matthew for two reasons: first, because we do not consider ourselves wealthy, and second, because we rationalize that the instruction was given to show that keeping the commandments alone is insufficient. Since we are not as wealthy, arrogant, or self-righteous as the "rich young ruler," Jesus' directive can't apply to us. But we are wrong.

ARE WE WEALTHY?

It is easy for us to consider ourselves less wealthy in comparison to so many others who have much more. We may think to ourselves, *I did not work for a fast-growing company where stock options led me to a nest egg that provided for an early and extravagant retirement,* or, *I wasn't lucky enough to pick the right stock which made me a millionaire,* or, *I have not sold a business and received a windfall payout,* or, *I do not even have a pension from a long career with a Fortune 500 company, or as a teacher or government employee.* But when we consider Jesus' conversation with the wealthy young man, we must admit that relative to the rest of the world, we are extremely wealthy.

Let's further address the false assumption that we are not wealthy. When we evaluate wealth, there are two factors to consider: income and net worth (I will use median numbers, those at the fiftieth percentile, since the average is skewed much higher by the super-rich who have extraordinarily high incomes and net worth). In 2020 the median household income in the United States was \$68,400,[23] which ranks in the top seventh percentile for household incomes globally.[24]

According to the Federal Reserve's Survey of Consumer Finances, the median household net worth of all US families is \$97,300.[25] A household net worth of \$97,000 ranks among the top

23. https://dqydj.com/average-median-top-household-income-percentiles/
24. https://howrichami.givingwhatwecan.org/
25. The Federal Reserve's Survey of Consumer Finances: https://www.federalreserve.gov/publications/files/scf17.pdf.

ten percent globally according to the Credit Suisse Global wealth report 2020.[26] Either way you slice it, since my annual salary exceeds $68,400 and my net worth exceeds $97,000, I must consider that I am wealthy, even rich, by any global measure. How about you?

Further, while I may not be so arrogant as to claim that I have kept all the commandments since I was a child, I might be arrogant enough to think, *I am more honest than so-and so,* or, *I am more generous than him,* or, *I tithe to church and support missions.* I might falsely conclude that because I've already done more than others, God would never ask me to sell my possessions to further His work . . . would He?

Many of us freely donate our used, worn out, and no-longer-wanted possessions. But I wonder if you have ever sold something valuable so that you could give or invest the proceeds in a way that will advance God's purposes. Have you ever redirected resources that you saved for a specific personal goal and instead invested them in a missional enterprise? I can think of several times when our family chose to do that; when our role as fiduciaries caused us to choose *not* to purchase something for ourselves so that we could bring blessing to others. One such time we were preparing to replace our twenty-year-old boat when we heard that a kids' camp needed a new ski boat for their summer waterfront program. It would have been easy to donate our old boat to the camp and buy a new one for ourselves. However, we purchased a Ski Nautique for the camp. Recently, we sold our practically new Toyota 4Runner to help a missional enterprise pay worker wages. In both instances, a charitable donation was the most effective method to advance God's kingdom.

At other times, making a longer-term investment was the most appropriate method for accomplishing God's goals. One such time, we refinanced our home so that we could use the equity to invest in the purchase of a missional cattle ranch working with the Roma (Gypsy[27]) people in Eastern Europe. In another situation we chose to lend money from our retirement nest egg (IRA) to start new missional businesses in the Republic of Georgia and in Indonesia.

26. Credit Suisse Global Wealth Report, 2020, p. 8: https://www.credit-suisse.com/about-us/en/reports-research/global-wealth-report.html.

27. These nomadic people from Northern India, who entered Europe between the eighth and tenth centuries, were thought to be from Egypt and thus mistakenly called "Gypsies" by Europeans. United States Holocaust Memorial Museum, "Roma (Gypsies) in Prewar Europe" (March 18, 2022): https://encyclopedia.ushmm.org/content/en/article/roma-gypsies-in-prewar-europe.

Our donor advised fund (DAF) was used to purchase equity to facilitate a reorganization for a business in Vietnam.

A financial advisor would not typically encourage you to sell or give away your possessions or to invest in such high-risk businesses. However, I hope to hear Jesus speak the words, "Well done, good and faithful servant," knowing they're not in reference to my accumulated net worth or compounded rate of return.[28] Instead, I hope His praise will be in relation to how well I deployed His assets to accomplish His purposes.

The world tells us that the one who dies with the most possessions wins, but will I be condemned if I "die broke" because I invested too much into high-risk missional businesses? I don't think so.

Instead, I hope His praise will be in relation to how well I deployed His assets to accomplish His purposes.

I can't shake the feeling that when Jesus talks about selling what we have, it applies to me and to all of us who are among the wealthiest in the world, not just the rich young ruler. Sure, I can always justify my lifestyle as being reasonable because I can point to so many around me who have more. But if I take an honest look at the resources that God has chosen to flow through my hands, I am forced to consider the following questions:

- Are there more resources that have gotten stuck in my net worth or more resources that are clearly deployed for God's goals?
- Do I simply give lip service to the notion that "God owns it all"?
- If an auditor reviewed my portfolio or nest egg, would it reveal a deliberate choice to invest in companies with intentional missional objectives, or might the evidence suggest that I should be convicted for embezzlement because I invest primarily to support my own lifestyle and comfort while investing nothing (or very little) in businesses that have clearly defined spiritual impact plans? (See Appendix C for SuperGreen Solution's Kingdom Impact Plan as an example).

28. A more complete discussion of these words and the parable of the talents is included in chapter eight.

- What percentage of my net worth (not the foundation or DAF that I funded, since these are already donated assets) has been invested in businesses that deliberately seek to expand God's kingdom, alleviate poverty, or eradicate exploitation of workers?
- Does my portfolio look any different than someone's who does not proclaim Jesus as their Savior?
- Does my obligation to be a fiduciary of His resources apply only to my tithe or donations or does it apply to every asset that I control: my bank account, my home, my retirement account, my automobile, and even my emergency cash reserve?
- As a fiduciary, should I immediately deploy, or at least make everything available, for His purposes when He asks?
- Does God expect me to always achieve market-like returns so that I can use some of the excess to donate to His work, or would He prefer that I immediately invest capital in ways that are focused on seeing the name of Jesus lifted up in difficult places?

What has grown faster over the past few years, your net worth or the portion of your net worth that is directly invested in businesses that have a clearly defined spiritual impact plan?

As a financial advisor, I know these questions are unconventional and are in opposition to typical investment practices such as maximizing profit and minimizing risk. But they are appropriate if I am a fiduciary of God's resources. Since a fiduciary has a legal obligation to attempt to accomplish the owner's objectives, our family has decided to not spend more each year on our own interests or toward increasing our net worth than we are willing to deploy for God's kingdom.

In 2020, for example, we decided to build a new garage and committed that we would donate, above our tithe, at least as much as we would spend building the garage to overseas businesses with deliberate redemptive objectives. The donation was sent to a

DAF which in turn quickly invested it into numerous missional businesses that are advancing God's kingdom in difficult places.

CONCLUSION

Current stock prices and home values have reached all-time highs. What has grown faster over the past few years, your net worth or the portion of your net worth that is directly invested in businesses that have a clearly defined spiritual impact plan?

Your answer will reveal whether you are behaving more like a fiduciary who freely invests in God's work or a Pit bull who holds tightly to its resources to satisfy its own appetite. Fortunately, with God all things are possible, even prying resources that can be invested for His great purposes out of the fierce grip of wealthy Christians.

QUESTIONS FOR STUDY

1. Have your personal investment goals been to maximize rate of return, minimize risk, and minimize taxes? Have your reasons for investing been to fund retirement or send your children to college, or to achieve short- and long-term goals like buying a home or business or taking a once-in-a-lifetime vacation? Are these goals and reasons for investing any different for you than they are for your non-Christian friends and neighbors?

2. Is there anything inherently wrong with the goals and reasons for investing cited above? What biblical passages come to mind that teach it is wise to save for the future, to provide for your family, and to make plans before undertaking major projects?

3. The author included Great Commission (making disciples); the Great Commandment (loving God and your neighbor); worshiping and glorifying God; and bringing justice, mercy, and *shalom* as God's goals for the world through His people. Then he poses the question, *Why don't our investment objectives match His purposes for those resources?* How do you react to that question?

4. Read Matthew 19:21-30. Explain what Jesus was requiring of the young man, how His disciples reacted to this teaching, and Jesus' encouragement to those who will follow Him.

5. In 2020 the median household income in the US was $68,400 and the median household net worth was $97,000, placing Americans in the top ten percent of wealth by global measures. Would God ask us to sell our possessions to further His work? How would you apply Matthew 19 to yourself if you were to have a conversation with Jesus about your commitment to follow Him with your wealth?

Personal Reflection

Recall that a fiduciary is not the True Owner. The author asks many provocative questions suitable for personal reflection regarding our goals and reasons for investing and the extent of resources that have been entrusted to us. Consider these and conclude if there is room in your financial plan for Jesus' goals.

Chapter 4

RIGHTEOUS BUSINESS

When the righteous prosper, the city rejoices. (Prov. 11:10a)

Most of us look at our investment statements to see whether the account value went up or down, but rarely do we give thought to the values, ethics, or morality of the businesses we invest in. As fiduciaries of God's resources, we have a duty to invest strategically with concern about whether specific businesses are advancing or ignoring God's kingdom, not simply if they are profitable.

ARE BUSINESSES RIGHTEOUS OR WICKED?

We only need to review the headlines to find evidence that businesses can be evil. In the late 1990s, the Enron scandal regarding faulty and misleading accounting led to the implosion of a Fortune 500 company which devastated employees and investors, wiping out their life savings. With the death of Bernie Madoff, we are reminded of the 2008 exposure regarding his appalling behavior. He swindled individuals, not-for-profits, universities, and other investors out of nearly fifty billion dollars through an elaborate Ponzi scheme. The respected company Volkswagen admitted in 2015 that eleven million of its vehicles were equipped with software that was designed and used to cheat on emissions tests. In 2016 Cambridge Analytica was in the news for using Facebook data from some fifty million users to interfere with the 2016 United States presidential election. In 2020 it was revealed that Wells Fargo created fake accounts in customers' names, generating over $2.6 million of unearned fees from customers without their permission.[29]

Nearly every day we hear about business fraud, greed, and corruption. If you don't know what values you are supporting through your investments, you support this behavior. As God's fiduciary, you are complicit when you invest in and turn a blind eye to the underlying fundamental business practices of the companies you invest in. Your ignorance of a dangerous work environment or exploitative labor practices funded by your investments does not relieve your responsibility for the harm that is incurred.

As God's fiduciary, you are complicit when you invest in and turn a blind eye to the underlying fundamental business practices of the companies you invest in.

In chapter one we discussed the fact that whether we invest directly in companies by purchasing their stocks or if we invest in them via a mutual fund—or if we have an IRA or 401(k) or nest egg of any kind—we are owners or lenders to these businesses. The warnings in the book of James discussed in chapter one are harsh toward business owners who don't treat workers fairly and who are greedy hoarders for their own benefit. Likewise, investors are complicit in the evil and corruption of the businesses that they own through their investments. Alternatively, investors deserve some credit for the goodness and life that is accomplished through the righteous businesses they invest in.

VALUES-BASED INVESTING: MAKING MORAL CHOICES

Sometimes when I speak about values-based investing, I use the following example to help people understand that investing has a moral component. I ask these questions:

29. Kathy Kristof, "Wells Fargo Fined for Opening Millions of Fake Accounts" (September 8, 2015): https://www.cbsnews.com/news/wells-fargo-pays-record-fine-for-customer-abuse/.

1. Would you be interested in investing in a mutual fund that has averaged over ten percent per year since 2002, even with the great bear market of 2008?
2. What if I told you that the fund is a blend of US and foreign large cap stocks and has beaten the S&P 500 by almost two percent annually since 2002?

That's an attractive track record. Are you interested?

If you had invested ten thousand dollars when the fund started in August of 2002, your investment would have tripled in value by August of 2016. What if I told you that it has a strict screening process for the selection of stocks which the manager considers "recession proof" due to their strong earnings and profits even during recessions? If you weren't interested before, are you now?[30]

What if I added that according to the fund's prospectus, it invests as follows:

> Under normal market conditions, the Fund will invest at least 80% of its net assets in equity securities [stocks] of companies that derive a significant portion of their revenues from alcoholic beverages, tobacco, gambling, gaming, publishing, and weapons manufacturing.

Investopedia describes the fund in this way: "[it is] a mutual fund . . . that focuses its investments on vice industries often considered socially irresponsible investments or 'sin stocks.'"[31] This blatant statement of how the fund invests its assets ought to get our attention. As followers of Christ and as fiduciaries of His resources—not our own—we have a responsibility to consider *how* profits are made, not just *how much* profit is made.

As followers of Christ and as fiduciaries of His resources–not our own–we have a responsibility to consider how profits are made, not just how much profit is made.

Where do we draw the line for what is acceptable or unacceptable to gain a profit? Is it acceptable to gain extra profits

30. This is not a solicitation of investment for a particular fund. Past performance is not a guarantee of future performance. Investors should always consult with their financial and tax advisor before making an investment.

31. https://www.investopedia.com/terms/v/vice-fund.asp

by taking advantage of people's addictions? What about gaining from companies who exploit workers, allow unfair labor practices, or pay below-living wages to produce products at a lower cost? Should we be concerned about investments that support or profit from pornography or abortion? What about higher profits gained by avoiding environmental regulations and polluting the environment? Is it acceptable for a company to pay bribes to avoid regulations?

As fiduciaries of the Master's resources, are there some investments that we should avoid? The answer is yes, but unfortunately, statistical evidence and my three decades of experience as a financial advisor confirm that most Christians do not select their investments any differently than non-Christians do.

How can we possibly reconcile this chapter's opening stories of corruption with the idea that businesses themselves and, by extension, investors in businesses, are considered sacred and not secular? Is it possible to see work, jobs, and business enterprise as part of God's design for the world, included in what He declared good when He created the world and something worthy of investment?

WHAT DOES RIGHTEOUS BUSINESS LOOK LIKE?

In the winter of 1995, a large fire broke out at Malden Mills in Lawrence, Massachusetts. The fire did not kill anyone but devastated a town already in desperate straits. The textile mill, one of the few large employers in the town, went up in smoke—a total loss, leaving Aaron Feuerstein, the owner, with few options.[32] If Feuerstein, a man in his early seventies, had decided to pocket the three hundred million dollars in insurance proceeds and retire, few would have blamed him. Even if he didn't want the sedentary life of a retiree, he could have taken this opportunity to re-invest in an offshore manufacturing operation for his company as most others in his industry would have done. After all, New England wages were among the highest in the world, and his trademark Polartec ® fleece could have been made anywhere, with cheaper labor and more profit. However, Feuerstein told *Parade* magazine, "I have a responsibility to the worker, both blue collar and white collar. I have an equal responsibility to the community. It would be unconscionable to put 3000 people on the

32. Rebecca Leung, "The Mensch of Malden Mills: CEO Aaron Feuerstein Puts Employees First," in *CBS News* (July 3, 2003). Retrieved May 17, 2021. https://www.cbsnews.com/news/the-mensch-of-malden-mills/.

streets and deliver a death blow to the cities of Lawrence & Methuen Mass."[33]

Feuerstein made two shocking decisions: he decided not only to rebuild the factory right there in Lawrence, but he also determined to keep all employees on the payroll during the reconstruction. The latter decision alone cost $1.5 million per week. In all, he paid out more than twenty-five million dollars, and he became known as the "Mensch of Malden Mills" because of his profound care for his workers at the expense of his net worth.[34] The Yiddish word *mensch* describes a person of "integrity and honor,"[35] who does what is right, because it is right, toward family or strangers, at home and in public. When people behave with honesty, integrity, consideration, and respect, they themselves prosper as does society at large. By spreading *mensch*-like behavior, we can make our society happier, healthier, and more successful. Proverbs 11:10 describes this kind of person, saying, "When the righteous prosper, the city rejoices."

Feuerstein was known as a wise businessman and would have known that the cost of his plan would be more than the insurance settlement. Apparently he used a different bottom line than just the one below the numbers, believing business owners do not have the right to oppress or take advantage of their workers.[36] On another platform, an award ceremony for business ethics, Feuerstein explained his motivation for making such a shocking and counter-cultural decision, quoting Jeremiah 9:23-24: "Let the rich man not praise himself, but rather, by demonstrating the will of God, show kindness, justice, and righteousness in his actions."[37]

WHAT ARE JUSTICE AND MERCY?

Which investment better suits your role as a fiduciary of God's resources—Polartec or the previously described fund? Fiduciaries of God's resources should aim to extend the kingdom of God by investing in businesses and management teams that at a minimum do no harm to the causes of Christ and, even better, proactively invest

33. *Parade Magazine* (September 8, 1996), 4–5. Used with permission.

34. https://www.cbsnews.com/news/the-mensch-of-malden-mills/

35. https://www.merriam-webster.com/dictionary/mensch

36. https://www.cbsnews.com/news/the-mensch-of-malden-mills/

37. "Keep this Book of the Law (Joshua 1:7-8), Part 2 of 'Get Ready,'" ENACTEDWORD, as quoted by Feuerstein (September 25, 2017): https://enactedword.com/2017/09/25/keep-this-book-of-the-law-joshua-17-8-part-2-of-get-ready/. Used with permission.

in companies that honor Christ and bring prosperity and blessing to their employees and community. When we make such choices, we live out God's instruction found in Micah 6:8 (ESV): "He has told you, O man, what is good; and what does the LORD require of you but to do justice, and to love kindness, and to walk humbly with your God?" Another version, lending a different word for kindness, is the NIV, which says to "act justly and to love *mercy*" (emphasis mine). As we will see, mercy is a specific type of kindness. Investing righteously requires a deeper understanding of justice and mercy in the context of business.

Investing righteously requires a deeper understanding of justice and mercy in the context of business.

Micah 6:8 is a summary of how God wants us to live. The text says to "do justice" and to "love mercy." You may think these are two entirely different things, but they are not. Mercy and justice go hand in hand. The Hebrew word translated as mercy is *chesedh,* and it describes God's unconditional grace and compassion. There are two Hebrew words translated as justice, which are *mishpat* and *tzedakah*. Both mercy and justice refer to how we are to treat the less fortunate, with justice generally emphasizing the action itself, while mercy emphasizes the attitude (or motivation) behind the action. The two together tell us that walking with God requires that we do justice out of compassionate love in action. It is not passive. We can and should apply these principles to our investment choices as well.

One of God's primary actions in the world is to identify with the powerless. He takes up their cause, loving and defending those who have the least social and economic power (see Deut. 10:18). As previously noted, there are two Hebrew words that are typically translated as justice. The first word, *mishpat,* occurs over two hundred times in the Old Testament. In its most basic sense, *mishpat* means giving people what they deserve, whether it's punishment for wrongdoing or defense and care when in a vulnerable state.[38] We know that God's character is frequently described as taking up the care and cause of the widows, orphans, immigrants, and poor (Ps. 146:7-9). Frequently God is identified as the Defender of these vulnerable groups.[39]

38. Timothy Keller, *Generous Justice* (NY: Penguin Group, 2010), 4.
39. See Exod. 22:22 and 23:9; Lev. 19:33-34; Pss 10:14 and 82:3-4 for examples.

But there is more to the biblical idea of justice than simply treating people equitably. The second Hebrew word translated as justice, *tzedakah*, usually points to a life of right relationships. The name of the Old Testament king Melchizedek, mentioned in the book of Genesis, literally means "king of righteousness" because it has *tzedakah* as its root.

I have generally applied the word *righteousness* to describe private morality or to the behavior of people who have a deep relationship with the Lord. But in the biblical context, these words grow in their application. They describe how we should conduct all relationships in family and society with fairness, generosity, and equity. Aaron Feuerstein was a righteous businessman because he did not separate his core values from the way that he managed his business.

Timothy Keller, in his book *Generous Justice,* explains the inextricable link between *mishpat* and *tzedakah.* He explains that *mishpat* (meting out punishment to those who do wrong and providing care for those who've suffered unjust treatment) is necessary only because we don't live out right relationships (*tzedakah*). His reasoning is that if we all lived as we should, our right relationship with God would result in good social order characterized by right relationships with everyone else. A world with perfect *tzedakah* (right relationships with everything) would eliminate the need for *mishpat* needed to make things right following injustice.[40]

Aaron Feuerstein was a righteous businessman because he did not separate his core values from the way that he managed his business.

Frequently in the Old Testament, *tzedakah* and *mishpat* are used together, creating one new concept out of the two ideas with implications for our society and how we invest. When *tzedakah* and *mishpat* are used together, they create the concept of *shalom* which means both "justice" and "peace." *Shalom* is a Hebrew word typically understood as peace. In truth it is a much richer word meaning harmony, wholeness, completeness, prosperity, welfare, and tranquility. In this context, wholeness is everything that undergirds people's well-being and security and even extends to restoration of relationships that have been broken. The biblical idea of *shalom* is the

40. Timothy Keller, *Generous Justice* (NY: Penguin Group, 2010), 10–11.

reason justice always must be "social,"[41] as Dr. Keller notes. When there is *shalom*, everything is as it should be, and the brokenness caused by the Great Fall in Genesis is restored.

Justice and Mercy Applied to Business

As a fiduciary of God's resources, wouldn't you like to ensure that your investments are consistent with *chesedh, mishpat, tzedakah,* and *shalom*? Businesses that balance the interests of all their stakeholders, including stockholders, employees, customers, suppliers, and even the surrounding community are hard to find. What follows is an example of a righteous company in the modern era. (Those who know me well are not surprised by the fact that I take an interest in a chocolate company.)

Milton Hershey founded the Hershey chocolate company in 1903 with the innovation of putting milk into the chocolate bar. The company prospered, as did all the dairy farmers in the surrounding countryside near Harrisburg, Pennsylvania. When the Depression hit and business fell apart, Hershey committed to not lay off his employees. Instead, he created his own public works projects in the town and put his employees to work building houses, an amusement park, a hotel, and a boarding school for orphans. The boarding school teaches orphans practical life skills within a supporting community. Hershey established a trust that provides operating revenue for the school. By depositing a large portion of Hershey company stock into the trust, the school is still funded to this day by the dividends and capital gains of the company.[42]

This is deep, passionate rejoicing: dancing-in-the-streets, ticker-tape-parade expressions of soul-soaring exultation.

The book of Proverbs tells us that "[w]hen the righteous prosper, the city rejoices" (Prov. 11:10). The root word *rejoice* in Proverbs 11:10 is particularly important. A unique term used only one other time in the Old Testament, it describes *ecstatic* joy, the exultation and triumph that people express in celebration of a great

41. Timothy Keller, *Generous Justice* (NY: Penguin Group, 2010), 11. Used with permission.

42. "Milton Hershey" (April 27, 2017): https://www.biography.com/business-figure/milton-hershey.

victory[43] such as winning the World Cup or being delivered from the hand of your enemy. This is deep, passionate rejoicing: dancing-in-the-streets, ticker-tape-parade expressions of soul-soaring exultation.

Amy Sherman, in her book *Kingdom Calling,* comments about this kind of rejoicing:

> By this we realize that the righteous, in their prospering, must be making a remarkably positive difference in their city. They must be stewarding their power, wealth, skills and influence for the common good to bring about noticeable, significant transformation in the city. Otherwise, what would be prompting the residents there to go crazy with gladness and gratitude? . . . Indeed, what the text teaches is that by the intentional stewardship of their time, talent and treasure, the *tsaddiqim* [righteous people] bring nothing less than *foretastes of the kingdom of God* into reality.[44]

As a fiduciary of God's resources, do you invest in businesses that exemplify the righteousness described in the book of Proverbs? Do your companies cause ticker-tape-parade-like dancing in the streets?

"The Wicked Have No Such Concern"

Proverbs describes this type of investing another way: "The righteous care about justice for the poor, but the wicked have no such concern," says Proverbs 29:7.

Compassionate care for the poor is not commonplace in today's business environment or in the investment world. Business and investor money flows to where it can be easily multiplied for maximum profit. A radical commitment to care about the needs of multiple stakeholders, not just the shareholders, is absent from most investment discussions. This might be because the "wicked have no such concern" for anyone except themselves.

A few years ago, I received a disturbing proxy from one of the mutual funds that I owned at the time. It was a core holding, a short-term bond fund that should have been benign regarding the types of investments that it was making. I was disturbed when I read

43. https://biblehub.com/hebrew/5970.htm

44. Amy Sherman, *Kingdom Calling: Vocational Stewardship for the Common Good* (Downers Grove, IL: InterVarsity Press, 2011), 17–18. Used with permission.

the proxy statement in which the board of directors recommended that I vote against a shareholder proposal that would "institute transparent procedures to avoid holding investments in companies that, in management's judgment, substantially contribute to genocide or crimes against humanity, or other egregious violations of human rights."[45] The board of directors was suggesting that the ends justify the means and that financial performance is to be regarded as paramount, regardless of how it is achieved. They were recommending that I should invest in companies that "substantially contribute to genocide or crimes against humanity, and egregious violations of human rights" to protect my own financial return. If you live in the United States and own one of the most popular short-term bond index funds, there is a high likelihood that you own this fund. It is extremely popular in large 401(k) and pension plans because of its consistent stability and performance.

To me, there is no clearer evidence that our current culture exemplifies Proverbs 29:7: "The righteous *care about* justice for the poor, but the *wicked have no such concern*" (emphasis mine). As a follower of Christ, I need to consider my decisions. Should I vote to protect my performance at the expense of other people's welfare, or should I care more about justice for the vulnerable and exploited than I do about my own financial return? The Word of God makes it clear that one action is righteous and the other action is wicked.

Traditional capitalism and the influence of Milton Friedman in the 1970s argues that the primary purpose of business is to maximize shareholder value. As we manage the Lord's resources as His fiduciaries, we need to care about others, not only ourselves. In ancient Hebrew, the verb translated "care about" is *yada,* which suggests an intense and deep level of care.[46] The same term is translated in Genesis as "to know" and is used to describe Adam and Eve's intimate relationship. So when the righteous "care about" justice for the poor, it means that they are intensely invested in seeing justice done for the poor. Their concern is deep, intimate, and passionate. Shouldn't our management of His resources cause us to seek optimized outcomes and maximized profit for *all* stakeholders—the community, the environment, and those who are in need—not just for a single stakeholder, the shareholder? Aaron Feuerstein knew that Polartec must be profitable, but he was also adamant that the business must

45. The name of this security is withheld to protect its privacy.
46. https://biblehub.com/hebrew/3045.htm

fulfill its social obligation to benefit the workers, community, and environment. Businesses must meet the needs of their employees by paying living wages, and they have a responsibility to care for the community where they operate.[47]

I have observed that in many ways, secular impact investors are more dedicated to influencing business toward the accomplishment of their social, environmental, or values-based outcomes than followers of Jesus are in making investments that influence godly outcomes. Impact investing which seeks positive Environmental, Social, and Governance (ESG) outcomes or achievement of the United Nations Sustainable Development Goals (SDGs) has gained traction since the 1970s and is now one of the fastest-growing sectors of the investment industry, and yet few Christians are even aware of the terms I am describing. Christian steward investors serving as God's *oikonomos* should be leading the charge for ethical investing which promotes human flourishing and advances the kingdom of God on earth. We must go above and beyond "impact investing" if we want to accomplish God's purposes with our investment monies.

CONCLUSION

Scripture tells us that "[w]hen the righteous prosper, the city rejoices" (Prov. 11:10). Have you considered your role as an investor? Do your investments cause cultural rejoicing? Are you simply giving a portion to support God's work or to help those who are less fortunate when your investments do well? Are you concerned about whether the "making of the money" brings blessing or pain? Do you invest in ways that actively "care about justice for the poor," or do the ends (profit) justify the means (the possible exploitation of the vulnerable or harm to the environment)? In the following chapter we will begin to explore what missional or redemptive investing looks like.

47. J. Kile, "Aaron Feuerstein" (November 19, 2010): http://moralheroes.org/aaron-feuerstein/.

QUESTIONS FOR STUDY

1. Are businesses righteous or wicked? What makes the difference? What difference does it make to a fiduciary of Jesus' resources?

2. Are there any "sin stocks" in your portfolio? If you were asked this question by your spouse, by your child, or by Jesus one day, how might you answer? If your answer is, "I don't know," what can you do now to give a definitive answer?

3. What biblical texts come to mind supporting the claim that work, jobs, business, and investing in business are part of God's design for the world? What biblical texts instruct the believer in their conduct as an employee, as a business owner, or as one who considers an investment and pursues it?

4. Define *justice*. Define *mercy*.

5. Review the concepts of *tzedakah* and *mishpat* and, used together, the concept of *shalom*. Consider what enterprises in your community might be an example of a righteous business that is seeking the peace and prosperity of its stakeholders—employees, customers, community—similar to Hershey or Polartec. What makes you think this is a righteous business?

6. Do the companies you have invested in care (*yada*, suggesting an intense and deep level of care) about justice for the poor? If you operate your own business, or have influence in a business, are there actions that you can take to pursue greater care for the poor and greater concern for the stakeholders of the business?

7. Read and discuss Proverbs 11:10-11 in the context of this chapter's discussion of righteous and wicked businesses.

Chapter 5

WHAT IS MISSIONAL BUSINESS?

In the last chapter I pointed out that some businesses can be wicked while others can be righteous. A business like Polartec represents what I would refer to as a "righteous" business, where the priorities of the owner clearly align with how God would have us organize and operate a corporation. On the other end of the spectrum would be pornographic production companies such as Vivid Entertainment or the not-for-profit corporation Planned Parenthood whose goals and operations are contrary to God's ordinances. I would refer to any such company as "wicked" since their primary purposes and values stand contradictory to a Christian worldview, and they do not promote the welfare of humanity as God admonishes believers in Christ to do. Many businesses fall somewhere between these two poles and are, at least on the surface, neither wicked nor righteous. As Christian investors we should know the difference and seek to invest in businesses whose values and standards for earning money are consistent with both God's character and His purposes. These considerations go deeper than simply seeking righteous companies. Fiduciaries of God's money are responsible to use it for His purposes. Let's dig deeper to understand the extra steps we can take to embrace this serious responsibility.

My journey into understanding my role as God's fiduciary began in 2003 when I made a trip to Krasnodar, Russia, on the Black Sea, to teach business fundamentals to university students. It was there that I learned firsthand how difficult it is for many people to lift themselves out of poverty, especially in places where the system is broken, corrupt, and stacked against the little guy. I thought, *How can I help to level the playing field for these young, motivated university students who must overcome so many roadblocks to succeed?*

I am an investor by training and vocation and an entrepreneur in practice, having partnered in many business startups. I know how important it is for small business owners to have honest, stable, and trustworthy capital. Since my time in Krasnodar, I have gained further understanding of the need for Christian investors specifically to participate in providing trustworthy capital in corrupt environments. Like-minded investors are desperately needed to support Christian business owners and to help level the playing field in difficult parts of the world. In frontier markets, where corrupt capital and business practices proliferate, Christian investors are needed so that Christian business owners can model business practices that promote human flourishing. Our role as God's fiduciary requires us to not only screen out and choose not to invest in companies that offend our moral beliefs, but also, and even more importantly, to proactively invest in companies and places where our values will reflect Christ and elevate the ethical bar in society.

BUSINESS AS MISSION AND COMMERCE AS A VESSEL FOR GOD'S KINGDOM WORK

When Eugene Peterson paraphrases the text from the book of John, saying, "The Word [Jesus] became flesh and blood, and moved into the neighborhood. We saw the glory with our own eyes, the one-of-a-kind glory, like Father, like Son, Generous inside and out, true from start to finish" (John 1:14, MSG), he gives us a vision for how earthly the presence of Jesus really is. Jesus wants to show up all over the globe, and commerce makes that possible everywhere.

Commerce is the language of the entire world, cutting across all social, economic, racial, age, and gender barriers. Every one of us must participate in the marketplace, and therefore there is no better place to build real, authentic relationships than here. Businesspeople go to where people are, identifying people's physical, financial, or spiritual needs, and offering solutions to meet those needs. We'll discuss Business as Mission (BAM) in this chapter. BAM is committed to expanding the kingdom of God through business enterprise. Investors participate in the Great Commission not only by donating to missions programs but also by strategically investing in missional enterprises around the globe, especially in least-reached places.

Investors participate in the Great Commission not only by donating to missions programs but also by strategically investing in missional enterprises around the globe, especially in least-reached places.

One of our most important duties as fiduciaries of God's resources is participating in the Great Commission where Jesus instructs His followers to "go and make disciples of all nations" (Matt. 28:19). We have been trained to do this through going ourselves or by donating to a missions organization to support a missionary who intends to become an incarnational witness to unreached people. But there is more to the directive than going or sending. Kenny Burchard offers a clarifying perspective on the idea of "going":

> The idea here is not "go on a mission trip" or "go somewhere." The participle [*going*] conveys a continuous action that is already happening right now, but that also continues to happen into the future. So, the idea is more like . . . "As you're going along in your life." The great commission is not a verbal command to go. . . . It is a command to disciple as you are already going. Going where? Answer: everywhere.[48]

Businesses, whether local or in a foreign country, are an effective and sustainable method of making disciples *while* we are conducting the normal business of life. It is like "moving into the neighborhood" because through business, we can build deep friendships with our employees, vendors, customers, and community. When we invest in BAM businesses, we seamlessly

48. Kenny Burchard, "Greek-Geeking the Great Commission in Matthew," in *ThinkTheology.org* (Nov 7, 2013): http://thinktheology.org/2013/11/07/greek-geeking-the-great-commission-in-matthew/. Used with permission.

integrate disciple making into the ordinary routines of everyday life. Unfortunately, many Christians believe there is a false dichotomy between what's "sacred" and what's "secular" and that business is secular while mission is sacred. We must shed this understanding. The late Dallas Willard, professor of philosophy at the University of Southern California, states,

> There truly is no division between sacred and secular except what we have created. And that is why the division of legitimate roles and functions of human life into the sacred and the secular does incalculable damage to our individual lives and to the cause of Christ. Holy people must stop going into "church work" as their natural course of action and take up holy orders in farming, industry, law, education, banking and journalism with the same zeal previously given to evangelism or to pastoral and missionary work.[49]

In the same way, we must abandon the misunderstanding that investing is secular and donations are sacred. From the first chapters of Genesis, God's design for human flourishing incorporated the management of resources, an early form of commerce. Business as Mission is not a new concept but rather is rooted in scripture and Christian practice since the Early Church modeled in Acts and in many of the writings of the apostle Paul. Mats Tunehag has written a helpful article clearly arguing that BAM has deep historical roots and a firm biblical foundation.[50] Therefore, capitalization of business through investment must be understood holistically as a necessary and critical part of Great Commission activity.

What Makes a BAM Business Different from Other Businesses?

There is not a single agreed-upon definition of a Missional Business, BAM Enterprise, or Great Commission Company. Some preferred terms are *redemptive business*, *transformational business*, or *spiritual impact business*. Regardless of what it is called, some common principles emerge:

49. Dallas Willard, *The Spirit of the Disciplines: Understanding How God Changes Lives* (NY: HarperCollins, 1988), 214. Used with permission.

50. Mats Tunehag, "Deeply Rooted for the Future" (December 23, 2020): http://matstunehag.com/2020/12/23/deeply-rooted-for-the-future/. See appendix for additional resources.

- They are businesses that are real, not deceptive platforms used to gain access to a "closed country" or "creative access" location. These businesses are profitable and sustainable while also having a clear and intentional focus on facilitating the expansion of God's kingdom "to the ends of the earth" (Acts 1:8).
- They are businesses focused on holistic transformation of individuals and communities through the multiple bottom lines of social, environmental, economic, and spiritual outcomes. These are sometimes called quadruple bottom lines or QBLs. Whether business owners adhere to church planting, disciple making, evangelistic, or incarnational witness strategies, they are concerned about the world's poorest and least-evangelized peoples.

Business as Mission is about reconciling everything broken by the Fall of humankind as described in Genesis. The Bible begins with God creating the world, giving life to Adam and Eve, assigning them tasks, and walking with them in the Garden of Eden. However, in the biblical account of events, this situation does not last very long. Deceived by a serpent, Eve eats the fruit of the forbidden tree, and Adam follows her lead. The result is what is historically called the "Fall" of humankind. The Fall affected social, environmental, economic, and spiritual spheres of human life as the subsequent curses fell upon that which God created "good." This resulted in the need for restoration in four main areas of brokenness:

1. *Social (Human Relationships):* God created Eve because it was not good for Adam to be alone, demonstrating God's intention for us to be in fruitful relationships with each other. With the Fall, relationships fractured and became contentious.

2. *Environmental (Creation):* God created a world that was both healthy and self-healing. It was balanced, integrated, and symbiotic. With the Fall, people's relationship with the rest of creation became antagonistic and exploitative rather than cultivating and nurturing.

3. *Economic (Abundance):* God gave Adam and Eve access to abundant resources for their wellbeing. He told them to be fruitful and multiply. With the Fall, resources became scarce, work became difficult, and business became selfish rather than altruistic.

4. *Spiritual (Connection with God):* Adam and Eve were created to be in a relationship with God. With the Fall, this relationship fractured.

Secular investors have been using the triple bottom line of financial, environmental, and social assessment to evaluate investment impact since the 1970s, but I was introduced to "purpose" as a fourth bottom line in a 2012 blog post by Mats Tunehag. He asked, "How can businesses serve *people*, align with God's *purposes*, be good stewards of the *planet* and make a *profit*?"[51] (emphasis mine). These four areas of people, profit, planet, and purpose align with the spheres of life listed above affected by the Fall:

1. *People (Social):* Addresses our relationships with one another in families, towns, and institutions.

2. *Planet (Environmental):* This is our relation to the natural resources made as part of Creation—resources which we are to steward, on God's behalf, for ourselves and future generations.

3. *Profit (Economic):* Pertains to the provision of goods and services to people. God's instruction to "be fruitful and multiply" applies not only to the reproduction of humankind as a species but also to the multiplication of all resources. Resources can be used, cultivated, multiplied, and traded to meet every need of man and woman, which is the definition of business. Business is about the creation and multiplication of resources to meet needs. Animal husbandry, grafting of fruit trees, creating medicine and vaccinations from natural elements, manufacturing, etc., all find their genesis in the Creation narrative.

4. *Purpose (Spiritual):* Purpose acknowledges our unique relationship with the triune God, our Creator. God's purpose for men and women is that we would bring Him glory (Isa. 43:7), and He invites us into a personal relationship with Him to fulfill that purpose.

51. Mats Tunehag, "Business as Mission: People, Purpose, Planet and Profit" (April 22, 2012): http://matstunehag.com/2012/04/22/business-as-mission-people-purpose-planet-and-profit/. Used with permission.

BAM Businesses Are Part of God's Redemptive Plan

God is on a mission to reconcile these four spheres of brokenness, and business can be a primary way of bringing this about. The apostle Paul reminds us that "God was reconciling the world to himself in Christ, not counting people's sins against them. And he has committed to us the message of reconciliation. We are therefore Christ's ambassadors, as though God were making his appeal through us" (2 Cor. 5:19-20). Investing in redemptive business is an amazing way to be an ambassador for Christ.

> ***Investing in redemptive business is an amazing way to be an ambassador for Christ.***

It is a big mission, and as followers of Christ we should be humbled that we have the privilege of participating in it. Churches everywhere rightly emphasize the spiritual aspect of the world's brokenness, namely our fractured relationship with God. However, there is seldom direct talk about healing the other three areas of brokenness or any acknowledgement that this kind of healing is also part of the mission to which God has called us.

The Business as Mission movement is shining a spotlight on the tremendous oppression that comes through poverty, hunger, lack of safe water, preventable diseases, absence of education, environmental degradation, and other social problems. These reflect the brokenness caused by the Fall, and missional business is uniquely positioned to facilitate healing.

The following story illustrates what an intentionally missional business looks like.

Central Asia, 2008

One critical consideration when making "missional impact investments" is choosing businesses whose owners are like-minded in their desire to use their businesses to expand the kingdom of God. This is a very clear differentiation from Biblically Responsible Investing (BRI), which is primarily reactive, seeking to screen out companies which are involved in activities that compromise Christian values. BAM investors invest in companies that are proactively furthering the kingdom of God through their commercial enterprise. In this context, I prefer to use the term *proactive values investing* (PVI) when creating impactful portfolios for Christians. PVI goes beyond BRI because it not only eliminates investments that offend our moral beliefs but also proactively includes investments that deliberately and intentionally seek to bring prosperity and blessing to all stakeholders. PVI deploys investment capital so that Jesus is purposefully made known and glorified. The following story illustrates how PVI serves to advance God's kingdom.

PVI goes beyond BRI because it not only eliminates investments that offend our moral beliefs but also proactively includes investments that deliberately and intentionally seek to bring prosperity and blessing to all stakeholders. PVI deploys investment capital so that Jesus is purposefully made known and glorified.

In 2008, during my first due diligence visit to a company in Central Asia, I began to build a relationship with the owner to make sure that our interests aligned. To say that he was intimidating when we met the first time is an understatement. This six-foot-six, 220-pound former athlete and mountain rescue climber was himself a mountain of muscle. He established and ran a printing publishing company for over a decade before we met. His company had become the fifth largest printing and publishing company in the country.

We examined the past financial performance of his company, the marketing and sales projections, products, market size, and competition. The development fund I served with was evaluating whether we should extend a four hundred thousand dollar loan to the company for the purchase of a new high-speed, four-color, Ryobi printing press. It was critical that the business could repay such a large loan and, just as important, that the owner was aligned with our objective of seeing the name of Jesus lifted up in a land where His name is rarely spoken. His response to the following question would indicate confirmation that he was "like-minded":

"If we help you buy a high-speed color printing press, what will be the most profitable use for that equipment?" I asked.

After thinking for a moment, my new friend responded that the most profitable use for that equipment would be to produce vodka labels and cigarette packaging. Then there was silence.

Had I traveled more than six thousand miles in thirty-six hours to invest in a business that wants to print *vodka labels* and *cigarette cartons*? Was this going to be the shortest meeting of my life in one of the most distant places to which I had ever traveled? I could invest in many companies back home and achieve the same results!

Following the long pause, however, a smile cracked the corner of his mouth, and he continued: "We will not be using the machine to make lovely vodka labels or tobacco packages. Doing such a thing would contradict with our belief that these products take advantage of people's addictions and that they are harmful to people and society. Our desire is to honor Christ with our printing."

He then explained his strategy. With the new Ryobi printing press, he could become the highest quality printer in Central Asia. He laid out a business plan for printing magazines that needed to have Western-quality, perfect-color shading on quality materials—periodicals such as bridal magazines, cosmetic brochures, and travel advertisements needing impeccable color tones. He explained that he was already in negotiations with both interior design and architectural magazine publishers, and he was on the verge of signing a contract with the government to print the first full-color, national encyclopedia for this country. These projects would provide similar or even better profit potential as printing vodka labels without compromising his Christian values.

Even more, his commitment to developing an upstanding company went even deeper and connected with the vision of a BAM company. While fifty percent of the company production time would be allocated to profitable business, the remaining production time would be used for printing Christian literature at cost and without profit (printing Christian literature was a legal enterprise in this country, and this business partnered with other organizations for the distribution of the literature). The result was a modestly profitable business that could simultaneously repay a loan and have a profound impact for the kingdom of God.

(On a side note, the owner of this company eventually became one of my closest friends—his daughter lived at our home for several months during the revolution and coup which took place in their country in 2010, we have vacationed together, and I became his de facto English tutor when we worked side by side for several months in Alaska.)

Investing in a business like this makes perfect sense to me when I consider my role as a fiduciary of God's resources. Sure, PVI presents a higher risk than investing in a stock or mutual fund at home. Sure, there could be a revolution; the borders could be closed, currency could freeze up, economic activity could collapse. In fact, all these things did occur. But, over the twenty years the business operated, it printed nearly eighty percent of all Bibles and other Christian literature in that region of the world, making hundreds of thousands of Bibles available in languages spoken in countries where Bibles must be smuggled. The business also repaid its entire loan faithfully as the Lord provided after the revolution was complete and business could be restored.

None of this was easy. In fact, there were many threats to the business, threats you would never need to think about if you simply invested the way your financial planner suggests. One night I forwarded the following email to my friends in America, asking them to pray for this business and for the safety of my friend, his wife, and his family. Several people responded to my prayer request wanting verification of its authenticity because it sounded like spam. Here is the email:

> *To: Undisclosed Recipients*
>
> *Subject: Urgent prayer request*
>
> *Dear friends:*
>
> *Please pray for AS now. For the past several months an angry neighbor with high political influence has been trying to have the business shut down. The neighbor used his influence to have every government agency called in to find fault (frequently bribed to do so). In October they hired armed guards to storm our building during the night shift with automatic weapons. The goal was to threaten and to scare our workers. All those efforts failed since no infraction was found by any of the government agencies. Last night things took a new turn. The neighbor hired a band of 30-40 ruffians/thugs and armed with submachine guns and Molotov Cocktails (bottles filled with gas), they came to S's house (just 50 meters from AS) and threatened to burn his house down if he did not stop the presses. The police were called in, but they did nothing to stop the mob, so there was no choice but to give in to their demands.*

Please pray for wisdom, peace, protection, love, and for God to get the glory and for his kingdom to continue to expand through the good news literature that we print. Especially pray for the personal safety of S and his wife E and his family.

-j-

PS – Today was the final day of an intensive 2-month course on "good news" translation. More details on that later…too busy now with urgent things to write.

(Sent: Friday, March 28, 2014, 2:47 p.m.)

(The postscript may be one of the most interesting aspects of the email since, over the years, distraction, disruption, conflict, illness, and calamity have frequently occurred just at the most critical time when presses were running to complete a major Bible printing or a Christian literature publishing project.)

Ask yourself, *Have you ever needed to pray about problems like this concerning your current portfolio options?*

What Will Influence a Culture More, Donations or "Moving into the Neighborhood"?

Christians tend to think that the only way they need to support God's purposes is through donations. In contrast, other religions and cultures gain influence in a society by investing in business and education which results in political influence and, ultimately, large-scale cultural impact.

I have come to agree with my friend who has lived in Central Asia since 1994. He says that for the most part, Christian organizations which seek to influence the culture have shown up underfunded, ill-prepared, and without a unified strategy. On the other hand, Muslims have come with significant financial resources and a long-term plan to gain influence in business, education, and politics.

I could clearly see in the span of ten years that the largest university, largest automobile dealership, largest hotel, largest manufacturer, and largest mosque have all been built in this city with financial investments and subsidies from the Middle East. The resulting change in the young adult culture is evident as they realize the best path to success and financial improvement is to attend the

Turkish University and to get a job that is sponsored by one of the large Middle Eastern companies.

Vision is having well-formed goals, an absolute necessity to anybody who is trying to accomplish anything. "Where there is no vision, the people perish" (Prov. 29:18, KJV). I must again agree with my friend when he says that many times it appears as though Western Christians have small vision, especially in contrast to Muslim influencers. Perhaps part of the reason that Christian missional projects are frequently disjointed and often small is due to a lack of collaboration, no unified strategy, or insufficient capital. Business as Mission strategies provide solutions to those deficiencies and open opportunities for larger, clearer vision.

In Proverbs 29:18, "perish" is the Hebrew word *yip·pā·ra'*, which connotes a feeling of unrestrained wildness,[52] like long hair blown in the wind. Strategic investment requires collaboration with shared vision and unified strategy. It cannot be wild and appear to be blowing in the wind without restraint. BAM businesses are demonstrating stable vision and strategy, integrating the principles of the Great Commission with their commitment to bringing reconciliation and restoration in social, economic, environmental, and spiritual spheres. It is time for like-minded PVI investors to join them.

CONCLUSION

Where are the Christian investors who willingly deploy resources to gain similar influence in the education, business, and politics of unreached countries? When will we learn to work collaboratively and invest strategically on a large scale to build the kingdom of God in difficult frontier markets?

> ***Let's "move into the neighborhood."***

As God's *oikonomos*, fiduciaries of His resources, do we consider the possibility of financial loss too risky? It seems risky if we are thinking that the resources are ours and to be used for our personal comfort, pleasure, and security. But, if we are serious about our duty to bring the Gospel to the least-reached areas of the world, there is no more effective or sustainable solution than making large-scale investments in businesses that can and will influence their local societies. Let's "move into the neighborhood."

52. https://biblehub.com/proverbs/29-18.htm#lexicon

QUESTIONS FOR STUDY

1. Consider the Great Commission mandate in Matthew 28:19: "[G]o and make disciples of all nations." In your faith community, what initiatives are generally considered Great Commission endeavors?

2. Discuss the perspective shared from Kenny Burchard on the idea of "going": "The participle [*going*] conveys a continuous action that is already happening right now, but that also continues to happen into the future. So, the idea is more like . . . 'As you're going along in your life.' The great commission is not a verbal command to go. . . . It is a command to disciple as you are already going. Going where? Answer: everywhere."

3. How can businesses be a tool that can serve God's purpose for making disciples while we are going about the normal affairs of life?

4. What makes something sacred and what makes something secular in God's eyes? Cite a biblical text to support your answer.

5. How might a Christian-owned business differ from a missional business? How might they be similar? How might stakeholders perceive the difference, if there is one?

6. Reflect on the brokenness resulting from the “Fall” of humankind in the Garden of Eden. What four main areas of brokenness ensued? Can business serve God’s purpose in the restoration of *shalom* in each of these areas? If so, how?

7. What will influence a culture more, donations or “moving into the neighborhood”? Why?

8. After reading this chapter, how might you reconsider your willingness to deploy resources to gain influence in the education, business, and politics of unreached countries?

9. How can Christian investors use PVI to collaboratively and strategically invest on a large scale to build the kingdom of God in difficult frontier markets? What risks do these investments pose?

10. How ready are you to “move into the neighborhood” with a deep, intimate, passionate concern (*yada*) for the world’s poorest and least evangelized peoples through business ownership as an investor?

Chapter 6

PLANTING TREES

Society grows great when people plant trees whose shade they know they shall never sit in.

THE REAL JOHNNY APPLESEED[53]

Nova, Ohio, is home to a nearly two-century-old tree, the last known tree to be planted by Johnny Appleseed. It produces small, tart, green apples, unlike ones found in grocery stores today. They were not grown for eating but for baking and making hard cider. Since dangerous bacteria polluted water on the frontier, cider gave the settlers something safe to drink.

A hero of American folklore, Johnny Appleseed was said to be a barefoot wanderer who wore a tin pot for a hat and carried a sack of apples. His legend testifies that he would leave a "start of trees" everywhere he went. Unlike Paul Bunyan and Babe, the Blue Ox, who are tall-tale fictions, Appleseed's legacy descends from a very real

53. All information on Johnny Appleseed was taken from the following sources: Killingsworth Environmental, "Behind the Rhyme: The True Story Of Johnny Appleseed" (September 25, 2018), https://thebiggreenk.com/johnny-appleseed/; Kristy Punchko, "9 Facts That Tell the True Story of Johnny Appleseed" (September 26, 2017): https://www.mentalfloss.com/article/62113/9-facts-tell-true-story-johnny-appleseed; "Johnny Appleseed" (May 20, 2014): https://www.biography.com/historical-figure/johnny-appleseed; https://1812blockhouse.com/history-tourism/the-legacy-of-what-may-be-the-last-johnny-appleseed-planted-tree/.

person named John Chapman, and his real life was far richer and more interesting than his legend. Chapman would likely be glad to see his seeds still bearing fruit nearly two hundred years later.

Chapman traveled widely, particularly in Pennsylvania and Ohio, pursuing his profession. While the legend of Johnny Appleseed suggests that his planting was random, there was actually a firm economic basis for Chapman's behavior. He established nurseries and returned, after several years, to sell off the orchard and the surrounding land.

In addition to being an entrepreneur, planting, growing, and selling his trees, he was devoutly religious. As a missionary for the "New Church" (also known as the Church of Swedenborg), he often stayed in people's homes, reading Bible stories and sharing his faith. His life demonstrated environmental stewardship, social goodness, and spiritual enlightenment for early American settlers. He seamlessly integrated his vocation and ministry, an admirable example for us. (However, while I do see his life as a teaching model, I do not endorse the theology of the Swedenborg Church).

There is no way to determine exactly how many millions of seeds he planted in the hundreds of nurseries he created in the territory south of the Great Lakes and between the Ohio and Mississippi Rivers, with some seedlings probably even traveling across the plains in covered wagons to western states. By some estimates, in forty-five years he planted more than twenty bushels of seeds, with each bushel containing an estimated three hundred thousand seeds, resulting in over six million apple trees during his lifetime. This was his service to God and to people.

Johnny Appleseed planted millions of trees whose shade he would never sit under and whose apples he would never eat. He invested his time, his expertise, and his resources for growth and compounding, not for himself but for the benefit of future beneficiaries. He understood his role as a fiduciary of God's resources, and he invested for eternity. He stewarded resources for the glory of God, and the blessings of his efforts extended to individuals, communities, and the new nation.

BIBLICAL CALL FOR GENEROUS SOWING OF FINANCIAL RESOURCES

Chapman's real-life story illustrates the apostle Paul's teaching on sowing and reaping in 2 Corinthians 9:6-10 where he says, "Whoever sows sparingly will also reap sparingly, and whoever sows generously will also reap generously" (v. 6). Paul's agricultural analogy helps us understand his beliefs concerning where our financial resources come from and how they ought to be deployed. Like a farmer, a generous giver/investor depends on God from start to finish: "[H]e who supplies seed to the sower and bread for food will also supply and increase your store of seed and will enlarge the harvest of your righteousness" (v. 10). God provides not only for the farmer's immediate physical needs in the form of a harvest of grain for his daily bread but also for his future needs in the form of seed for next year's planting.

Since God routinely does this for the farmer, He is surely able to do the same for us, as businesspeople and as investors, provided we seek to serve as His fiduciaries. God supplies our seed (investment) and even increases it so that we can be generous on every occasion (vv. 10-11). We should not assume that the increase is for improving our personal standard of living or indulging our own appetites. The term Paul uses for "generous" is *haplotes* which denotes the singleness of a noble character, a pure heart, or a sincere intent.[54] It signifies open heartedness with our possessions, the perfect opposite of self-indulgence.

God provides not only for the farmer's immediate physical needs in the form of a harvest of grain for his daily bread but also for his future needs in the form of seed for next year's planting.

The general principle is the more we sow generously for God's purposes, the greater the harvest will be—not for our own benefit but *so that* an increasing harvest of righteousness will be achieved. Applying these principles to us as investors, the more assets we thoughtfully and prudently deploy for kingdom purposes, the more profitable the eternal harvest will be.

You may have been taught previously that the seed (your assets) must be protected for next year's harvest (future growth opportunities). Christian investors or businesspeople are typically the first to express concern over deploying too much seed, thinking that they must be "good stewards," protecting the seed so that it can grow more crops in the future. The thinking goes that if you give

54. https://www.biblegateway.com/resources/commentaries/IVP-NT/2Cor/Results-Generous-Giving

away too much, you will not have resources to produce more income in the future, crippling future donations.

While this reasoning may have some value relative to excessive donations, I would argue that God supplies the resources for us to give, and this line of thinking is not relevant to the concept of *investing* in missional enterprises. The act of investing itself is a valid way of planting seed for future harvest. Although investing in impactful frontier market businesses carries higher risk of financial loss than traditional investments, with proper business planning and accountability it is possible to achieve financial return in addition to the social, spiritual, and environmental impact so desperately needed in our world. So, investing in this way does not necessarily deplete the "seed" in the same way that donations might. Missional investments, in fact, should grow and multiply themselves, recycling financial resources continually so that impact is achieved over decades or centuries, not just a single time as most charitable donations do.

Missional investments, in fact, should grow and multiply themselves, recycling financial resources continually so that impact is achieved over decades or centuries, not just a single time as most charitable donations do.

THE COVENANT FUNNEL

Accumulating wealth and passing it on through the generations has been the historical pattern of investing. Dynasty families grew their estate and investment holdings then consolidated the wealth and property to transfer it to the next generation, with the firstborn male child often receiving special privileges. Prominent among those privileges was a double portion of the estate as an inheritance and the father's blessing. Great families of wealth were created and sustained in this way.

Abraham is an excellent biblical example. Historically, similar inheritance practices were followed by the Caesars of Rome, the Tudors, Rothschilds, Vanderbilts, Kennedys, and many others. These families amassed great wealth and focused the transfer of wealth to subsequent generations with the express purpose of preserving the dynasty. Many Americans take the same view of their wealth and savings. Granted, few Americans have the same kind of wealth to pass on as the examples I have cited, but, whatever we do have, we hold with the same fervor as these famous dynasties.

One of my greatest concerns is that believers in the American Church are trained to take a similar perspective with our financial planning. We save, store, and invest to protect ourselves or make our families "self-sufficient." We strive to preserve our standard of living by building retirement nest eggs, 401(k) plans, portfolios, and bank accounts so that we can achieve financial independence and then pass it on to the next generation. It is not unusual for these practices to define our understanding of "stewardship" in contrast to a biblical understanding of the role of the Lord's *oikonomos*.

One of my close friends uses the term *covenant funnel* to describe the difference between the cultural system of wealth accumulation for generational transfer and a biblical model for handling financial resources. Over and over the text of scripture shows us a new understanding for how Christians should handle wealth accumulation and transfer. Rather than a two-step process of amassing wealth and passing it to the next generation, scripture adds a third important step for believers, telling us that we are blessed with resources so that we can be a blessing to others. God's blessing comes to us in a variety of ways with financial blessing being one of the most obvious. Our call is to allow God's resources, especially financial, to flow through us and not get stuck in our hands.

We are blessed with resources so that we can be a blessing to others.

It is very clear that God's covenant with Abraham forever changed the idea of wealth accumulation. The writer of Genesis tells us, "Now the Lord said to Abram, 'Go from your country and your kindred and your father's house to the land that I will show you. And I will make of you a great nation, and I will bless you and make your name great, *so that you will be a blessing*'" (Gen. 12:1-2, ESV, emphasis mine). The purpose of God's blessing in our own lives is *so that* we can funnel God's resources to be a blessing to others.

Additional verses illustrating this principle include Genesis 41:56-57, in which Joseph stored up grain during times of abundance *so that* Egypt became a blessing to other nations. Malachi 3:5 tells us the Lord will testify against those who deprive the vulnerable of fair wages and justice and those who do not bring blessing with financial resources. Likewise, Jesus warns in Matthew 6:19-21 to not store up treasure on earth, because our hearts are always drawn to where we invest financially.

Eugene Petersen paraphrases 2 Corinthians 9:12-13 in this way to describe our responsibility to use financial resources to bring blessing:

> Carrying out this social relief work involves far more than helping meet the bare needs of poor Christians. . . . This relief offering is a prod to live at your very best, showing your gratitude to God by being openly obedient to the plain meaning of the Message of Christ. You show your gratitude through your generous offerings to your needy brothers and sisters, and really toward everyone. (2 Cor. 9:12-15, MSG)

Investing, not donating, is the most effective method for bringing perpetual and sustainable blessing to those who are in need and to bring the Gospel to those who have not heard it. Dallas Willard states,

> People who have assimilated the character of Christ into all areas of life and society…clearly see that giving is only a part and by no means the largest part of stewardship before our Lord. [They] understand it is part of their responsibility to control the world's possessions in a way that ministers to all.[55]

The best way to alleviate poverty in the long term and to bring restoration to broken communities is through vibrant Christian businesses that shine the light of the Gospel and bring healing and blessing.

The Bible issues a stark warning to us through the apostle John's words to the Church at Laodicea, which applies very well to many contemporary Christian investors:

> I know your deeds, that you are neither cold nor hot. I wish you were either one or the other! So, because you are lukewarm—neither hot nor cold—I am about to spit you out of my mouth. You say, "I am rich; I have acquired

55. Dallas Willard, *The Spirit of the Disciplines*, p. 214. Used with permission.

> wealth and do not need a thing." But you do not realize that you are wretched, pitiful, poor, blind and naked. (Rev. 3:15-17)

It is not wrong or evil to have wealth. However, seeking to accumulate wealth for our own indulgence, comfort, and security so that we can say, "I do not need a thing because I am financially independent," seems to be the character flaw that John warns against. We are, in fact, managing God's resources as His fiduciaries. Therefore, we must look beyond our temporal goals and set our eyes on eternal outcomes by bringing the good news to all nations. Is it possible that when we focus on our own financial goals rather than addressing the material injustices and spiritual poverty around us that we are poor and blind? We are temporary managers of the resources that He puts in our hands. They are to be used for His glory and His eternal purposes such as furthering His kingdom and bringing blessing to the nations. As God's *oikonomos*, our investments need to look more like Johnny Appleseed's investments which continue to bring blessings two centuries later—not only to his own family but to communities across North America.

A JOYOUS PORTFOLIO

I have heard preachers use the acronym J.O.Y. to describe the order of priorities in our lives, with J = Jesus, O = Others, and Y = Yourself. They conclude that a joy-filled life is one that puts Jesus first, others second, and yourself third. If you look at your portfolio in this light, would it be a JOYous one, honoring and proclaiming Jesus as its first and most important priority, then seeking to bring blessings to others as its second priority, leaving you to benefit as the third priority? If you are like most investors, your portfolio probably reflects the opposite order. We are schooled to believe that the top priority for investing is seeking personal gain, to bring blessing to ourselves by increasing our wealth, or to derive a steady income for retirement. A minority of investors make "doing good" a second priority by instituting social, environmental, or even biblical screens to promote blessing or at least to avoid doing harm. Few investors consider how their investments can be used to accomplish Great Commission outcomes or to lift up the name of Jesus in places where His name is rarely spoken.

Few investors consider how their investments can be used to accomplish Great Commission outcomes or to lift up the name of Jesus in places where His name is rarely spoken.

When we save and invest, we should ask ourselves the following difficult questions:

- Am I making this financial decision to gain self-sufficiency, or do I have a plan for how my savings will ultimately be used to bless others?
- Do I seek to minimize support of companies that oppose my core beliefs?
- Do I consider what investments are available that will have a direct impact on blessing others and building the kingdom of God?
- When I consider passing my wealth to the next generation, do I factor in my children's ability to steward the resources as fiduciaries of God's assets?
- Keeping in mind that being a fiduciary is a job, much like the CFO of a business, I need to remind myself that few CFO positions automatically pass to a son or daughter. Has God entrusted me with resources to bring blessing to others now or automatically pass that responsibility to the next generation?
- There is overwhelming human suffering around the globe and billions who have not yet followed Jesus as their Savior. Is God trusting me with resources that can be deployed now for His kingdom, while I am alive?

Here is an example of a modern-day business that has an eternal view toward blessing.

Highland Harvesters: Growing Apples to Grow People

Highland Harvesters (HH) is an agribusiness that grows and processes fruit for the flourishing of people and communities across Ethiopia. It was established in 2014 in southern Ethiopia, near the town of Chencha. They have planted over forty-eight thousand apple trees of many varieties that can be grown in the highlands of southern Ethiopia.

The nation of Ethiopia is incredibly diverse. With the second highest population in Africa, it contains 123 unique people groups speaking eighty-six individual languages. The southern region is the most diverse and arguably least developed, both economically and spiritually. Fifty-two tribes live in this region, and most of the thirty-four unreached people groups in Ethiopia are found here. Extreme poverty and conflict characterize most of their history.

While still having some of the highest poverty rates in the world, Ethiopia has experienced some of the highest economic growth in recent years. This has led to significant poverty reduction for the country, but wealth has not been distributed equally. Urban dwellers have tripled incomes and gained access to more and more basic human services, but the rural poor have become poorer and still lack access to basic human necessities such as safe water and food.

In this context of extreme poverty, conflict, and spiritual darkness, Highland Harvesters started the first commercial apple orchard in Ethiopia. The orchard is located at an intersection of three people groups: the Bele (*bay-lay*), the Dorze (*door-zay*), and the Shamma. These groups have fought against one another for generations, with their oral histories consisting primarily of accounts of conflicts against one another. They each live in extreme poverty. The Bele people, being the most impoverished and least developed, still lack access to electricity, safe water, roads, and basic health services in their village.

HH was established for the express purpose of supporting these three tribes economically, socially, and spiritually. HH secured a long-term renewable lease through the Ethiopian government and received 31.5 hectares of land that was previously the killing fields, the site of numerous battles and bloodshed between these three tribes. HH envisions reconciliation, forgiveness, and prosperity taking root in this community. The shoots and buds of restoration are already becoming visible as members of all three tribes now work together, planting and cultivating apple trees as well as reading the Bible and worshiping together in the orchard.

Economic Impact: HH's agriculture experts employ and train rural Ethiopian women and men to operate a sustainable agribusiness which produces food, alleviating hunger and providing economic benefit to the country. They have a permanent staff of forty-seven plus one hundred seasonal workers. The main orchard will produce hundreds of tons of apples each year and establish a market for Ethiopian-grown apples. Highland Harvesters is training and equipping smaller family orchards with current best practices for pruning and growing to increase the yield and revenue for local farmers. In time HH will build, scale, and grow a supply chain so that logistics will be more beneficial for local farmers.

Social Impact: In the words of one manager, "We use apples to grow people." Some of HH's social impact goals are poverty reduction and improved access to basic needs such as safe water, education, and health services. Food shortages and malnutrition reign supreme in Ethiopia. Agribusiness has the potential to have a huge impact on the health and well-being of the people. Employment opportunities are scarce in this rural area, and orchards require large numbers of unskilled laborers so job creation will lead to more vibrant, growing rural communities.

In 2020 Ethiopia experienced locust infestations and weather abnormalities of biblical magnitude, causing severe famine. HH provided direct food support to alleviate some of the pain during this difficult time, and they continue to work diligently to quell the age-old conflicts between the Bele, Dorze, and Shamma tribes. The farm is neutral ground where members of the different tribes can work alongside one another, breaking down the historical negative prejudices they hold.

The farm is neutral ground where members of the different tribes can work alongside one another, breaking down the historical negative prejudices they hold.

Environmental Impact: Although much of Ethiopia has experienced disastrous environmental damage over the past few decades, HH strives to be an example for healthy land stewardship for the entire country. HH leased thirty-one hectares of land and set about clearing the scrub brush and unproductive trees to make space for more environmentally friendly and productive apple trees. Orchard management seeks to protect and add value to the local land by stewarding it for health and productivity. Irrigation, soil management, and terraced planting to prevent erosion are rejuvenating what was previously unproductive wasteland.

Spiritual Impact: The southern highlands of Ethiopia continue to be the home to Africa's highest concentration of unreached people groups (UPG). Youth With a Mission (YWAM) describes UPG in this way: "An Unreached People Group (UPG) is a group of people that have very few, if any, local believers. This group has their own language, culture, worldview, and ways of behaving. They may have heard the gospel. A few people might have even become Christians. But they can't reach the rest of their own people group without outside help."[56]

Employees are the lifeblood of Highland Harvesters' business and ministry. As previously noted, the orchard employs people from the Bele, Dorze, and Shamma tribes. The Dorze people are an unreached people group, and Shamma people have a small Christian presence but are largely "unreached." HH has strong influence in these communities, and, as they add more employees, their spiritual influence continues to grow. Workers at Highland Harvesters start each workday with devotions and prayer, led by one of the Christian managers. In addition, the management team hosts a smaller group devotion twice a week, and all employees are invited to participate in a weekly Bible study focused on discipleship. Twice a year, HH hosts a half-day-long Fellowship Day with speakers, worship, games, fun, and plenty of food for everyone. It is a wonderful celebration for the families and the entire community.

Highland Harvesters and its investors are a living picture of people who plant trees whose shade they know they will never sit in. Knowing that it takes at least five years before an apple tree sapling grows to where it can start producing fruit, their investment horizon is a long one, extending to "when the Lord returns." Building an orchard with tens of thousands of trees, irrigation, cleaning and processing facilities, cold storage, and distribution infrastructure is not easy and demands a long-term perspective. The risks are high. Drought, floods, war, pestilence, and disease are all problems that have already occurred. An investor who is seeking to increase their own personal net worth will likely determine that this investment carries too much risk. But for God's fiduciary, seeking to see the name of Jesus lifted high among people who have great need and who have not yet heard the Gospel, this seems like a great investment. Johnny Appleseed couldn't have known that one of his trees would still be producing fruit centuries later. Similarly, whether the Lord returns tomorrow or centuries from now, the lands of Highland Harvesters

56. "Definition of an Unreached People Group (UPG)": https://www.ywamfrontiermissions.com/unreached-people-groups/what-is-an-unreached-people-group-upg/#:~:text=Definition%20Of%20An%20Unreached%20People%20Group%20(UPG)&text=For%20short%2C%20these%20groups%20are,may%20have%20heard%20the%20gospel. Public domain.

could be producing apples and bringing blessing to the people of the southern Ethiopia highlands.

CONCLUSION

Planting trees whose shade I will never sit under requires surrender of my own goals. It requires sacrifice. "He who sows sparingly will also reap sparingly, and he who sows generously will also reap generously" (2 Cor. 9:6-7). I am inspired by the example of missionaries who, over one hundred years ago, literally packed their belongings into their own coffin, knowing they would likely come home "horizontally, not vertically." These brave souls were sowing seeds of the Gospel in sub-Saharan Africa, a region known in the missionary community as the "White Mans [sic] Graveyard" due to the high mortality rate of Western missionaries from malaria, yellow fever, and other fatal diseases.[57]

Sowers of seeds in this region eventually established the Sudan Interior Mission (SIM), and the following excerpt from Walter Gowan, one of the founders of SIM, from a last letter sent home to his mother, tells the story of a man committed to the work at hand with the full knowledge he'd never see the fruit. Dying of malaria in August of 1894, he said this:

> *Written in view of my approaching end, which has often lately seemed so near but just now seems so imminent, I want to write while I have the power to do it.*
>
> *Well Glory to God! He has enabled me to make a hard fight for the Soudan [sic] and although it may seem like a total failure and defeat it is not! We shall have the victory & that right speedily.*[58]

Are you ready to plant some trees?

Gowan did not see immediate fruit or harvest, but today, over one hundred years later, almost half of all Nigerians (the modern-day nation where SIM established its first base) are Christians. That's 95.4 million people.

A wise person plants trees whose shade he or she will never sit under. A wise person invests for eternal outcomes that he or she will never see in this life.

Are you ready to plant some trees?

57. Lenny Miles, "Pack Your Coffins....Let's Go!" (Posted: April 10, 2013): https://milesinmissions.wordpress.com/2013/04/10/pack-your-coffins-lets-go/. Used with permission.

58. Lenny Miles, "Pack Your Coffins." Used with permission.

QUESTIONS FOR STUDY

1. Was Johnny Appleseed the legend, named John Chapman, a businessman or a missionary?

2. Read 2 Corinthians 9:6-11. Who supplies the seed for the sower, and who provides the increase? What purpose has God indicated for the increase? Explain how these principles apply to God's fiduciary.

3. Compare the above teaching with financial educators who teach that preservation of capital and seeking personal gain is the utmost priority for investors. What challenge does the author make to traditional financial wisdom regarding "stewardship" in contrast to a biblical understanding of the Lord's "*oikonomos*"?

4. What is the three-step process of the "covenant funnel," and how does this differ from secular generational transfer of wealth? Does God's purpose in blessing Abraham (Genesis 12:1-2) differ from His purpose blessing you with financial resources?

5. Why did Jesus warn His followers in Matthew 6:19-21 not to store up treasures on earth?

6. Discuss your view regarding investing and donating as effective methods for bringing blessing and the Gospel to those in need. What does the following statement made by Dallas Willard mean to you: "[P]eople who have assimilated the character of Christ into all areas of life and society…clearly see that giving is only a part and by no means the largest part of stewardship before our Lord. [They] understand it is part of their responsibility to control the world's possessions in a way that ministers to all."

7. Has anyone ever challenged you with the idea that when you save and invest you should ask yourself several difficult questions to test your motivations and your obligation as God's fiduciary, questions such as,

   a. Am I investing to gain self-sufficiency or with a plan for how my savings will ultimately be used to bless others with Great Commission outcomes as a priority?

   b. Have I selected righteous businesses and excluded wicked businesses in my investments?

   c. Are there available investments that seek the prosperity of others and build the kingdom of God?

d. Am I properly planning for the transfer of my wealth?

e. Is God trusting me with resources that should be deployed for His kingdom now while I am alive, or are resources getting stuck in my hands?

8. In the narrative about Highland Harvesters, what significant issues were revealed that might cause a fiduciary to choose to invest or not to invest in this business?

9. The ancient proverb repeated in this chapter is summarized, "Society grows great when people plant trees whose shade they know they shall never sit in." Eugene Peterson's *The Message* paraphrases Galatians 6:7-8 as follows: "Don't be misled: No one makes a fool of God. What a person plants, he will harvest. The person who plants selfishness, ignoring the needs of others—ignoring God! —harvests a crop of weeds. All he'll have to show for his life is weeds! But the one who plants in response to God, letting God's Spirit do the growth work in him, harvests a crop of real life, eternal life." Are you ready to plant some trees?

Chapter 7

A DANGEROUS PRAYER

Do not be daunted by the enormity of the world's grief. Do justly, now. Love mercy, now. Walk humbly, now. You are not obligated to complete the work, but neither are you free to abandon it.[59]

I PRAYED A DANGEROUS PRAYER

I vividly remember the afternoon many years ago—a bright, sunny, hot day, unusual for Upstate New York where I live. Because we need to make the most of such rare, beautiful days, I was on my riding mower cutting our lawn. Mowing is one of my favorite activities because it is one of the few things in my life that I can work on and finish (at least until the next week). It's also a time when I can listen to music, sermons, or audiobooks undisturbed for several hours. On this day, I was listening to a series about Nehemiah and leadership.

Nehemiah's story, about the rebuilding of Jerusalem in the mid-fifth century BC, took place while Nehemiah was cupbearer to King

59. This quote is often attributed to the *Talmud* but is more accurately described as a loose translation of a commentary on a portion of the *Pirke Avot*, which is itself a commentary on Micah 6:8. See *Wisdom of the Jewish Sages: A Modern Reading of Pirke Avot* by Rabbi Rami Shapiro, (December 7, 2020), https://inwardoutward.org/do-not-be-daunted-dec-7-2020/.

Artaxerxes I. Over one hundred fifty years earlier, Nebuchadnezzar and the armies of Babylon had invaded Israel and carried many of the Jewish people into slavery. Eventually the Jewish people were given the opportunity to return to Jerusalem, but not all of them did. The temple at Jerusalem had been destroyed and needed to be rebuilt, but the Jewish community was dispirited and defenseless against its non-Jewish neighbors. Hanani, one of Nehemiah's brothers, had recently returned from Judah, and Nehemiah questioned him about the Jewish remnant and Jerusalem itself. Distressed at news of the desolate condition of Jerusalem, Nehemiah obtained permission from Artaxerxes to journey to the land of Israel to help rebuild its ruined structures. The king granted him permission, legal documents, a royal escort, and the title "governor" to guarantee the assistance of Persian officials. Nehemiah journeyed to Jerusalem and alerted the people to the necessity of repopulating the city and rebuilding its walls. Nehemiah encountered hostility, but under his direction, the Jews succeeded in rebuilding Jerusalem's walls in only fifty-two days.

Usually we are amazed by Nehemiah's leadership skills and how he successfully persuaded the discouraged Jews to rally and accomplish an amazing feat. But what struck me that day was Nehemiah's reaction when he first heard the desperate news about Jerusalem. The text says that Hanani told his brother that their people were "in great trouble and disgrace. The wall of Jerusalem is broken down, and its gates have been burned with fire," and when Nehemiah heard these things, he "*sat down and wept*" (Neh. 1:3-4, emphasis mine).

I am not an emotional person. I don't cry often, so the words struck at my core. I continued to mow but paused, then replayed the audio several times, listening to Nehemiah's response. I eventually shut off the lawnmower and asked myself if I cared about anything enough to sit down and cry. Sure, I love my wife and kids and family, and I will cry when they are hurt or in great need, but is there anything that I would cry about simply because it matters to God? Do I care that much about anyone else's needs? Do I care about orphans or widows or people who lack enough healthy food to stay alive? How about girls who are exploited or the vulnerable in society or any of the other many things that God cares about? Do I care enough about the lost—those who do not know Jesus—to sit down and weep?

The answer was simple: I don't think so.

I had heard about situations and people in desperate need. I had learned about the unreached people groups of the world and, with my wife, had generously funded many missionaries and mission projects. I had attended the Perspectives™ on the World Christian Movement course on world missions. I had been on missions trips and visited poor countries, but none of these experiences had ever forced me to sit down and cry. As I resumed mowing the lawn, I began to weep. Why was my heart so hard that I hadn't cried for the things that broke God's heart? I realized at that moment that if I'm consumed by the cares of my own life, I don't have time to care—really, deeply, honestly, and painfully care about the issues that God is passionate about.

I prayed in response to this realization, *Lord, break my heart for the things that break Your heart.* Unlike Nehemiah I didn't fast and pray in the days following this experience, but I did repeat that simple prayer every day for months, maybe even a year, until I began to feel God's sadness and pain.

It has been years since that afternoon encounter with Nehemiah, and still God continues to answer that prayer by continually stirring a passion for the most vulnerable and least reached. The prayer challenged my status quo, my contentment with all that I have, and my complacency about serious problems around the globe. There is a bubble around many Americans that allows us to disregard less fortunate parts of the world. Perhaps you have heard the saying, "When America sneezes, the world catches a cold," which aptly captures not only our influence on the world but also our ignorance and indifference concerning the world's troubles. Consumed with my own life, my own issues, and my own problems, I was no different.

It took time for God to soften my heart, but now I cry when I hear stories of those who are lost without access to the Gospel, especially when they live in harsh and hostile situations. However, the emotion is only the first step. Once your heart begins to break for the things that break God's heart, you can't sit back and do nothing. You are compelled to take uncomfortable and sacrificial action. It is not enough to just post about the plight, we must do something. American Christians have great mountains of resources that are rarely deployed to alleviate the physical and spiritual poverty that exist in other parts of our world. We are not obligated to fix every problem, but neither are we free to ignore them.

My story is not an isolated example. I have talked to many men and women around the world who have had similar experiences that shook them to their core and broke their hearts for the things that break God's heart. Sometimes it is an unexpected life-threatening illness that causes a successful businessman or woman to take inventory of what really matters in life. Perhaps it is a cross-cultural experience that reveals the face of poverty or makes the brokenness experienced by those who are lost without a savior real. In the absence of such a heart change, it is difficult to persuade an investor to use their hard-earned savings to help those in need.

The prayer asking God to break my heart for the things that break His heart has launched me on a sacrificial journey with my family, faith, and funds that I never would have experienced if I followed my own advice as a financial advisor. I pray that you will willingly offer the same prayer and let God's answers dangerously threaten your status quo.

The prayer asking God to break my heart for the things that break His heart has launched me on a sacrificial journey with my family, faith, and funds that I never would have experienced if I followed my own advice as a financial advisor

A FREEDOM BUSINESS IN NEPAL

As part of my role serving with a Christian economic development fund, I sometimes visit businesses that the fund invests in. A few years ago, I decided to learn more about the scourge of human trafficking and the exploitation of young girls while also seeking examples of successful economic solutions available to break the cycle. The fund made an investment in a business in Nepal that works with both survivors and those at risk of human trafficking. These types of businesses are called freedom businesses and exist to fight human trafficking or exploitation. I know that Jesus weeps at this situation, and I wanted my heart to break along with His.

If possible, I try to include family members when I travel to see projects. On this trip I decided to bring my two young adult daughters. Our plan was to visit several freedom businesses and see firsthand the source of the human trafficking problem. Here is an excerpt from an email that I sent home during our trip:

> *My daughters and I have just returned to Kathmandu following a 5-day trek in the mountains of Nepal, a 5-hour*

drive from Kathmandu over a mountain range on some very treacherous roads. I was amazed that the big Nissan 4-wheel drive got through some of the places without tipping over on rocks, or getting stuck in the mud, or falling off a cliff where it was obvious that landslides are common during this, the rainy season.

After our rugged ride we hiked an additional 5 miles to a very remote village at about 7000 feet above sea level. No electricity, no bathroom—lots of mud and very primitive. I have visited many impoverished areas all over the world, but I have never spent several days and nights in these conditions.

Even more striking than the extreme poverty is this: just 4 years ago you would not have found a single teenage girl in this village. All of the girls had been sold—trafficked into prostitution—by the time they were 12. This region has the highest rate of trafficking in the country, with girls mostly sent to India.

Today, the exploitation has been almost completely eradicated thanks to some ingenious businesspeople who recognized the economic roots of trafficking. After a devastating 2015 earthquake they helped Nepalese families rebuild their homes, but quickly realized that would not be enough to change the drastic situation. There needed to be economic change to protect the young girls. The businesspeople raised capital to build "homestays" in many rural and remote villages like the one we visited. Almost all of them are primarily accessible only by foot.

A homestay is a rustic hostel, usually made from concrete block and sheet metal roofing and siding, offering several simple guest bedrooms with cots and a small common area to share meals. They offer reverse osmosis canisters for refilling water bottles after a long day of hiking in the hot and humid environment, and solar-powered LED lights (helpful for removing leeches from our feet, ankles, and lower legs that hitchhiked and burrowed through our socks as we walked through the soaking wet tall grasses on the trails between villages). Each homestay is owned and managed by a single family selected by the village elders. In addition to creating homestays, the organization worked

> *with the government and villagers to establish hundreds of miles of eco-friendly hiking trails between villages and over the mountains in this remote region. The hiking trails and homestays have become a popular destination for trekkers and hikers from around the world with foot traffic and tourism bringing economic prosperity to the homestay owners and to others through tourism-generated revenue. Each village has experienced significant economic renewal.*
>
> *This visit has been a meaningful lifetime memory for me and my girls—especially wonderful was seeing a little girl quickly hold my daughter Christy's hand on one of our day hikes. When this beautiful girl with deep brown eyes, matted hair, and a dirty red dress began to cry as we left her village the next day, we all cried. She had clearly experienced a little bit of heaven and the love of Jesus through the playful love that Christy showed her. Thankfully, this young girl, age 7 or 8, is no longer at risk of being exploited or trafficked because her family has living-wage revenue from their homestay. Many others do not need to sell their daughters because they can earn a living by selling a chicken to the hikers for dinner, or by selling trinkets in a makeshift gift store, or by participating in other income-producing opportunities related to tourism. As we left the village, we took a picture with the little girl and her family including her 16-year-old sister—the first teenage girl in this village in many years. It made me think about my girls: would I have sold them if our family had lived in this village 5 years ago and had no other sources of income for survival?*

It was an honor to meet the business owners that are making such a life-changing impact in these rural communities and to invest in their projects. As a fiduciary of God's investment resources, I am satisfied that these investments are deployed for His glory, productively embodying the Gospel, and providing a clear quadruple bottom line (QBL) impact with social, economic, environmental, and spiritual gains.

The actions of these businesspeople were risky, requiring steps of faith to start a new business enterprise in the wake of a natural disaster with no guarantee of success. There was immediate need for relief, but there were also systemic economic problems that needed to be resolved to protect young girls in the future. Both needs required sustainable economics solutions. As described in chapter two, charity by itself can provide immediate relief from catastrophic events but can rarely deliver long-term solutions that can eventually be self-funding and self-sustaining. God's heart breaks for the people, conditions, and circumstances like these. Investing is making a difference.

One of the most powerful impacts of this story, and God's gift to me, was how this experience opened my daughter Christy's eyes. Before we began our trek into the remote mountain villages, we had spent several days visiting other freedom businesses in Kathmandu. We learned about the circumstances that drive families to sell their daughters, we visited the "red light district," we saw brothels, and we talked with and toured numerous businesses that are successfully retraining young women and providing dignified and fair-wage employment so they can rebuild after their previous life of enslavement.

On the third day of our mountain trek, having visited at least three villages, a light bulb went on in my daughter's mind. She looked at me and said, "Dad, we have been in three villages. Why are there no teenage gir . . . ," and before she could finish the word *girls*, her mouth dropped. "Oh," she said after a long pause, ". . . those businesses in Kathmandu, you know, the freedom businesses, those are there for the girls who are no longer here, because they were sold into slavery." I cried when she had that realization, and I cry even now as I write this. I am glad that God is breaking my daughter's heart for things that break His heart.

CALLED TO MORE

Being a fiduciary encompasses far more than my finances. God entrusts every resource of time, talent, and treasure for His glory. It is easier for me to invest if I have a focus—a calling—regarding how and where to use them. A calling is most fulfilling when it utilizes all personal resources toward accomplishing an inner passion. God continues to break my heart and stir passion in me. I allow Micah 6:8 to inform the way I serve the Lord with my skills, abilities, training, experience, and relationships, especially in the realm of finance: "He has shown you, O mortal, what is good. And what does the Lord require of you? To act justly and to love mercy and to walk humbly with your God."

When I first adopted this verse, I was primarily focused on learning to act justly and to love mercy. While studying the context and implications of this, I came across a Jewish commentary on the verse which says, "Do not be daunted by the enormity of the world's grief. Do justly, NOW. Love mercy, NOW. Walk humbly, NOW. You are not obligated to complete the work, but neither are you free to abandon it."[60]

"Do not be daunted by the enormity of the world's grief. Do justly, NOW. Love mercy, NOW. Walk humbly, NOW. You are not obligated to complete the work, but neither are you free to abandon it."

The commentator assumes that the reader is overwhelmed by the vastness of the world's problems, depravity, and suffering. Yet prior to praying the dangerous prayer, I think I was like most people who live in affluent societies. I was ignorant and ambivalent about the grief around the globe. We in the West are privileged to live distanced from daily life-and-death situations. This is a luxury that is not experienced in much of the world. If we allowed the truths of the suffering around the world to sink in—people going day and night without enough food to eat; young women trapped, drugged, and abused; people dying without ever hearing the good news of Jesus—we would rightly be overwhelmed.

While fully believing that the ultimate resolution to these troubling problems lies squarely within God's sovereign power, we have an obligation to *learn* about the world's griefs and then to allow our hearts to be *moved to action,* offering what we can out of our abundant resources. Although it is easy to be lackadaisical in our response to overwhelming problems, the commentator reminds us not to delay. Our response is urgently needed NOW. The Lord's *oikonomos* deploys resources without delay to fulfill God's purposes on earth. Once we've seen and learned how we can participate, we are obligated to continue. Ignorance and apathy are inexcusable.

60. Pirkei Avos, "(Ethics/Chapters of the Fathers) 2:16," from Jewish Education: The Source for Everything Jewish (November 20, 2017): https://jewish-education.tumblr.com/post/167722479419/do-not-be-daunted-by-the-enormity-of-the-worlds.

CONCLUSION

I have spent many years being a missional investor, partnering with businesses in frontier markets, visiting them and getting to know the culture and story of each one. At times I am completely overwhelmed by the enormity of the injustices, the human needs, and those who are lost. I wake up in the middle of the night trying to solve the problems I encounter. I have grown to appreciate the ancient truth: *"You are not obligated to complete the work, but neither are you free to abandon it."* Thank goodness I am not obligated to complete the work, but I must not be so self-absorbed that I ignore it. I believe that God's heart breaks when His children hoard wealth and do not release it to alleviate the pain, suffering, brokenness, and spiritual hunger prevalent in the world. Making others aware and helping them to deploy assets to further God's kingdom on earth is my calling and service.

Do you wrestle with these same inner conditions that I have shared? Is your heart breaking for the things that break God's heart? Have you wept because of the enormity of the world's grief? If not, could it be that you are ignoring God's call to restore and reconcile a broken world? Investing in a freedom business might be a great place to start.

QUESTIONS FOR STUDY

1. In this chapter the author shared several deeply personal transformative moments in his walk with God. Describe a significant situation when you and God had a personal encounter and the outcome of that encounter. Have you had an experience that shook you to the core, that broke your heart for the things that break God's heart?

2. How would you describe a *calling*? To fulfill a calling, what personal resources would you put into use? Share an experience when you heard God calling you to a specific action or pursuit.

3. How do you react to broadcast news of devastating suffering in far-off nations? If that need is closer to home, does it change your reaction?

4. The author discusses the Jewish Talmud commentary on Micah 6:8: "Do not be daunted by the enormity of the world's grief. Do justly, now. Love mercy, now. Walk humbly, now. You are not obligated to complete the work, but neither are you free to abandon it." Are you overwhelmed at times by the problems around the world? Why or why not? What tangible actions are you taking to alleviate poverty, exploitation, and injustice? How are you promoting shalom through Gospel proclamation?

5. Do you think God is elated, indifferent, or grieved by how you use and deploy the resources He has entrusted to you? What practical steps can you take to make investments that address issues that break God's heart?

Chapter 8

THE PARABLE OF THE TALENTS

History is replete with stories of businesses whose employees and culture reflect the values and personality of their founders. Successful CEOs train their executive managers to imitate the behaviors which made their business successful in the first place. As a result, management teams and executives usually employ the same tactics they have learned from the CEO and other senior leaders.

If the founders exhibit noble character qualities such as integrity, honesty, generosity, compassion, and broad benevolence to employees, customers, and communities, it is likely that the management teams, employees, and corporate culture will reflect the same values. However, when business founders exhibit selfish, ruthless, greedy character traits, it is highly likely that their businesses, management teams, and employees will reflect and employ the same unscrupulous traits. Successful business leaders replicate themselves so that their personnel emulate their behaviors and achieve the same success and profit as they themselves have.

TWO INFLUENTIAL BUSINESS CULTURES: ONE NICE, ONE UGLY

Founded in 2007, Evive integrates big data with predictive analytics to help people optimize their work benefits. The company is passionate about making an impact on people's daily lives, and their team is no exception. In an interview with Built in Chicago in 2018, user interface (UI) designer Andres Gonzales observed that while the company had doubled its size in the previous two years, it had not lost its focus on impact. Gonzales admits that during his interview process, he felt the conviction of founder, Peter Saravis, toward impact, and that alignment gave him confidence in Evive as the place for him to settle. They share a collective commitment to make an impact and improve people's lives.

McKenzi Higgins, a technical account analyst at Evive, described in the same interview a partnership opportunity between Evive and the Greater Chicago Food Depository to fight hunger. Higgins admires Evive's commitment to a goal outside its own organization.

Additionally, Evive created a "going green" initiative to reduce their ecological footprint that further reveals their company culture. From the founders to the management team to the employees, Evive reflects the values instilled by top leadership. They are committed to creating a better world and impacting the lives of others, and their team acts on their passions to support those values.[61]

Standard Oil sits in contrast to the health and positivity of Evive. Most of us recognize the name of the founder of Standard Oil, but time has erased the memory of his character and influence. Relative to ruthlessness in business, few businesspeople in history can compare to Standard Oil founder, John D. Rockefeller. Rockefeller favored corrupt business practices such as bribing politicians and entering into agreements with the railroad companies that were illegal and unethical.[62]

The company used underhanded business tactics to crush its competition, allowing the company to reap where it had not scattered and harvest where it had not sown seed. Some of Rockefeller's cutthroat business practices included the following:

- Pricing oil as low as necessary to drive smaller refiners out of business, forcing them into bankruptcy or to sell to Standard Oil at deep discounts.

61. Brian Nordli, "For the love of benefits: How Evive's team rallies around its mission" (September 28, 2018): https://www.builtinchicago.org/2018/09/28/spotlight-working-at-evive.

62. "Story of the world's first billionaire and the most hated man in America," from Stockifi (April 17, 2021): https://stockifi.wordpress.com/2021/04/17/story-of-the-worlds-first-billionaire-and-the-most-hated-man-in-america/.

- Buying up all the components needed for the manufacture of oil barrels to prevent competitors from being able to store their product or to get it to market.
- Demanding and cutting secret deals with the railroads, allowing the company to distribute its product at greatly reduced costs compared to competition and takeover targets.
- Dispatching thugs to break up competitors' operations that could not otherwise be controlled.[63]

While Rockefeller demonstrated religious behavior through active involvement in church affairs and generous financial support, this appearance contradicted his aggressive pursuit of profit and ruthless business practices.[64]

THE PARABLE OF THE TALENTS

Jesus frequently used financial and business stories to convey a deeper spiritual truth. In one instance He uses the character of a ruthless businessman, one reminiscent of Rockefeller, to illustrate what the kingdom of God is like. Sometimes people misunderstand the story, thinking that it is primarily about making a good financial return, but it is really about something completely different.

In the parable of the talents, found in Matthew 25:14-30, a master departing on a journey entrusts three servants with varying amounts of his wealth. When he returns, we learn the results of the stewards' actions over the time that the master has been away. The first two stewards have doubled the amount they had been entrusted with while the third returns only the original amount he had been given to manage. The master praises, rewards, and assigns more work to the first two servants in response to their actions. But he condemns the third and sends him away.

I have heard many people over the years discuss this parable and use it to defend their position that stewardship is about making a "market-like return." Or they argue that the primary teaching of the parable is that we should use our resources to maximize return so that we can give away some of the profits to support "the Lord's work." It is a mistake to think the parable is a proof text defending the notion

63. "John D. Rockefeller: The Ultimate Oil Man," from U-S-History.com (n.d.): https://www.u-s-history.com/pages/h957.html.

64. "John D. Rockefeller" (n.d.).

It is a mistake to think the parable is a proof text defending the notion that the primary role of a good steward is to achieve financial returns.

that the primary role of a good steward is to achieve financial returns. While it is true that we often misuse the money God entrusts to us, the same is true of many other resources such as our natural abilities, our intellect, our influence, our health, our status, even our knowledge of the Bible. A key point of the parable is that we must employ every resource to accomplish the Master's purposes, but it is not the only point.

I have heard others use the parable to justify accumulating wealth so they can retire in comfort. Many Christians mistakenly assume that this parable supports the American ideal of achieving financial independence to live lives of leisure in retirement. This is another false interpretation since the servants were rewarded with much greater responsibilities and more work, not an extended vacation or early retirement. The text does not indicate a bonus or pay raise or other personal reward. The words the master offers to the first two servants, "Well done good and faithful servant" (Matt. 25:21), are not meant to be praise for a compounded rate of return on investments or the amount of wealth accumulated here on earth. Instead we will hear, "Well done good and faithful servant" if we use all our resources deliberately to increase the kingdom of God on earth, making disciples to the ends of the earth, and providing relief, support, and comfort to those who are vulnerable and in need.

While understanding this parable challenges us, we cannot allow a historical misunderstanding of it to cause us to fail in faithfully executing the mandate God has given, which is to use His resources with clarity of purpose and confidence in building His kingdom. Let's not get distracted by the large amount that was entrusted to the servants or that they "doubled" the investment. These are minor factors—and in truth, it is not difficult to double an investment if you have sufficient time. Instead let's focus on three important lessons this parable teaches us in our role as God's fiduciaries:

1. An *oikonomos* of God's resources knows God intimately and invests as God would invest.

2. An *oikonomos* does not allow fear to interfere with pursuing the Master's goals.

3. An *oikonomos* is not lazy and purposefully deploys resources that are entrusted to them.

Let me explain these further.

First, in God's kingdom, we must know our Master, understand the Master's character, and match or surpass His practices. It is hard for me to equate the master's business practices displayed in this parable as ones we should emulate. Like so many modern-day greedy, unscrupulous businessmen, this master sought personal gain, no matter the tactic. He expected his trained servants to do what he would with his money, which was to make a profit. The servants who knew their master and acted in the same way that he would were praised accordingly, but the servant who knew the character of the master but did *not* act the way the master would have acted was condemned.

We should not assume that the master in this parable is a holy man reflecting God's character. The last servant and the master agree that he is a hard man who harvests where he has not sown and gathers where he has not scattered (Matt. 25:24). This would describe God in a way which can hardly be defended by the rest of scripture. Considering what the Bible teaches, I would expect Jesus to be a righteous businessman, not ruthless. His character and that of His business would bring prosperity, transformation, justice, and rejoicing to the community and not extract profit at any cost. A righteous businessman would bring a foretaste of the kingdom of God.

A businessman like the master in this parable would be more like John D. Rockefeller—one who on the outside attended church faithfully and donated large sums to his church and other philanthropic causes while simultaneously using business practices that reflected ruthlessness. Rockefeller's managers (stewards), as part of the largest company in the United States at the time, understood and conducted business in the same manner that Rockefeller would himself, like the first two servants in the story.

In the kingdom of heaven, fear does not control actions.

Second, we are mistaken when we deduce that the third servant is punished because he did not make a profit. The master condemns the third servant for being *fearful*. He knew the master's character but was afraid of him and so did not behave in a way that the master would have behaved or would have expected a servant of his to behave. In the kingdom of heaven, fear does not control actions.

The Lord is benevolent so we can trust in His righteousness and not fear Him. The third servant knew the master's character the same way that the first two servants did, but due to fear, he decided to take actions that were not characteristic of the master. The master agreed that he was hard, even ruthless. Fear that prevents us from taking action to accomplish our Master's purposes is condemned. An often-repeated commandment in the Bible is, "Do not fear." In fact, the phrases "fear not" and "do not fear" occur at least one hundred times in scripture. God makes it clear that since He is in control, we should not fear. Typically we try to control as much in life as possible, especially when it comes to money, but we fool ourselves when we think we can control our lives or even our financial well-being. I have observed over a long career that even those who do everything right with systematic saving, wise budgeting, and competent investing can be brought to nothing with an unexpected, uncontrollable business loss. Think COVID-19. Or a catastrophic health issue comes at a time when health insurance coverage is lost due to circumstances out of their control. Or it could be financial devastation due to fraud or market conditions. Think Enron, WorldCom, or Bernie Madoff, for example.

When we think we can control these things, we are arrogant, and we are wrong. If we attempt to control our financial future, we end up making irrational decisions out of fear. Some people are paralyzed by fear of making an investment due to fear of loss even when circumstances are not tragic or dire. The third servant suffered from this fear and was condemned for it.

How fearful are you? Do you consider missional investing in frontier markets, among unreached people groups, too risky? I have lost count of the number of times that Christians have told me exactly that, saying, "Missional investments are too risky. Please ask me to invest later, after the company is stable and earning a consistent profit." God does not need Christians to invest in missional companies *after* they are stable and earning a profit—non-Christians will be more than happy to invest at that time. Wealthy Christians can "de-risk" QBL investments by being the first to invest in difficult places, facing the risk of loss with courage so that God's kingdom can be built in unreached places. Christians seeking to maximize financial return with minimal risk are investing for their own benefit with fear and self-interest as their primary motivators. The Lord's *oikonomos* are not to be motivated by fear. They are willing to assume additional risk to proactively extend God's grace to those who do not yet know Him.

They are willing to assume additional risk to proactively extend God's grace to those who do not yet know Him.

Finally, as God's *oikonomos,* we should not be lazy with the resources God has given us. Laziness is an unwillingness to work or use energy. It can also be described as showing a lack of effort or care. The third servant was too lazy to seek opportunities for investing the provided resources so that the master's goals could be accomplished. He was condemned and cast out as a result. Perhaps he thought it was too much work to hire and manage workers to cultivate a field so it would produce productive crops. Or maybe it was too much work to deposit the money at the bank to earn even a little interest.

As a professional money manager and personal investor, I can tell you that both investing and giving require the hard work of research, due diligence, and accountability to do them well. When it comes to missional investments, an investor must spend a lot of time learning the culture where they are investing, getting to know the entrepreneurs in whom they are investing, and holding the investee companies accountable to the terms of the loan or investment. This has required up to a hundred or more days per year traveling for my colleagues and me as we meet with and monitor the missional investments in our portfolios.

It takes time and thoughtful investigation to partner with others who have more experience in making missional investments, but the eternal impact is priceless.

We cannot be lazy if we want to serve as the Lord's *oikonomos*. We need to get out of our comfort zones by either doing the work ourselves or by building relationships with advisors and others who are experienced in making QBL investments. If we are lazy, we will continue to invest in the ways we always have, following the advice of advisors who invest as the secular world suggests and maximizing personal financial return with minimal risk. It takes time and thoughtful investigation to partner with others who have more experience in making missional investments, but the eternal impact is priceless.

Have you been lazy with the financial resources you control? Is your investing characterized by ignorance of the exploitative or corrupt business practices used by many publicly traded investments but choosing them anyway? A diligent, hard-working *oikonomos* investigates alternative investment strategies that align with God's values and achieve His purposes. Furthermore, lazy investing extends to following the financial guidance of an advisor who does not share your Christian values or worldview, especially if they see their primary role as increasing your net worth, not helping you deploy resources for the True Owner.

CONCLUSION

As the Lord's servants, His *oikonomos*, we are fiduciaries of the resources He has entrusted to us. Because we are familiar with His character, we must invest wisely. Aligned with His purposes, we are called to fearlessly deploy resources to fulfill his Great Commission mandate and energetically pursue opportunities that accomplish His goals. Such courage builds the kingdom of heaven on earth. Ignorance, fear of loss, and laziness are not acceptable for those who wish to hear, "Well done, good and faithful servant."

QUESTIONS FOR STUDY

1. Read and discuss Matthew 25:14-30. Compare and contrast your previous interpretation of this passage with any new insights gained from this chapter's review of this parable. Questions to consider:

   a. Is this parable primarily about making a good financial return?

   b. Does this parable justify the American ideal of achieving financial independence to live a life of leisure?

   c. What were the first two servants commended for and what was their reward: a raise, a vacation? What was the third servant condemned for?

   d. Does the master in this parable represent God? Why or why not?

2. Ask yourself, as God's fiduciary, if you know God intimately and invest as He would invest.

   a. Do you allow fear (specifically in your investments) to interfere with the goals of the Master, the True Owner? Might you be condemned for having invested as the world does, generally ignorant of the composition and character of the companies you own in your portfolio?

b. Might you fall short of the commendation, "Well done, good and faithful servant," for having failed to generously deploy financial resources over which you have control in pursuit of fulfilling God's Great Commission mandate?

3. Gauge your heart-readiness to consider the enormity of the world's grief and your commission from God to be His ambassador and fiduciary in pursuing the reconciliation and restoration of a broken world.

Chapter 9

PROACTIVE VALUES INVESTING BASICS

I hope that in the previous chapters you have been persuaded that your role as an *oikonomos* extends far beyond financial competence and charitable giving. The mandate of the Lord's fiduciary is to deploy resources to fulfill His purposes as laid out in the Great Commission and the Great Commandment. To act justly, we need to overcome our areas of ignorance, as well as our emotional fears, idolization, and falsely placed dependence on investments as our source of happiness and safety. Recognizing that God is our provision, we can trust Him to meet our needs while we deploy resources for His purposes.

This chapter discusses the practical steps that a person can take to begin to invest a portion of their investable assets into missional enterprises, thereby managing God's resources well. (Although the examples provided are of American financial mechanisms, the principles apply to wealthy Christians worldwide. Depending on where you live, you will need to consider what mechanisms exist within your own national financial structures and laws.)

This and the following two chapters are more technical in nature and address the details and practical actions required for those who wish to implement proactive values investing (PVI) strategies into their portfolios either through an advisor or by do-it-yourself means. Chapters twelve through sixteen return to less technical but critical scripture insights for how missional investing is appropriate in the way we approach retirement and estate planning.

UNDERSTANDING INVESTMENT CATEGORIES

In practical terms, investable assets fall into three categories defined by how they are treated from a tax point of view. First are after-tax investments; then pre-tax investments, usually called "qualified" assets; and third, monies given to a charitable entity such as a trust, foundation, or donor advised fund (DAF). Think of each category like an umbrella: the umbrella defines how everything underneath it will be taxed. Under each umbrella are the actual investment types as described in chapter one. Bank instruments, stocks, bonds, mutual funds, real estate, and alternative assets can be held under any one or all the umbrellas. But while the underlying investments are the same, they will be treated differently from a tax standpoint depending on which tax umbrella they fall under.

Umbrella One: After-Tax Investments

After-tax investments are the most common and easiest to understand. Under this umbrella, bank instruments pay interest and are subject to ordinary income tax each year. Stocks, bonds, and mutual funds may earn dividends each year which are subject to ordinary income tax, and if you sell them, any gain is subject to capital gains tax. If you are reading this, then you probably have after-tax investments since according to the Federal Deposit Insurance Corporation (FDIC), ninety-five percent of Americans have at least one bank account[65] and forty-six percent own a mutual fund.[66] Investments can easily be directed into missional enterprises using after-tax dollars by simply writing a check.

Umbrella Two: Qualified (Pre-Tax) Investments

Qualified investments are investments that you deposit into an account before paying taxes. This would include traditional IRAs and retirement accounts such as 401(k) or 403(b) investments. They

65. "How America Banks: Household Use of Banking and Financial Services," from the Federal Deposit Insurance Corporation (December 17, 2021): https://www.fdic.gov/analysis/household-survey.

66. F. Norrestad, "Share of households owning mutual funds in the United States from 1980 to 2020" (January 11, 2022): www.statista.com/statistics/246224/mutual-funds-owned-by-american-households/.

are tax-deferred because you do not pay tax on them each year as they grow. Under this umbrella, interest from bank accounts and dividends from stocks, bonds, and mutual funds are tax-deferred, meaning you do not pay tax on the earnings until you withdraw the money. At the time of withdrawal, you will be subject to ordinary income tax on the entire amount withdrawn because you never paid tax on the original deposits (they were made pre-tax) and you never paid tax on the earnings (tax-deferred). According to the Bureau of Labor Statistics, thirty-eight percent of the US workforce participates in a 401(k) plan.[67] The US Census Bureau confirms a similar participation rate for individual retirement accounts (IRAs).[68] It takes a little more effort to make investments into missional businesses using qualified dollars, but it can be done by using a "self-directed" IRA. It is recommended that you seek counsel from an advisor who is familiar with self-directed IRAs and how they are used to invest in privately held, not publicly traded, investments.

Umbrella Three: Charitable Investments

Most Americans do not have a charitable investment account. I describe them here because they may be a useful tool in a year when you experience a windfall financial event such as receiving a large bonus, exercising stock options, selling a business, receiving a settlement, or winning the lottery. Charitable investments are held in foundations or pooled charities such as community funds or donor advised funds (DAFs). For tax purposes, these are funds that have already been given away. The investor has already received the charitable tax benefit but may still retain some power to recommend how the funds will be used to achieve charitable purposes, either now or in the future.

In 2019 there were 873,228 DAF accounts in the United States.[69] While that may seem like a lot, based on a population of 328 million, only .2 percent of the US population—roughly two out of every one thousand people—are wealthy enough to have a DAF account. To say that these folks are rare is an understatement, and yet in the realm of missional impact investing, they are usually the only

67. Financial Samurai, "The 401(k) Participation Rate Is Shocking" (November 4, 2018): https://www.financialsamurai.com/the-401k-participation-rate.

68. https://www2.census.gov/library/publications/2010/compendia/statab/130ed/tables/11s0552.pdf

69. https://www.nptrust.org/philanthropic-resources/charitable-giving-statistics

ones approached as potential funders for missional enterprise. This is unfortunate because God desires that we all serve as His *oikonomos*. We are all fiduciaries of the Lord's resources. God owns one hundred percent of the resources, assets, and investments that we control during our lifetime. They are not our own. But we act like only the wealthiest Christians—those who have deposited resources under umbrella three—are called to serve as the Lord's *oikonomos* with their investments. Every one of us is the Lord's *oikonomos* and has a duty to manage His resources for Him—not just our donations and tithes but our after-tax and qualified retirement holdings as well.

God owns one hundred percent of the resources, assets, and investments that we control during our lifetime. They are not our own.

Unfortunately, Americans have been conditioned to think that only charitable resources can or should be used to achieve social, economic, environmental, and spiritual goals. I strongly believe that each fiduciary of God's money should employ all three categories (after tax, pre-tax, and charitable monies) to further His kingdom and to achieve these QBL outcomes. As I have previously stated, charitable donations are not more sacred than investments, and investments are not more secular than donations. All financial resources can and should be used for furthering God's kingdom on earth.

How is this done, practically speaking? Finding, vetting, and monitoring missional investments is not easy. It is wise to connect with a person or organization who has experience investing in frontier markets for the purpose of achieving QBL outcomes. It is also helpful to work with a financial professional who can advise on the tax implications of various strategies. An advisor who has experience building both traditional portfolios and kingdom impact portfolios can coordinate an overall plan which matches your personal financial needs with your desire to be a faithful *oikonomos*. Look for advisors who have traveled overseas to coach and mentor Great Commission companies and who have invested their own money into QBL investments. They are best equipped to advise you on the risks and rewards of such investing.

USING AFTER-TAX MONIES

After-tax investments can be the easiest for making a missional investment. You simply select an organization or missional enterprise to invest in, then write a check. Most investments are made as loans to the missional enterprise, but it is possible to own stock (equity ownership) in a missional business as well, depending upon the most appropriate structure for both the enterprise and the investors. Obviously, the enterprise itself must have a legal structure (usually an LLC) that is responsible for tax reporting. The enterprise should issue tax statements each year on earnings or losses that you may receive from these investments. It can get very complicated when dealing with entities in foreign countries, so a US-based LLC is often recommended. You should consult your tax and legal advisor before making a direct investment of this sort.

Alternatively, there are several US- and foreign-based organizations that "pool" like-minded investors' capital and seek out businesses that are achieving QBL outcomes, then make investments on behalf of their investor community. You can invest in these organizations which serve as general manager and will provide annual performance and tax reports for you. Sometimes these groups make investments that are loans to the business entity or sometimes they will invest in the equity (stock) of the business. Investors who participate this way gain the added benefit of diversification within the investment group as well as the inherent benefit of the due diligence and accountability processes that are put in place by the funding organizations. Some of these organizations have management teams with over a hundred cumulative years of experience coaching, working, mentoring, and investing in missional enterprises in frontier markets. These are great resources for the average investor and can be used for after-tax, pre-tax, or charitable investing.

USING QUALIFIED (PRE-TAX) MONIES

Using qualified (pre-tax) investments such as IRAs and 401(k) s can be an excellent method for deploying resources to achieve kingdom goals. Since these types of accounts are tax deferred, they are easier to manage from a tax point of view since there is generally no income tax due each year on the earnings inside of the account.

Qualified Charitable Distributions (QCDs)

Sometimes, older American investors do not need to maximize such accounts for their own benefit because they have other retirement income sources such as a pension, part-time work, social security, or rental income which are sufficient to support their lifestyle. These investors are forced to take income they do not need in retirement so that the government can collect taxes. Required minimum distributions (RMDs) force account holders to withdraw from these accounts after they turn age seventy-two, whether they need it or not. For these individuals, a provision in the Internal Revenue Code which created Qualified Charitable Distributions (QCD) allows retirees over age seventy-two to make distributions to charities which are not only counted toward satisfying their RMD for the year (up to one hundred thousand dollars) but also are excluded from their taxable income. This is truly a win-win from a financial standpoint, from a tax standpoint, and for missional enterprises that need investors. Consult your tax advisor to determine if a QCD is right for you.

Self-Directed IRAs

An investor does not have to be retired to use their IRA to invest in businesses that are seeking to fulfill the Great Commission. They can begin investing in missional businesses immediately through a self-directed IRA. The difference between self-directed and other IRAs is the types of assets that are owned in the account. Regular IRAs typically house only stocks, bonds, mutual funds, and other relatively common, publicly traded investments. Self-directed IRAs, as their name implies, permit investors to hold private placement investments that are not publicly traded on an exchange. For example, you could invest in real estate, precious metals, currencies, a privately held company, or a missional enterprise. I began using a self-directed IRA many years ago when my wife and I would meet brothers and sisters in Christ who, for one reason or another, could not secure a bank mortgage to purchase a house. We began holding low-interest mortgages for these friends as part of our duty as the Lord's *oikonomos*. My IRA is, after all, owned by the Lord and should be used to help His children. Later I began to use my IRA to fund missional businesses across the globe for the same reason.

You may not have heard of a self-directed IRA. This is most likely because most financial advisors, because of compliance restrictions placed on them by their broker dealer, are unable to recommend to their clients or advise them on how to use IRA monies, or self-directed IRAs specifically, to achieve God's purposes. But it is possible for Christian investors who desire to invest in proactive, missional businesses to invest their IRAs, 401(k)s, and other qualified (pre-tax) investments in QBL investments by using a self-directed IRA. Furthermore, rolling money from a traditional IRA to a self-directed IRA can avoid income tax because the investor is not making a taxable withdrawal but simply transferring from one type of IRA to another.

I know individuals whose self-directed IRAs have provided a mortgage to a Christian school; supplied loans to businesses in Eastern Europe, Central Asia, and North Africa; purchased equity ownership in a tourist resort in Southeast Asia; and many other intriguing mission-minded investments.

One final note on self-directed IRAs. They can be disqualified as a tax-advantaged account if you don't follow all the IRS regulations with precision. An advisor who is experienced in making these kinds of transactions is critical for understanding the potential tax pitfalls, including self-dealing rules and unrelated business income rules that are associated with the use of self-directed IRA accounts.

USING CHARITABLE MONIES

A word of caution for those who have been entrusted with so many resources that they have benefited by establishing a private foundation, charity, or donor advised fund. In my experience, many in this category have fallen into a self-serving mindset, treating these accounts as though they still own the resources, feeling justified in investing these resources in traditional ways to accomplish typical goals like reducing risk, seeking market-like returns, and deploying only earnings or a portion of earnings to the Lord's work. The Bible clearly teaches that the Lord owns it all. Even more important, the assets that have been given to such an account have already received large tax benefits because they have been donated to achieve charitable purposes. There are an estimated $141.95 billion in assets in DAFs and an estimated

> ***Christians have utilized tax strategies to benefit themselves, and yet few actually deploy the principal to achieve God's purposes.***

one trillion dollars in private foundations.[70] If we assume that evangelical Christians comprise roughly forty-one percent of the population,[71] that would mean that there are nearly $468 billion of Christian donations sitting in foundations or DAF accounts. These Christians have utilized tax strategies to benefit themselves, and yet few actually deploy the principal to achieve God's purposes. Instead, these account owners and managers have chosen to create perpetual endowments which slowly drip resources toward God's goals.

What do you think Jesus will say about this when He returns? Will He be as angry as He was with the money changers in the temple who took advantage of the law to benefit themselves (Mark 11:15)? Will He ask why we did not consider the urgency? "The harvest is plentiful, but the laborers are few; therefore, ask the Lord of the harvest to send out laborers into his harvest" (Luke 10:2). This is a familiar text for all who prioritize the Great Commission. But what sometimes goes unnoticed is the *urgency* of Jesus' words. If crops are not harvested when they are ripe, they will spoil. Every farmer and backyard gardener knows this. A harvest delayed by vacation, illness, or apathy will be lost. There is no way to justify hoarding resources and not deploying them when these monies have already been donated and have already received a generous tax benefit because they are designated for charitable purposes. Since God owns it all, how can Christians disburse these resources sparingly, preserving them for perpetuity rather than supplying them to meet the immediate needs of today? How will we answer the question of why nearly *five hundred billion dollars* remains idle or was invested in companies with unethical, immoral, or anti-Christian values, when there are billions of people who have yet to hear His name? There is no good reason why one hundred percent of these holdings should not be invested in ways that further the kingdom of God on earth. This might be a

---

70. Eileen R. Heisman, "National Philanthropic Trust is proud to publish our 15th annual Donor-Advised Report," from The 2020 DAF Report (2021): https://www.nptrust.org/reports/daf-report/?gclid=CjwKCAjw87SHBhBiEiwAukSeUevhkkWvf6eCat7Qg8j2JDwLP6y_OCYZQyN5HKHzpFqauieDh-EM5xoCGq4QA-vD_BwE. Published amount for 2017 in Giving USA 2018, increased by 0.8 percent. Increase reported as an increase in asset values for 2018, in Giving USA 2020, p. 97. That value for 2018 was decreased by 5 percent to allow for grants made, and that was increased by the 28.7 percent in the Standard & Poor's 500 Index for 2019, to yield $1.016 trillion.

71. Frank Newport, "5 Things to Know about Evangelicals in America," from Gallup Polling Matters (May 31, 2018): https://news.gallup.com/opinion/polling-matters/235208/things-know-evangelicals-america.aspx.

good time to review chapter six regarding a common justification for not sowing seeds. Many falsely argue that the resources (seed) must be protected for future opportunities. I find this contradictory when in fact these resources have already been given away and have received generous tax benefits so that they can accomplish the charitable outcomes that they were donated to support.

Similarly, there are $18.9 trillion of IRA and 401(k) assets in the USA. Assuming the same forty-one percent is owned by born-again Christians, there are $7,750,000,000,000 (nearly eight trillion dollars) of assets hoarded in retirement accounts. That is more than fifteen times the amount in charitable accounts, and they are rarely invested in a manner that seeks God's purposes. We treat them as our own, resisting the spiritual truth that they are God's, and we are His *oikonomos*.

Christians must deliberately invest in to achieve God's eternal purposes rather than focusing on achieving temporal gains.

Our fiduciary responsibility requires us not to hoard them and treat them as our own but rather to deploy them in ways that will achieve God's eternal purposes. Jesus' teaching in Matthew 6:19-20 (NASB) is very clear: "Do not store up for yourselves treasures on earth, where moth and rust destroy, and where thieves break in and steal." These are temporal matters that should not consume our attention. "But store up for yourselves treasures in heaven, where neither moth nor rust destroys, and where thieves do not break in and steal." We should focus on God's eternal objectives. Nearly eight trillion dollars seems like a lot of temporal focus! Christians must deliberately invest in to achieve God's eternal purposes rather than focusing on achieving temporal gains.

STRATEGIES FOR A KINGDOM PORTFOLIO

Traditional financial planners frequently cite a basic rule of thumb for balancing investments to reduce risk as you age. They suggest you invest a percentage of your portfolio equal to your age in safe, "fixed" investments. For example, at age thirty, you should invest thirty percent of your portfolio in safe investments like bonds and seventy percent in volatile investments like stocks. But by age sixty, you should have shifted your portfolio so that it consists of sixty percent bonds and forty percent stocks. See table below:

Traditional Investing *Rule of Thumb: Invest a percentage of your portfolio into bonds based on your age*		
Age	**% Bonds**	**% Stocks**
25	25	75
35	35	65
45	45	55
55	55	45
65	65	35
75	75	25
85	85	15
In retirement you should reallocate your portfolio assets, not just your annual savings.		

Table 1

I suggest using a similar rule of thumb as Christians to balance our portfolios based on our personal needs *and* our fiduciary duty to fulfill God's objectives. Consider allocating ten percent of your investments to QBL investments when you begin your career in your twenties. Then use a strategy that increases this percentage by ten percent every ten years based on your age and the likelihood that your discretionary income will increase as you get older.[72] A missional investing progression would look like this:

72. Disclaimer: These "Rules of Thumb" are for general illustration purposes only and should not be relied upon as a recommendation for individual investors. Investments in QBL investments carry higher risk than traditional investments. Investors should consider their specific calling as God's steward investor and consult their investment advisors and tax professionals to determine the amount that is appropriate based on their specific age, income, net worth, risk tolerance, and missional objectives. Investing in QBL investments should not be done in isolation without consideration of how they properly integrate into a person's entire financial and life plan, entire portfolio, and net worth.

Missional Investing *Rule of Thumb: Invest a percentage of your annual savings into QBL investments based on your age*		
Age	**% QBL**	**% Traditional**
25	10	90
35	20	80
45	30	70
55	40	60
65	50	50
75	60	40
85	70	30
In retirement you should reallocate your portfolio assets, not just your annual savings.		

Table 2

This strategy provides a nice framework for balancing our duty to care for our family and to deliberately invest with God's goals as a high priority. As His *oikonomos,* we should have a strategic plan to deploy His resources effectively and abundantly.

A REAL-WORLD EXAMPLE

My friends Charlie and Miranda[73] are now in their mid-seventies. We have been working together for many years, and they have grown passionate about stewarding their resources by investing to build God's kingdom through transformational enterprise. At first, they used charitable donations and a DAF to help fund micro enterprise businesses in Haiti, Morocco, and Ethiopia. Over the years, they heard the stories I would share about Business as Mission projects in frontier markets and decided they wanted to do more. They began to use their IRA as a resource for furthering God's kingdom. Prior to their retirement, I helped them perform an "in-service" rollover from their company 401(k) plan to a self-directed IRA. The IRA now

73. A fictional couple whose story represents a composite of my actual clients, businesses, and investment choices.

holds investments in a chain of cafes in southeast Asia, an organic ranch in eastern Europe, and most recently, equity in a solar/efficient energy global franchise brand. These and other investments made through their self-directed IRA are furthering God's kingdom in difficult places, allowing entrepreneurs to be the incarnation of Christ in cultures where Jesus' name is rarely spoken.

These and other investments made through their self-directed IRA are furthering God's kingdom in difficult places, allowing entrepreneurs to be the incarnation of Christ in cultures where Jesus' name is rarely spoken.

Balancing their personal needs with a desire to deploy resources to make disciples, we have coordinated a robust portfolio, including traditional and missional investments. They are gradually increasing the percentage of their estate invested strategically for God's purposes as their own personal needs are diminishing. In addition to DAF and IRA investments, this family has also made after-tax investments into two different pooled funds, combining their resources with other like-minded investors who provide patient and purposeful capital to dozens of BAM businesses in creative access locations. With this added diversification, they now have missional investments in the Americas, Europe, Asia, and Africa.

Furthermore, we have had numerous discussions about estate planning and the best ways to include their children in missional investment strategies. They are planning ahead to make sure that their children understand their view of stewardship and are aware of the investments they have made. In the future we plan to do a "family summit" to explain the role of the Lord's *oikonomos* and do a deep dive into family investments so their children understand and are prepared to continue the mission-minded investments when their parents can no longer do so.

I am proud of my friends. They have taken steps of courage as they worked hard to understand God's call on their lives and their financial resources. I would expect them to hear the words, "Well done, good and faithful servants," when they enter His glory.

As Charlie and Miranda's story shows, I am not talking about them giving away their resources—although that may be appropriate in some cases. I am talking about how they have invested their net worth in greater percentages into missional businesses as they aged. This means accepting a higher risk than their former traditional stock, bond, and mutual fund portfolio had, and it requires that they trust the Lord. After many years of self-sufficiency and "financial independence," they are learning what it means to pray, "Give us this day our daily bread" (Matt. 6:11, NASB). They make this request for themselves and for the business owners whom they support. The result is a greater focus on achieving God's goals rather than appeasing their own interests. I believe that their investing goals and practices provide a nice illustration of balancing their duty to care for their family and to deliberately invest in kingdom enterprises.

In addition, Charlie and Miranda demonstrate a thoughtful approach for their children's future as well as respectful plans to disciple them in the process of kingdom-thinking. Some might argue that in principle, parents need to provide an inheritance for their children, believing that it is their duty to make sure that their children are better off financially than they were. For these people, I suggest considering my friend's example and asking if it really is good stewardship to pass along all our net worth to our children.

[*Note:* Charlie and Miranda's guidance came from an advisor with knowledge and experience in traditional investment, tax, and estate planning strategies. The advisor also possessed the broad network of global relationships necessary for developing a portfolio of missional businesses in many frontier markets where Jesus is not well known. Therefore, the advisor was qualified to help them to coordinate both their eternal and temporal goals. The "Next Steps" section provides guidance for readers to determine if their advisor has adequate qualifications to guide them on a similar path.]

CONCLUSION

What percentage of your after-tax investments have you allocated to missional investments? What percentage of your qualified (pre-tax) retirement accounts have you invested in companies that are seeking QBL outcomes? If you are among the wealthiest (those who have established a charitable investment account), are you hoarding the principal and only slowly deploying it toward kingdom investments? Will you pray for God to confirm His purpose for the corpus of your charitable account? Can the corpus be deployed by investing it into missional enterprise *now*?

QUESTIONS FOR STUDY

1. We're ready now to explore practical steps that we, as God's *oikonomos*, can use to fulfill our call toward pursuing the Great Commission and Great Commandment mandates. The *who*, *what*, and *why* questions have been posed and discussed. As fiduciaries entrusted with resources that belong to God, how then can we deploy His resources to accomplish His goals?

2. Are you one of the ninety-five percent of Americans with a bank account? Are you one of the forty-six percent who own a mutual fund? Are you one of the nearly fifty percent of all workers who have received a tax break by depositing money into a pre-tax retirement account (401(k), IRA, 403(b), 457(b))? Have you used the tax breaks that come from creating a donor advised fund or foundation? Investments can be made into missional businesses from all these types of accounts. Have you ever made a "missional investment"? If not, why not?

3. A small fraction of Americans has established charitable investment accounts—about .2%. From your understanding of what is required of God's *oikonomos*, is it likely that God desires that only wealth deposited into charitable investment accounts should be made available for His use? Why or why not?

4. What is a Qualified Charitable Distribution (QCD) and who can utilize this tax-advantaged strategy to make charitable donations? How does this work in tangent with required minimum distributions from tax-advantaged retirement accounts? Is this charitable giving tax break only for the very wealthy? Why or why not?

5. Discuss how "self-directed" IRAs can enable both *oikonomos* investors seeking current tax breaks and those who have already amassed a nest egg in pre-tax retirement accounts to pursue investment in missional quadruple bottom line (QBL) investments. Why might retirement savers not have heard of self-directed IRAs?

6. What scriptural warning might be applied to those who take significant tax breaks for deposits to charitable funds but then keep the money invested in a traditional manner to maintain control of the principal, primarily seeking growth rather than disbursing the funds for charitable or missional investment purposes now? Can that be construed as hoarding? Consider how that warning might also apply to your assets and investments.

7. Have you wrestled with the idea of balancing your duty to care for your family and to deliberately invest in kingdom enterprises? What percentage of your income have you allocated to charitable giving annually? What percentage of your after-tax investments and what percentage of your qualified pre-tax investments have you invested in missional businesses? What change in strategy or investments will it take to represent the True Owner in a way that pleases Him?

Chapter 10

RISK AND RETURN FOR THE STEWARD INVESTOR

Summary of Action: Medal of Honor Recipient Lt. (SEAL) Michael Murphy: For actions during Operation Red Wings on Jun. 28, 2005:

On June 28, 2005, deep behind enemy lines east of Asadabad in the Hindu Kush of Afghanistan, a very committed four-man Navy SEAL team was conducting a reconnaissance mission at the unforgiving altitude of approximately 10,000 feet. The four SEALs . . . were scouting Ahmad Shah – a terrorist in his mid-30s who grew up in the adjacent mountains just to the south. . . [Ahmad] Shah led a guerrilla group known to locals as the "Mountain Tigers" that had aligned with the Taliban and other militant groups close to the Pakistani border. The SEAL mission was compromised when the team was spotted by local nationals, who presumably reported its presence and location to the Taliban.

A fierce firefight erupted between the four SEALs and a much larger enemy force of more than 50 anti-coalition

> militia. The enemy had the SEALs outnumbered. They also had terrain advantage. They launched a well-organized, three-sided attack on the SEALs. The firefight continued relentlessly as the overwhelming militia forced the team deeper into a ravine.[74]

The four men were pinned down trying to reach safety. However, despite the intensity of the firefight and suffering grave wounds, Lieutenant Michael Murphy risked his own life to save his teammates' lives. Moving away from the protection of the mountain rocks, he exposed himself, a deliberate and heroic act that deprived him of cover and made him a target for enemy fire. While under fire, Murphy contacted the Quick Reaction Force at Bagram Air Base and calmly provided his unit's location and the size of the enemy. Receiving a shot in the back that caused him to drop the transmitter, he retrieved it, completed the call, and continued firing at the enemy. His actions on this deployment cost him his life but saved the life of one of his teammates. Upon receiving the Medal of Honor for their son's sacrifice, Murphy's parents characterized his sacrificial actions not as those of a hero but those of a leader.[75]

Leaders complete their mission. They take risks that others would never take. Leaders step out in obedience to a higher authority to accomplish the primary objective, even if it requires sacrifice on their own part. A fiduciary of God's resources must be willing to lead by taking risks that others are unwilling to take to achieve His purposes.

DEPLOYMENT, RISK, AND SACRIFICE

Deployment, in military terms, can describe sending troops into duty or can refer to "activities required to move military personnel and materials from a home installation to a specified destination."[76] Deploying a person from a "home" to a destination often in conflict, in disruption, or at war, is a movement from safety to risk.

Consider that in one act of obedience (being born incarnate), Jesus raised the stakes for any of us who really dare to follow His example. Jesus was "deployed" by God the Father from His home installation, in heaven, to the unsafe, conflict- and sin-filled combat zone of earth.

74. "Lt. (SEAL) Michael Murphy: For actions during Operation Red Wings on Jun. 28, 2005," https://www.navy.mil/MEDAL-OF-HONOR-RECIPIENT-MICHAEL-P-MURPHY/.

75. Bill Robinson, "Whitworth University 2008 Graduate-Commencement Address" (May 17, 2008): https://www.whitworth.edu/cms/administration/president-emeritus-bill-robinson/speeches--messages/2008-graduate-commencement-address/.

76. https://www.military.com/deployment/deployment-overview.html

He ultimately laid down His life to accomplish the primary purpose for which He was deployed: the reconciliation of people to their Father.

For the incarnation of God to have any bearing on our understanding of business and stewardship, we must recognize that sacrifice and risk are inescapable. Deployment, risk, and sacrifice stand as foundational elements of incarnation. Jesus left a throne for a manger, a king's life for a nomadic one. He left the realm of immortality to eat, sleep, and fellowship with time-constrained humans, then consummated those departures in the most brutal and humiliating of all deaths. The incarnation of Christ should inspire us to be sacrificial risk takers. It is the only way to be missional businesspeople and fiduciaries of the Lord's resources.

The Pitfalls of Fear and Greed

Ken Haman, managing director at AllianceBernstein, one of America's leading institutional wealth management firms, concluded that for the majority of wealthy investors, there is a negative correlation between the accumulation of wealth and feelings of anxiety about their financial well-being.

Fig. 2: Relationship between wealth and anxiety

Figure 2[77] illustrates this relationship between wealth and anxiety: when a person has little or no money, they typically have high anxiety, which motivates them to accumulate wealth. As wealth grows, fear and anxiety initially lessen, but by the time a person or family reaches the median wealth of their peers, anxiety quickly levels off. Now it requires more wealth to maintain that same feeling of safety. There is a perception that more wealth will keep anxiety low, but anxiety and fear increase steadily as wealth increases. The fear changes from a fear of survival to a pressure to maintain a lifestyle, apprehension over the complexity of their financial or business affairs, and anxiety over losing what they have.

In general, Christian investors behave the same as their non-Christian counterparts when it comes to making investment decisions. This observation is confirmed by Amy Sherman in her book *Kingdom Calling: Vocational Stewardship for the Common Good.* Sherman summarizes research by Michael Lindsay, who interviewed over three hundred evangelicals who had achieved significant success in the fields of politics, business, entertainment, media, and others. Lindsay set out to understand the intersection of faith and work in the lives of these individuals. Lindsay's research demonstrates "little evidence . . . of how these evangelical leaders' lifestyles differ from those of their secular peers" (ref. in Sherman).[78]

"The vast majority of evangelicals perched atop their career ladders in various social sectors displayed a profoundly anemic vision for what they could accomplish for the Kingdom of God."

Sherman points out Lindsay's observation that these affluent individuals live their materialistic lifestyles without examination. Few questioned the ratios of their generous compensation packages to their lower-level employees (ref. by Sherman). Sherman goes on to say Lindsay found that "*less than half of the business executives reported that their faith influences how they invest their money*" (emphasis mine).[79] Sherman summarizes Lindsay's careful research by stating that "the vast majority of evangelicals perched atop their career

77. Figure 2 is based on content from Ken Haman, "Using Science to Become Better Investors," AllianceBernstein (July 2018). Used with permission.

78. Amy Sherman, *Kingdom Calling: Vocational Stewardship for the Common Good* (Downers Grove, IL: InterVarsity Press, 2011), 15. Used with permission.

79. Sherman, 15–16. Used with permission.

ladders in various social sectors displayed a profoundly anemic vision for what they could accomplish for the Kingdom of God."[80]

Investor decisions are often motivated by fear and greed. This is true for Christians and non-Christians alike. Fear and greed may seem harsh, but what better words describe investment decisions that seek to minimize risk and maximize financial return for a single stakeholder, the investor? In contrast, holistic investing requires that investors seek to optimize the interests of other stakeholders, including customers, employees, the community, the environment, even God. God's *oikonomos* should commit to provide a safe work environment and living wages for employees, reduce corruption, increase justice in the community, and care for rather than exploit the environment. Christ's example of incarnation among us calls us to take higher risk than non-Christians to achieve God's purposes. Consumerism and materialism evoke an opposite response where investors seek to maximize comfort and security for themselves alone.

Fear is a powerful motivator, as you may recall from our discussion about the fearful servant in Jesus' parable. People will do irrational things to avoid loss. In fact, studies have shown that the pain of losing is twice as strong as the joy of winning.[81] So the feeling of pain we experience over losing five hundred dollars is equal, but opposite to, the feeling of joy that we experience from gaining one thousand dollars. Some would say, "I don't want to take any risk because I have worked so hard to earn what I have." I personally understand and can attest to this fear. But in light of eternity and our roles as managers and not owners, shouldn't we confront such fear as we seek to become missional investors? John Piper suggests, "By removing eternal risk, Christ calls his people to continual temporal risk."[82]

Greed, an overwhelming urge to have more than I really need, is a natural outgrowth of fear. We have been conditioned and taught from an early age to accumulate, store up, save, and even hoard. Watching kids at a birthday party furiously grabbing for candy from a piñata is an obvious example. Adults are more subtle. Accumulating to reach financial independence is an expected goal for us. Greed is the invisible sin of our times because although it is prevalent, no one

80. Sherman, 16. Used with permission.

81. https://thedecisionlab.com/biases/loss-aversion/

82. John Piper, "A Call for Christian Risk" (May 29, 2002): https://www.desiringgod.org/articles/a-call-for-christian-risk. Used with permission.

thinks they themselves are greedy. Milton Friedman taught us in the 1970s that the ultimate measure of a company's success is the extent to which it enriches shareholder value.

When asked, *What are your primary goals for your investments?*, most Christians respond like any other investor: "High return and low risk." But there is a better way.

Embracing Risk and Trust

Most traditional investors seek investments that will provide maximum financial return per unit of risk taken. However, what if we considered a new paradigm for viewing our investment decisions, one that seeks to accomplish God's purposes rather than grow our resources to reduce anxiety, fear, or risk?

Legacy Ventures Partners uses a nine-square grid to help determine if an investment should be added to its missional portfolio (Figure 3):

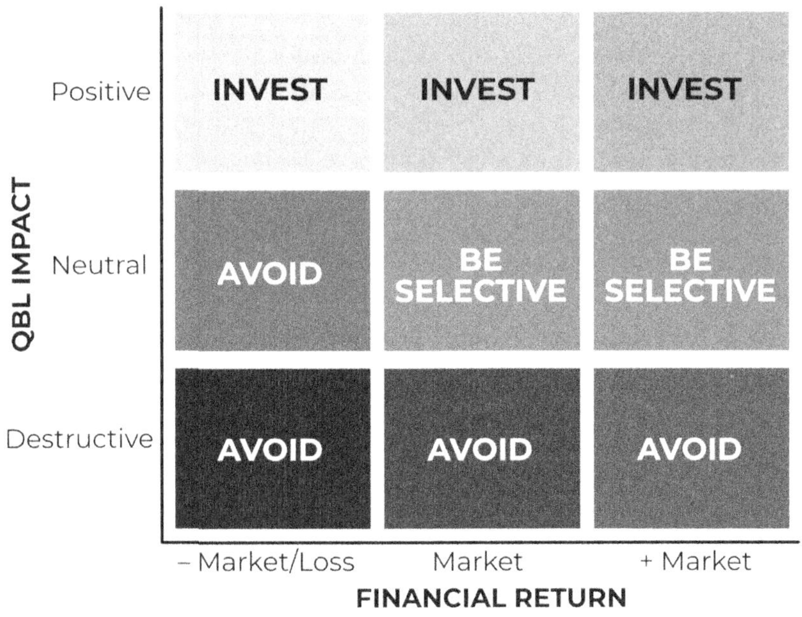

Fig. 3: Missional portfolio considerations

The horizontal axis represents financial return, and the vertical axis represents impact across quadruple bottom line (QBL) outcomes (economic, environmental, social, and spiritual). Investments on the right represent those with higher financial returns compared to those on the left, which are considered "concessionary" because they will likely achieve below-market returns, return of principal, or even financial loss. Vertically, investments across the top have high QBL impact in contrast to the negative impact of those on the bottom.

God desires us to take added risk to expand His kingdom. We are working for Him when we assume higher risk and lower return for the sake of higher kingdom impact. Are there Christians who are willing to take on higher *risk* by deploying investments into harsh business environments, among unreached people, to achieve a compelling and significant spiritual impact?

More than thirty years of professional observation causes me to believe that Christians are trailing secular impact investors who proactively seek to accomplish their non-financial objectives such as environmental, social, and governance (ESG) change via their investments, even if it means lower return. In their 2018 annual survey of impact investors, the Global Impact Investing Network (GIIN) reported that over one-third of secular impact investors have indicated that they are satisfied with below-market returns or even a simple return of capital if they achieve their impact objectives.[83]

Greed and fear motivations derive from a worldly perspective, especially in our materialistic and affluent world. God's wisdom is often the opposite of what we naturally believe. The apostle Paul tells us that "the person without the Spirit does not accept the things that come from the Spirit of God but considers them foolishness, and cannot understand them because they are discerned only through the Spirit" (1 Cor. 2:14). Jesus taught "the last will be first"; "he who is greatest among you shall be your servant"; and "whoever desires to save his life will lose it, but whoever loses his life for My sake will save it" (Matt. 20:16, 23:11; Luke 9:24). Does this apply in the realm of finance? Does God's wisdom seem foolish to us?

Let's consider generosity and confidence, the opposites of greed and fear (Figure 4):

83. Global Impact Investing Network (GIIN), "2018 Annual Impact Investor Survey" (2018), 3.

Worldly Perspective	**Greed** Maximize Shareholder Return	**Fear** Avoid Risk
Godly Perspective	**Generosity** Optimize Stakeholder Outcomes	**Confidence** Deploy with Purpose

Fig 4: Investing motivations

The core values of generosity and confidence should replace fear and greed when we make investment decisions as the Lord's *oikonomos*. Christian investors can season their investment choices with generous confidence that emulates the character of the True Owner. When we base our missional investment decisions on what we were taught in our MBA classes first, and second on accomplishing God's purposes, we are being foolish stewards.

OUR STORY

Proactively investing in ways that result in God being glorified has brought my wife and me great satisfaction, even when risk is much higher and returns are much lower than a typical risk-adjusted portfolio. In addition to below-market, low-interest mortgages and personal loans held for brothers and sisters in Christ who could not otherwise own homes or cars, we are able, by God's grace, to deploy investment dollars into business projects that serve to accomplish QBL outcomes.

As previously mentioned, we invested in an apple orchard project and a coconut oil production facility. Another of our investments is in a biotechnology company on the Indian subcontinent that has patented a biological treatment for municipal wastewater. The process delivers treated water suitable for non-potable (i.e., agricultural) use by installing its bioremediation process, which takes advantage of the microbes and plants from the local environment to remove toxins and biologically treat wastewater. We have also invested in a honeybee business in Central Asia, an IT company in West Asia, and an ecotourism resort in Southeast Asia. All are seeking profound kingdom impact among the most vulnerable and least reached.

We are committed, as God's fiduciaries, to patient capital investments that seek multiple bottom-line outcomes. We're not looking for an attractive financial rate of return for our own benefit. We seek to share the risks, the burdens, and the benefits of our investments with other stakeholders. Our investment decisions are informed and influenced by optimization of positive outcomes for all involved. Proverbs 16:8 reminds us, "Better is a little with righteousness, Than vast revenues without justice" (NKJV).

CONCLUSION

As God's fiduciaries we must set aside the natural tendency toward risk aversion. We should generously deploy resources into investments that accomplish God's purposes instead. Stephen Neill, in his book *A History of Christian Missions*, declares that early Christians knew that at some point, they'd likely confront losing their life if they acknowledged their faith.[84]

God's fiduciaries must be committed to deployment, not risk avoidance.

God's fiduciaries must be committed to deployment, not risk avoidance. We must embrace risk engagement, not just risk management. Storing up treasures in heaven means proactively deploying our saved capital not simply to maximize our rate of return but to accomplish the multiple eternal bottom lines of the Master.

When is the last time you asked yourself,

- Would a review of my portfolio reveal any substantial difference or increased risk-taking (to accomplish kingdom impact) than a non-Christian's portfolio?
- Do I consider God the primary stakeholder in the investments I select?
- Am I ready to invest my assets—RRSP, IRA, 401(k), TFSA, ISA, Pension Scheme, Super or other retirement accounts, even a DAF or Family Foundation corpus—for QBL impact and not just financial return?

84. Stephen Neill, *A History of Christian Missions* (NY: Penguin, 1964), 43.

- Am I truly God dependent or have I become self-reliant in my financial decisions?

Being the Lord's *oikonomos* requires us to intentionally deploy investments for optimized impact, with a view to spiritual outcomes and financial return, not simply to maximum financial return or risk avoidance for ourselves.

This type of life-or-death risk taking seems crazy, but as John Piper says, "This was normal. To become a Christian was to risk your life. Tens of thousands did it. Why? Because to do it was to gain Christ, and not to was to lose your soul."[85]

85. Piper, "A Call for Christian Risk": https://www.desiringgod.org/articles/a-call-for-christian-risk. Used with permission.

QUESTIONS FOR STUDY

1. Define the word *deploy* and discuss what deploying financial resources means to you.

2. Share a story when you have committed and deployed financial resources for the purpose of kingdom impact that required personal sacrifice or risk.

3. Common motivators for both Christian and non-Christian investor decisions are fear and greed. Discuss how this statement from John Piper can influence a Christian to confront fear as they seek to be God's fiduciary in the realm of missional investing: "By removing eternal risk, Christ calls his people to continual temporal risk." Cite any biblical texts that come to mind that provide similar instruction or encouragement to press on in the face of risk or fear.

4. Read Matthew 19:16-30. Which commandments did the rich young man acknowledge to Jesus that he had kept since he was a boy? "Do not covet" was not a commandment that Jesus had cited. Why do you suppose Jesus stated that the young man needed to "go, sell your possessions," to follow him (v. 21)? How was greed or covetousness impacting this rich young man's genuine and earnest desire to follow Jesus?

5. Discuss the nine-square grid's value as a tool to help change the basis of investment decisions toward accomplishing the purposes of God rather than expanding our own wealth in a vain effort to reduce anxiety and risk.

6. Environmental, social, and governance (ESG) impact investments seek to accomplish meaningful change in these areas. Global Impact Investing Network reports, "One third of secular impact investors have indicated that they are satisfied with below-market returns or even a simple return of capital if they achieve their impact objectives." What is your reaction to this finding?

7. Review Figure 4 and draw a conclusion regarding your investing motivations. Have your motivations been largely influenced by a worldly perspective or a godly perspective?

8. Consider the statements, "God's fiduciaries must be committed to deployment, not risk avoidance," and, "Storing up treasures in heaven means proactively deploying our saved capital not simply to maximize our rate of return but to accomplish the multiple bottom lines of the Master." Look again at Matthew 19:21. What did Jesus state that the rich young man should do with the proceeds from the sale of his possessions, and what benefit would that provide for the rich young man?

Personal Reflection

Would a review of my portfolio reveal a substantial difference or risk taking (to accomplish kingdom impact) than a non-Christian's portfolio? What evidence is there that I consider God as the primary stakeholder in my selection of investments? Are the primary objectives for my portfolio temporal gains or eternal outcomes? Am I choosing to be God-dependent, and am I ready to prove my desire to seek spiritual impact as well as financial return with the investable assets He has entrusted to me as His fiduciary?

Chapter 11

IN SEARCH OF THE OPTIMIZED QBL PORTFOLIO

OPTIMIZING A PORTFOLIO

Constructing a portfolio that achieves QBL outcomes through its underlying investment is not easy. I have served as a money manager and financial advisor for more than three decades. Most people would call me a professional investor, but my professional expertise is better described as an asset allocator. There is a simple difference between the two. Investors invest money to achieve a single outcome—usually to make more money. Asset allocators invest money into a variety of investments to balance and achieve multiple objectives at the same time. For example, a client of mine may need to produce income for retirement while simultaneously growing their portfolio to keep pace with inflation. These are two very different objectives which require different types of investments and management strategies. An investor representing a client (usually a fund manager) will seek to achieve income or growth, but not both. On the other hand, an asset allocator acting for a client will employ multiple types of investments and strategies to accomplish these competing objectives of income and growth simultaneously because this is what the client requires.

My friend Peter Shaukat uses the words *maximization* and *optimization* to distinguish the difference between investing and allocating. Maximization refers to the act of making a single thing as great as possible. If you are interested in the maximization of profits, you want to get as much money as possible out of your investments. You do not care about any other measures of success. An investor must be a good maximizer to achieve their client's objectives. On the other hand, optimization refers to manipulating a variety of variables to create the most efficient solution for achieving multiple outcomes at the same time. If you are interested in optimizing a portfolio, you will combine a variety of asset classes to achieve the best risk-adjusted returns. An asset allocator is not seeking maximum return but the best return per unit of risk taken.

As the Lord's *oikonomos*, we must be asset allocators. Our job is to allocate the capital God entrusts to us among a variety of projects and methods to optimize QBL impact. IBEC Ventures created a short video with Mats Tunehag which offers a simple visual explanation of this concept called, "Wall Street vs BAM Street."[86] Capital is not free—it has a cost, and the cost must be respected by investors and investee companies alike. Balancing stakeholders and outcomes is critical in developing a truly optimized QBL portfolio. An *oikonomos* must be a trustworthy allocator of capital, not just an investor.

How then should we think about investing for impact versus investing for risk-adjusted return? As fiduciaries of the True Owner's resources, we must first make sure our investment objectives reflect the True Owner's goals. It is not appropriate to assume that maximizing the financial rate of return is the most important goal for God's fiduciary. Prioritizing the economic rate of return for shareholders over the Master's other bottom lines is self-centered and falsely assumes that the investor, the one with capital, is to be prioritized over all other stakeholders.

Each Investment Is Not Evaluated Alone but by How It Contributes to the Overall Portfolio

Modern Portfolio Theory, although usually applied to managing portfolio risk, can provide an excellent model for us as we construct

86. "BAM Street - Mats Tunehag" (2016): https://vimeo.com/152713984.

portfolios that accomplish QBL objectives. Harry Markowitz, the winner of the 1990 Nobel Prize in Economics, is also known as the father of Modern Portfolio Theory (MPT) for the portfolio construction model he published in *The Journal of Finance* in 1952. Markowitz emphasized that the competing objectives of reducing risk and achieving higher financial return go hand-in-hand. MPT continues to be one of the most important and influential economic theories. It is foundational to current portfolio management because it helps risk-averse investors construct portfolios that optimize expected return based on a given level of risk.

MPT provides us with this major insight concerning investment capital: an investment's risk and return characteristics should not be viewed in isolation. The rate of return of a specific investment is less important than how that investment behaves in the context of the entire portfolio. Therefore, to optimize performance, a portfolio must be constructed using non-correlated investments that enhance the portfolio's risk-adjusted return to optimize performance. MPT offers the possibility of constructing an "efficient frontier" of optimal portfolios, offering the maximum expected return for a given level of risk. The following story will help illustrate the insight noted above.

Negative Correlation and the Efficient Frontier

When we were newly married, my wife and I planted flowers at our new house. After planting hundreds of tulip and daffodil bulbs, we soon learned the principle of "non-correlation." Our flower beds were brilliant with color in April and May, but they were just patches of dirt filled with the remnants of dead tulips and daffodils the rest of the summer. We learned a valuable lesson. If you plant flowers with characteristics that correlate to different months in their blooming cycle, flowers will grace your home continuously. If not, you may have a great return at the start but dirt and wilted foliage at the end.

In the same way, every investment has its own characteristics. An experienced investor expects lower returns from bonds than stocks because bonds carry lower risk. Different combinations of securities will produce new risk-return relationships that are entirely different from each individual investment. It may surprise you to learn that the careful addition of higher volatility investments like stocks (higher risk) can reduce risk (measured by standard deviation) in a portfolio of bonds. The Efficient Frontier (Figure 5) represents the best of the bond/stock combinations—producing the maximum expected return for a given level of risk.

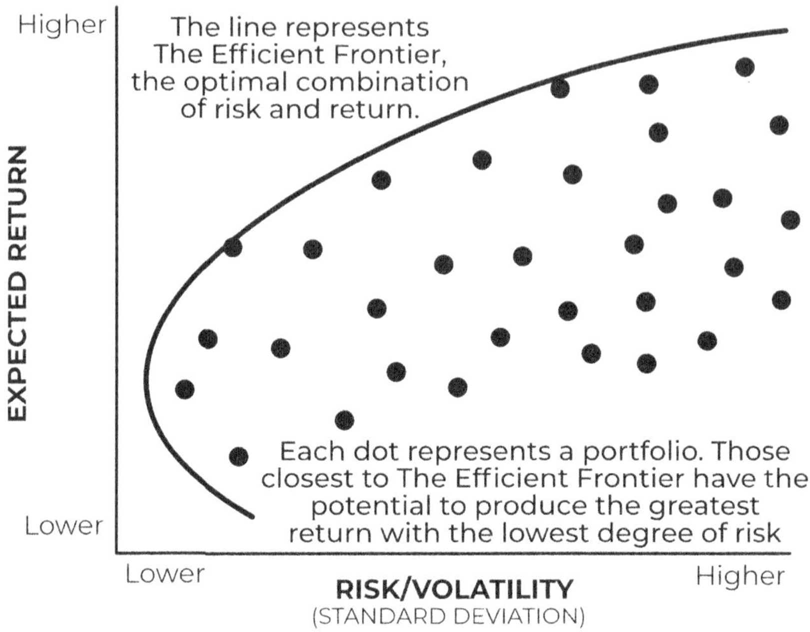

Fig. 5: The efficient frontier

Like planting flowers that bloom at different times, combining the two non-correlated asset classes enhances overall performance. This is called an *optimized risk-adjusted portfolio*. Sophisticated investors also recognize there is a multitude of different asset classes (large cap, small cap, emerging markets, government bonds, junk bonds, cash, etc.), each offering its own performance characteristics. An entire portfolio moves to the top left of the Efficient Frontier chart when these classes are properly combined, which results in optimized risk-adjusted returns. The whole becomes greater than the sum of its parts.

It's perplexing to hear Christian stewards stating that impact investments must achieve "market-like" returns. That's like saying a portfolio must always achieve a return equal to the S&P 500 index. Few savers are willing to stomach the potential forty percent losses that a pure stock portfolio typically experiences, so most allocate their capital among different asset classes to reduce volatility. Similarly, each impact business will have different characteristics relative to QBL outcomes. As the Lord's *oikonomos* we should focus on outcomes that are of greatest importance to the Master: justice, mercy and kindness, humility, holistic transformation, and so on, not just financial return.

Grace and generosity apply to our investment decisions as much as they do to our charitable endeavors. Some companies will inherently achieve greater environmental impact. Some will be in more profitable sectors or more developed markets, which makes it easier to achieve accelerated financial growth. Some businesses will require more laborers, which can provide for a higher degree of social and spiritual impact. Some geographic regions will have lower "expected" returns in each category due to economics, corruption, environmental policies, natural disasters, or persecution. We cannot expect every missional business to measure the same in all areas. By combining a set of investments, each with different strengths and weaknesses across multiple bottom lines, we can create a portfolio that is optimized to achieve holistic impact.

By combining a set of investments, each with different strengths and weaknesses across multiple bottom lines, we can create a portfolio that is optimized to achieve holistic impact.

It is important to note, however, that as the Lord's *oikonomos and* as allocators of His resources, we should expect a minimum level of "return" from each declared bottom line in our portfolio to optimize the overall results. Minimum requirements might include establishing financially healthy businesses that operate on ethical principles (economic); creating dignified jobs with fair compensation and human interactions that are just and merciful (social); caring for the natural world so as to minimize harm and to restore degraded air, water, and land (environmental); and designing, executing, and monitoring a spiritual impact plan that brings blessing and transformation to individuals, families, local communities, and nations (spiritual). While anticipating such a "return," we must be quick to acknowledge that the QBL characteristics at any given company will not only vary from those at any other but also will be variable over time within the company in question.

EVALUATING POTENTIAL QBLS AND BUILDING A HOLISTIC PORTFOLIO

MPT requires a portfolio manager to evaluate each investment by how it contributes to the overall portfolio rather than viewing its characteristics alone. In the same way, missional investors should pay attention to each individual company's contribution to the overall portfolio objective of holistic QBL impact. God's fiduciaries should not use the same measuring stick for every individual investment, as if they expect every business to score equally on each bottom line.

My colleagues and I have begun to develop a "spider web assessment tool" (Figure 6) by which we can assess a company's current position and progress toward achieving QBL impact. By plotting each company's QBL characteristics on a graph, we can easily visualize which QBLs are strongest and which ones are weakest.

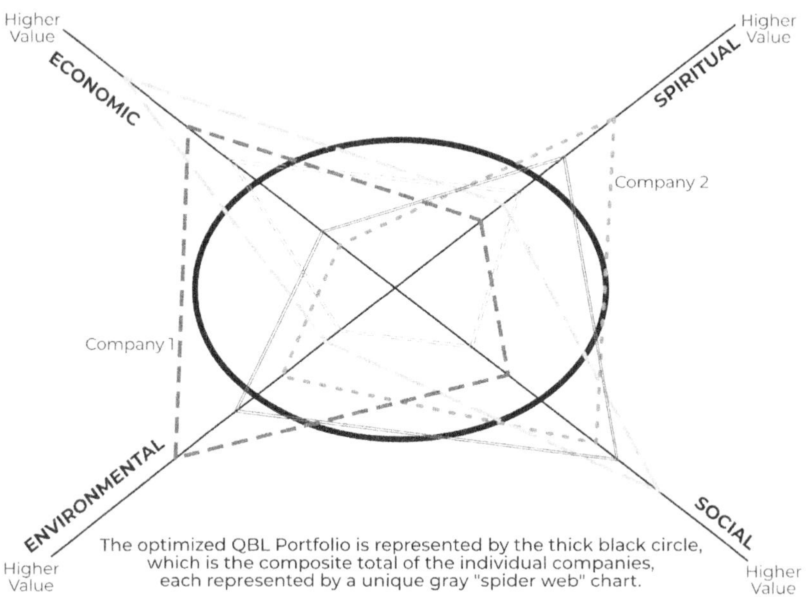

Fig. 6: The optimized QBL portfolio

The assessment tool is useful in helping businesses create strategies to improve each of their four bottom lines. In this diagram, Company 1, an environmental consulting firm (dark gray, long-dashed line), scores highly on *economic* and *environmental* impact, but due to its small size and few employees, it has less opportunity for *spiritual* and *social* impact. In contrast, Company 2, an organic agriculture business (light gray, short-dashed line), scores very high on *spiritual* and *social* impact because it employs many workers from unreached people groups providing discipleship opportunities, yet it is struggling financially due to corruption which has hindered its ability to sell products in a fair and profitable manner. By combining the individual "spider web charts" from the dozens of transformational businesses in our portfolio, we can assess the QBL results for our entire portfolio, optimizing the strengths of each company to offset the weaknesses of other companies so that the portfolio as a whole achieves QBL impact.

Comprehensive QBL impact can be accomplished in a portfolio even when individual companies are stronger or weaker in any given category. Like the principles learned from MPT and "optimized" returns, steward investors should not expect each missional business to look the same relative to each bottom line. Instead, by assessing the QBLs for each business and combining multiple companies, particularly those with varying strengths and weaknesses, we can create more fully optimized QBL portfolios.

INVESTING AND ALLOCATING ARE NECESSARY SKILLS IN BUILDING A QBL PORTFOLIO

The body of skills and knowledge necessary to allocate your investments to achieve God's purposes may seem overwhelming. Optimizing a portfolio of missional businesses to achieve QBL outcomes is not simply throwing a token investment into an online microfinance fund such as Kiva (although that may be a starting place). A successful *oikonomos* must allocate investments very differently than a traditional investor because their desired outcomes are different.

Portfolio construction principles such as MPT apply to impact investing but in non-traditional ways. Some might be tempted to invest in a missionary who is raising capital to start a coffee shop in a Middle Eastern country. Some appropriate questions for an investor to ask are, *What market research has been done to confirm that there are enough coffee drinkers in an area where most people prefer tea? Is there competition? What skills and experience does the missionary have that will equip them for success in this business? What are the projected expenses, revenues, and profit of the business, and can it afford to repay loans?*

An allocator on the other hand will ask the same questions but add some additional and very different questions such as, *How will each bottom line be measured, and how do these anticipated outcomes affect the overall performance of the portfolio relative to each bottom line? Is my present portfolio overweighted in a particular geographic region, industry, or currency? Does this investment add value to the portfolio as a whole? Will this business have a cyclical cash flow with expected high-income months and expected low-income months? Can an investment be structured to match the company's cash flow cycle and simultaneously provide cash flow to the fund at times when other businesses may have difficulty making payments?*

CONCLUSION

Most people think that being a steward involves simply living on a budget, saving for retirement, and tithing. The job of the Lord's *oikonomos* is more complex and difficult. It is wise to seek guidance from others who have already walked this path and can help you fulfill your duties as God's fiduciary.

QUESTIONS FOR STUDY

1. Compare and contrast the ideas of portfolio maximization and portfolio optimization.

2. When we pursue a portfolio that seeks to maximize the financial rate of return as the most important goal, who is the pre-eminent stakeholder? Are God's goals represented? Explain why or why not. Would a financial advisor support or caution the investor for choosing this goal?

3. Living on a budget, saving for retirement, tithing, and generous giving are financial practices of stewards. Has the concept that God's fiduciaries should also invest for impact versus exclusively investing for risk-adjusted returns ever been posed to you before reading this book? What other financial advisors, Christian authors, or personalities have expressed this idea?

4. What are the four bottom lines for a quadruple bottom line business? Identify the stakeholders for these businesses. If you choose to invest in a QBL business with lower-than-average market returns and high spiritual and social impact, who is the pre-eminent stakeholder? Are God's goals represented? Explain why or why not.

5. How would your financial advisor react to your decision to choose the goal of impact investing versus a maximized financial return? Would you expect your advisor to support this decision, caution you, or react in another way?

6. Suppose you invested in a Business as Mission company that was unprofitable and eventually closed. Would this change your advisor's reaction? What biblical text would you share with someone who earnestly sought to deploy resources in a Kingdom Business and saw that business cease? What might Jesus say in response to such an outcome? How might your advisor's and Jesus' response differ if the venture was a traditional, non-impact business?

7. What is Modern Portfolio Theory and how does it serve as a model for constructing a QBL investment portfolio?

8. Review and discuss the spider web assessment tool. How does plotting each company's QBL characteristics on a chart help with creating a portfolio that fully optimizes QBL impact? Which bottom line (if any) would make a QBL business likely to be one that you would select, as God's fiduciary, to deploy capital to support the business's growth and development?

9. Are you more apt to be a lone ranger or a partner in pursuing investments in kingdom impact businesses? Why?

Chapter 12

MAMMON'S INFLUENCE ON CAPITAL AND INVESTMENT

Many live as enemies of the cross of Christ. Their destiny is destruction, their god is their stomach, and their glory is in their shame. Their mind is set on earthly things. But our citizenship is in heaven. (Phil. 3:18-20)

I have observed throughout my career that capital, wealth, and riches exhibit a particular personality that influences how investors use them. This chapter explores the qualities of capital operating in the world system.

When the apostle Paul contrasts those living as enemies of the cross of Christ, whose minds are set on earthly things, with those whose citizenship is in heaven, he establishes a stark distinction between earthly and kingdom-minded individuals. However, this concept extends beyond just individuals to include institutions and systems that behave in earthly versus kingdom ways. Unfortunately, our beliefs and practices regarding investing and capital itself have been dangerously perverted by an earthly mindset leading to a lopsided economic system dominated by earthly minded capital.

HOW CAN CAPITAL BE EARTHLY MINDED?

Capital (our financial resources), like physical money, is neutral, but it takes on characteristics depending on what system it is operating out of. The apostle Paul reminds believers in Ephesus that "we do not wrestle against flesh and blood, but against the rulers, against the authorities, against the cosmic powers over this present darkness, against the spiritual forces of evil in the heavenly places" (Eph. 6:12, ESV). Capital can be influenced in the same way that we can be influenced by either the Spirit of God or the spirit of our enemy. Two systems—the world's system and God's system—compete to influence capital. Jesus highlights this struggle when He teaches about mammon, saying, "No one can serve two masters; for either he will hate the one and love the other, or else he will be loyal to the one and despise the other. You cannot serve God and mammon" (Matt. 6:24, NKJV). While many Scripture translations use the word *money* in place of *mammon*, I believe the word *mammon* better captures the tension between the actual tangible asset, money, and the factors that influence our relationship with, beliefs about, and attitude towards that asset. Like the writer of Proverbs who personifies wisdom as a lady, Jesus here personifies mammon. Jesus suggests that mammon bears qualities in opposition to the qualities of wealth in God's kingdom and even in opposition to God Himself.

As a result, our view of capital has been tainted by mammon's influence. While interpretations of the word *mammon* range from a simple description of wealth, riches, or money to a belief that Jesus is referring to an ancient Syrian god, it is reasonable for us to use a generally accepted definition that strikes a balance between these extremes and to look at mammon as the *personification of wealth, money, riches, or capital.*

What Does Mammon Look Like?

I have a large, fine art photographic print created by fashion photographer Michael Belk, titled, "Can't Take it with You: A lesson on retained earnings."[87] Belk, who left his high-powered career to bring Jesus Christ to life through the lens of his camera, created a compelling collection of fine art photography depicting the messages of Jesus, showing His relevance by depicting first-century Jesus

87. Michael Belk, *Journeys with the Messiah: The Parable Edition* (Santa Rosa Beach, FL: Journeys with the Messiah, LLC, 2011), 20–21.

interacting with twenty-first-century personas such as Wall Street executives, Italian fashionistas, common people, even people with questionable character. The specific photograph hanging above my desk depicts a funeral procession walking through a hillside cemetery led by a forward-looking priest, followed by four men struggling to bear a coffin clearly over-filled with gold coins that are spilling onto the ground. Behind the coffin-bearers walk five mourners, and behind them stands Jesus—half-turned away but looking with intensity toward the procession. He seems to be the only figure wrestling with the obvious irony of a burial procession for a gold-filled coffin.

To me, this compelling photograph effectively illustrates the modern obsession with accumulating wealth on earth. Jesus addresses this obsession quite directly with His teaching in the Gospel of Matthew in what is certainly one of the most popular verses about wealth, as He sets up His challenge of serving either God or mammon: "Do not store up for yourselves treasures on earth, where moths and vermin destroy, and where thieves break in and steal. But store up for yourselves treasures in heaven, where moths and vermin do not destroy, and where thieves do not break in and steal. For where your treasure is, there your heart will be also" (Matt. 6:19-21).

Understanding "where our heart is" and whether it's influenced by Jesus' teaching about mammon is foundational to establishing a proper view of deploying capital for kingdom purposes.

Understanding "where our heart is" and whether it's influenced by Jesus' teaching about mammon is foundational to establishing a proper view of deploying capital for kingdom purposes. Unfortunately, many conversations about wealth and capital get derailed by the question, *Is money good or evil?*

Money itself is neutral. It is neither good nor evil. Money is a resource, a tool which can be used for *either* good *or* evil. But the conversation must continue beyond the morality of money and get at the core of what spirit is influencing how a person, society, or culture thinks about capital. Only when we recognize that the spirit holding power over the earthly use of capital is that of mammon will we see the debasement it has caused.

MAMMON, FALSE ASSUMPTIONS, AND SPRING FLOWERS IN WINTER

There are basic principles for how things operate in the world. If our assumptions are not based on truth, our system will eventually break down. The apostle Paul admonishes the Early Church not to "conform to the pattern of this world, but [to] be transformed by the renewing of [their] mind[s]" (Rom. 12:2). If we think as the world thinks about wealth, capital, and investing, we needn't change a thing. Conformity is as easy as paddling downstream. But, if we are committed to thinking about capital as God does, our minds need to be transformed. We make a mistake when we minimize the personality of mammon and how it influences the character qualities of capital, an error which may seem small at the moment but can have serious consequences over time. Consider the astronomers and scientists of Julius Caesar's day who misunderstood the solar system and therefore built a faulty calendar.

In 46 BC Julius Caesar built his calendar on the incorrect but prevailing assumption that the earth was the center of the solar system. The resulting miscalculation of the length of the solar year meant the calendar became unsynchronized with the seasons. In time, it seemed as if the flowers of spring were blooming in the wrong month. The sixteenth-century pope Gregory XIII was concerned about this effect, not because the calendar was incorrectly predicting when flowers should bloom but because it meant that Easter, traditionally observed on March 21, continued to fall further and further away from the spring equinox. In response, an Italian scientist, Alysus Lilius, proposed an ingenious solution that successfully synced the calendar and the seasons. But even his solution, which the Gregorian calendar adopted in the sixteenth century, does not sync perfectly with the solar year—it is off by eleven seconds per year—and by the year 4909, the Gregorian calendar will be a full day ahead of the solar year.[88]

If calendars built on false assumptions lead to spring flowers blooming in winter months, how much more important is it to avoid making capital deployment decisions on false assumptions, especially assumptions influenced by the worldly spirit of mammon? Misallocation of capital results in uneven distribution, with capital piling up where it

88. Jennie Coehn, "6 Things You May Not Know About the Gregorian Calendar" (August 22, 2018): https://www.history.com/news/6-things-you-may-not-know-about-the-gregorian-calendar.

is not needed and scarcity of capital where it is needed most. This results in poverty, exploitation, and 3.23 billion people with little or no access to the Gospel of Jesus Christ.[89] It is worth learning what assumptions we have about money and capital, so we become kingdom-minded investors who use capital strategically and sacrificially to serve others in love and to advance God's kingdom priorities.

HOW MAMMON HAS INFECTED CAPITAL

Business cannot start without capital. Startups in the United States or other developed economies are typically begun with personal resources, home equity loans, or help from family and friends. Some call this "family, friends, and fools financing." As the business matures, it seeks outside capital from traditional sources such as banks, lenders, angel investors, private equity, or venture capital.

The same process is true for missional enterprises. But the group of investors who support investment into missional enterprises must not be influenced by a mammon spirit. They must see capital very differently than an investor who operates exclusively with an earthly economic perspective. Considering Jesus' warning not to store up treasure on earth, I would like to highlight the character qualities of capital as defined by the world's economic systems, personified by mammon, and how these qualities influence its deployment.

The following attributes identify investment capital with mammon-focused characteristics that seek to prioritize the investor's temporal gain:

1. *Expensive:* Mammon is expensive for missional enterprises, expecting high financial returns based on what is best for the investors. Market-rate returns are expected, with higher returns always expected for increased risk.

2. *Impatient:* Mammon is impatient, expecting clear and timely exit strategies so capital is returned to investors promptly. The world's economic system expects that capital will be returned to investors within five to seven years so that investors can re-invest the capital into another high-return opportunity.

3. *Frugal:* Mammon is frugal toward missional investments but extravagant toward its own self-interests. It expects to

89. "What Is a UPG?": https://globalfrontiermissions.org/gfm-101-missions-course/the-unreached-peoples-and-their-role-in-the-great-commission/.

provide just enough capital so that the business can "cash flow" itself as soon as possible—it will release as little capital as possible to minimize risk and to maximize return for the investor.

4. *Risk Averse:* Mammon is risk averse. It does not like to take risks, minimizing potential losses to the investor by structuring deals that transfer as much risk as possible to the entrepreneur and away from the investor.

5. *Imperialistic:* Mammon is imperialistic. It always wants to maintain control, so investors set up their investments to maintain their ownership or influence over the companies invested in for as long as possible.

6. *Selfish:* Mammon is selfish, expecting that investment capital itself will take priority over the needs of all other stakeholders.

The spirit of mammon subtly permeates how Christian investors look at capital, causing them to believe that the investor is the most important stakeholder. As a result, investors with this mindset have greater difficulty considering investments in closed countries which seek multiple bottom-line outcomes.

The lack of capital flowing from rich countries to poor countries drew the attention of Nobel Laureate, Robert E. Lucas. The Lucas Paradox is the name for his finding that although the expected return on investment might be high in many emerging or frontier economies, capital does not flow there because of the high level of uncertainty associated with those expected returns. Reasons for the imbalanced flow include inadequate infrastructure, a poorly educated labor force, corruption, and a tendency to default on debt from abroad, among other factors. As of January 2021, by share of total world equity market valuations, the largest and most developed countries control over eighty-five percent of the resources of the global capital markets. This means that less than fifteen percent of market capitalization is allocated to the countries that need capital investment the most to develop their economies—which would alleviate poverty and the myriad troubles that accompany it.

Mammon is frugal toward missional investments but extravagant toward its own self-interests.

Does our investing reflect God's economic design? Or has mammon's influence confused the purpose, qualities, and distribution of capital so that we exploit it for personal gain rather than using it as a tool to bring *shalom* to a broken world?

God's *oikonomos* has a different responsibility, and capital in the hands of His fiduciaries must carry different qualities from the world's system and from how most traditional secular investors think. Recognizing that God is the True Owner, obedience to God's purposes is the goal—not increase for ourselves. In the next chapter we will explore the qualities that better define how fiduciaries of God's resources should characterize their investment capital and specifically how these qualities are being used by the investors who capitalized Heritage Farm and Ranch in Romania.

ROMA PEOPLE, EASTERN EUROPE

It's a forty-five-minute drive from the Romanian city of Oradea to the village of Șuncuiuș, a community that seems stuck in a bygone era. The curvy road is dotted with neatly stacked hay mounds. Horses graze in uncut yards, and occasionally you'll pass a cow tied to a fence. Old Transylvanian farm buildings painted in pastel colors and Soviet-era buildings, broken and vacant, line some of the streets. But a far less tranquil picture presents itself at the village outskirts, where a squalid Roma (Gypsy) settlement extends across a muddy hill.

When it rains, the dirt roads leading to the Roma settlement turn into a muddy bog. Most families lack the financial means to update the interior of their tiny houses, so dirt floors are common. It's not unusual for a mother, father, and many children to live under a dilapidated roof covering a single-room home measuring just four square meters (around forty-four square feet). A cast iron wood stove used for both cooking and heating sometimes fills the room with smoke as water for tea is boiled in a blackened pot. Speaking of water, the only source is a village well, accessed by walking down the deeply rutted road where a sea of mud awaits everyone. A young boy and his sister stand in the mud, which nearly spills over the top of their rubber boots as they attempt to draw water using a hand pump. In short, the settlement is a rural slum.

Romania's Roma communities live in abject poverty, the likes of which nobody would expect in present-day Eastern Europe. They remain the most persecuted and left-behind people group in Europe with a thirty-five percent literacy rate, a second-grade education on average, seventy percent unemployment, and an average income of two hundred dollars per month.

Heritage Farm and Ranch—Bihor Region, Romania

Heritage Farm and Ranch was born out of the prayers of two graduates from Emanuel University in Oradea, Romania. Cristian is a theology graduate and bi-vocational pastor who works on his family farm, and Ioan is an energetic business professor who has been involved in several entrepreneurial ventures and now serves as dean of the Emanuel Business School.

Together with their team, they envisioned care for the Roma people and bi-vocational revenue for missionaries, pastors, and church leaders who serve in these impoverished rural areas. Heritage Ranch and Farm is an agriculture business, focused on producing healthy, organic vegetables and meat products in the northern region of Romania near Oradea. Demand for organic products is increasing exponentially in Europe, and Romania is no exception.

Organic agriculture is not easily mechanized so it requires a lot of labor. Heritage now owns more than three hundred acres of ranch land for raising organic beef, chicken, and pork, and manages over fifty greenhouses which produce organic vegetables such as lettuce, cucumbers, tomatoes, squash, and eggplant. By equipping and training Roma people to become experts in the field of organic farming, many of the systemic problems of unemployment, poverty, and education are mitigated. Farming and faith are generational and are most successfully passed from one generation to the next through families. As Roma families are transformed through holistic vocational training and discipleship, the light of Jesus and economic prosperity are breaking through. Villages and communities are being transformed, and the reputation of Roma society is changing from being known as thieves and gamblers to being Europe's highly esteemed, successful, and ethical organic food experts.

It has been more than five years since Heritage began, and it is showing some positive results while staying focused on the long journey ahead to make the business sustainable and to see generational change in Roma communities.

Economic Impact: Although Romania gained European Union (UE) member status in 2007, foreign sponsorships have not provided the hoped-for economic solutions for rural Romania and Roma villages. Unemployment plagues the communities, leaving local churches unable to financially support their leaders. Heritage now employs pastors from four rural churches so they can support their families as bi-vocational ministers.

Having established a solid, large-scale, farm-to-market relationship with several large grocery retailers, Heritage is beginning to build a network of cooperative farms to meet the growing demand for organic products while providing living wages and self-sustaining employment for hundreds of families.

Social Impact: Stigmatized because they are Roma, it is very difficult for Roma people to find employment. These insurmountable obstacles in Roma communities result in generational illiteracy and poverty. Heritage is establishing farm operations near Roma villages and hires primarily Roma people to work at their farms.

Domestic features that most people take for granted are missing in most Roma homes. Financial resources allow employed Roma to make much-needed home improvements such as installing concrete floors, repairing leaking roofs, adding much-needed insulation for the harsh winter temperatures, and installing plumbing for running water supply. Living wages also allow families to purchase healthier food, providing added benefits for children because a well-nourished child living in a safe home is more likely to improve their academic performance.

Environmental Impact: Organic farming can be profitable, and organic food appeals to consumers as both a healthy and ethical choice. Beyond money and ethics, though, organic farming practices result in numerous environmental benefits.

Organic farming reduces the use of pesticides which in turn reduces contamination to the soil, water supply, and air. The result is a reduction of millions of pounds of persistent and harmful pesticides that would otherwise enter the environment annually, a stark contrast to conventional mass-production farming. Natural cultivation practices, crop rotation, and soil management are far better than chemical management. A nine-year study by USDA Agricultural Research Service (ARS) shows that organic farming builds up organic soil matter better than conventional, no-till farming.[90]

---

90. Don Comis, "Organic Farming Beats No-Till?" accessed September 7, 2021 (July 10, 2007): https://www.ars.usda.gov/news-events/news/research-news/2007/organic-farming-beats-no-till/.

Dwindling water supplies and poor water health are also very real threats. When the water supply is at risk, people and the planet suffer. Heritage's CEO notes that one major threat to Romania's rural water sources and rivers is runoff from harmful pesticides and toxic fertilizers used by non-organic farms. Heritage is proud of their efforts to keep the water source safe.

Spiritual Impact: From its inception, Heritage has provided income for the CEO who simultaneously serves as pastor of two rural churches. Unlike most pastors, he does not receive compensation from the church but instead is a financial contributor to the churches he serves.

The Gospel is lived out in word and deed in all farm operations. Lives have been changed and baptisms have been conducted among those who are ministered to. Those who have turned to Christ have changed their lives and no longer steal, beg, or cheat to make a living. Simultaneously, Heritage has provided up to seventy-five thousand dollars of produce annually to a ministry to disabled and homeless people in one Roma community.

CONCLUSION

I believe in capitalism (trade and industry controlled by private owners for profit, rather than by the state), but individuals have been so heavily influenced by the "spirit of mammon" they don't recognize the flawed decisions they make while allocating capital. Can any of us actually believe that earthly economics are perfectly operating the way that God designed them to operate? The earthly system is broken. The evidence is twofold: our habit of prioritizing the needs of a single stakeholder, the investor, and uneven distribution of capital around the globe. A kingdom-minded investor should use capital differently, both strategically and sacrificially to serve others in love and to advance God's kingdom priorities.

How was Heritage capitalized? Let's turn the page and look at the qualities of kingdom capital and how it is being used in funding Heritage Ranch.

QUESTIONS FOR STUDY

Capital: Money and possessions, especially a large amount of money used for producing more wealth or for starting a new business. Example: "*She leaves her capital untouched in the bank and lives off the interest.*"[91]

Mammon: Material wealth or possessions especially as having a debasing influence. Example: "*you cannot serve God and mammon*"[92]

1. Read Philippians 3:18-20 and Matthew 6:24 and discuss the author's statements:

   a. "Unfortunately, our beliefs and practices regarding investing—even capital itself— have been dangerously perverted by an earthly mindset leading to a lopsided economic system dominated by earthly-minded capital."

   b. "Our view of capital has been tainted by mammon's influence."

   Explain why you agree or disagree with these statements. In your discussion, identify which spirit (the spirit of the kingdom of heaven or the spirit of mammon) you see mostly at work in your country and world today in the realm of investing.

91. https://dictionary.cambridge.org/us/dictionary/english/capital
92. https://www.merriam-webster.com/dictionary/mammon

2. What spirit has primarily been influencing your personal allocation of capital? If a worldly mammon spirit has contributed to your understanding of how capital ought to be allocated, what solution does God offer in Romans 12:2 to counter that corrupt influence?

3. Review the six attributes of investment capital personified by mammon as applied to missional enterprise investments and agree or disagree with the author's statement, "The spirit of mammon subtly permeates how Christian investors look at capital, causing them to believe that the investor is the most important stakeholder."

4. What is the Lucas Paradox? What would change if the Spirit of God fully influenced the qualities of capital entrusted to His fiduciaries around the world?

Chapter 13

SIX QUALITIES OF KINGDOM CAPITAL AND INVESTMENT

The "kingdom of heaven" is a central theme running throughout the Gospel of Matthew, with the phrase being used over thirty times in the book. The kingdom is offered to those who put God's kingdom before their own self-interest, creating tension between the "kingdom economy" and the "earthly economy." Business in God's hands is a powerful tool to advance God's kingdom, and this is possible because the character qualities of capital in the kingdom of heaven are different from the character qualities of capital in the earthly system.

The character of God infuses capital with His attributes so that each time we invest in a Christ-centered business, the capital plays a critical role in fulfilling God's goal of seeing His kingdom come on earth as it is in heaven. When the character of capital is influenced by mammon's spirit, it gets sidetracked to earthly priorities, and the capital becomes derailed from building heavenly treasure. The practical implication is that Christ-centered businesses get overlooked for investment, even by Christian investors. In frontier markets, where agents of the Gospel are in short supply, so too is the capital needed to grow small and medium enterprises (SMEs).

Each time we invest in Christ-centered businesses that earn a return while accomplishing eternal spiritual and social missions, we play a role in God's redemptive plan on earth.

God's *oikonomos* can accomplish something very few investors can by reaching the least and the last, applying a different mindset regarding capital. They are influenced by a different spirit and are intent on seeing lives transformed with the Gospel through businesses that deliver excellent products or services and that help employees live out their God-given purpose in the workplace. Each time we invest in Christ-centered businesses that earn a return while accomplishing eternal spiritual and social missions, we play a role in God's redemptive plan on earth.

CHARACTERISTICS OF CAPITAL IN THE KINGDOM ECONOMY

1. *Affordable:* Kingdom capital is affordable. It balances the needs of all stakeholders. Financial costs are balanced with special attention paid to the borrower's needs so that the business can survive and thrive—the investor is not more important than the entrepreneur.

2. *Patient:* Kingdom capital is patient. It understands that missional enterprises in frontier markets will take a long time to plant and grow. Capital is invested with a distant horizon in view—five, ten, twenty years, even until the Lord's return.

3. *Liberal:* Kingdom capital is liberal. It understands that a shortage of capital in emerging market startups could be a death sentence to a new enterprise. Therefore, it ensures that enough capital is available.

4. *De-Risking:* Kingdom capital is de-risking. It willingly takes financial risk to accomplish spiritual objectives and helps to de-risk these unusual investments for future investors.

5. *Catalytic:* Kingdom capital is catalytic. It provokes and facilitates change that benefits other stakeholders.

6. *Serving:* Kingdom capital is serving. It invests with a primary goal of building people and community.

Although these character qualities align differently than traditional investment capital, these qualities do not negate the necessity for strong due diligence before investing and strong accountability protocols after an investment has been made. The next section will explore in detail what these qualities of capital mean with regards to missional deployment in balance with responsibility and due diligence.

The following table illustrates the side-by-side comparison of traditional and kingdom capital characteristics:

Mammon Maximizes results for the investor	**Kingdom of Heaven** Optimizes outcomes for all stakeholders to build God's Kingdom
Expensive	Affordable
Impatient	Patient
Frugal	Liberal
Risk Averse	De-Risking
Imperialistic	Catalytic
Selfish	Serving

Fig. 7: Character of capital

KINGDOM CAPITAL IN THE EYES OF AN OIKONOMOS IS...

Affordable

There isn't a level playing field in frontier markets, especially for those who seek to do honest, transparent business, paying taxes and fair wages. Interest rates are frequently fifteen to twenty percent at banks and even higher from hard money lenders. Offering affordable capital for Christian business owners seeking to influence culture and raise the moral bar for business ethics and finance may be one of the few ways that investors can help to level an uneven playing field caused by corruption or government policy. When the cultural norm is paying bribes rather than taxes, a lower interest rate from like-minded Christian investors can help believers pay honest taxes and fair wages and practice honest bookkeeping in their business. This can elevate the whole culture.

There are two frequently mistaken assumptions regarding making capital affordable for missional purposes. The first is the expressed need for an investment to achieve "market-like" returns. To start, what "market" should be used to determine what "market-like" even means? It is unfair to expect Western-type, risk-adjusted returns when investing in broken or infant-stage economies. The risks involved in these kinds of investments are enormous. Corruption, political instability, hyperinflation, wars, currency devaluation, erratic climate, insufficient skilled labor, dishonest entrepreneurs, language barriers, poor legal systems or ownership rights, loss of visa for the entrepreneur, family illness, or cultural norms and expectations that are extremely different from Western culture—the list goes on and on. The Lord's *oikonomos* must think differently when investing in such environments. It is nearly impossible to expect that an investor will be financially rewarded for taking the necessary risks in such extreme settings. God's *oikonomos* invests so that community transformation and spiritual awakening can take place.

There are good reasons for Christian stewards to invest in well-developed companies which generate consistent and stable "traditional Western" market-like returns. For example, stockholders can influence a company culture or its business practices. But, for early-stage companies in undeveloped countries, God's *oikonomos* may need to sacrifice personal financial return to provide a stable foundation for these vulnerable companies.

The second mistake is calling these investments charity because investments into a missional enterprise can result in a lower rate of return. A better description is concessionary capital. Concessionary capital is any investment that receives a below-market rate of financial return. This kind of investment is described by some as charity because it acts to subsidize the enterprise. I disagree because there is virtually no industry on the planet that has not been "subsidized" with grants or concessionary capital at one point in its history. Many governments, lobbyists, and special interest groups around the world subsidize industries, companies, or programs that are important to them. The United States government, to manipulate supply, pays farmers to grow certain crops and then pays other farmers not to grow crops or even to leave land unplanted. Japan has subsidized their automobile industry for decades to make their automobiles globally competitive. Parts of the international airline industry have also benefited from subsidies with one Middle-Eastern-based airline receiving subsidies in the billions of dollars, allowing it to grow in defiance of market forces, affecting competition, and creating an unfair advantage for itself.[93]

Recent subsidies include the 2008 bank and automotive bailouts based on a government belief that some businesses were "too big to fail." Alternative energies such as wind and solar are heavily subsidized by government grants and tax credits. The successful tech industry has grown because of government and academic subsidies and grants to develop such technologies as the internet, micro and nano chip technology, and smart technologies. Activists subsidize their own agendas through academic grants and favorable corporate investment. It is hard to argue that a portfolio of US Fortune 500 companies has not benefited from, or been supported and influenced by, concessionary capital in the past.

In light of such strong evidence that the global economic system benefits from concessionary capital, shouldn't the Lord's *oikonomos* make investments that are financially affordable and beneficial to small businesses that are planted to grow in hard places so that QBL outcomes can be achieved? Choosing to invest in certain industries or geographic locations to protect investors and maximize return while avoiding companies that have potential for higher spiritual impact limits opportunities to expand God's kingdom.

In light of such strong evidence that the global economic system benefits from concessionary capital, shouldn't the Lord's oikonomos make investments that are financially affordable and beneficial to small businesses that are planted to grow in hard places so that QBL outcomes can be achieved?

93. Bart Jansen, "'Outrageous': Emirates CEO Says Airline Isn't Subsidized" (June 20, 2015): https://www.usatoday.com/story/news/2015/06/30/emirates-ceo-clark-persian-gulf-subsidies-dispute-aa-delta-united/29502997/.

The apostle Luke recalls a parable that Jesus tells about a "shrewd manager" which Jesus concludes with this explanation: "The people of this world are more shrewd in dealing with their own kind than are the people of the light. I tell you, use worldly wealth to gain friends for yourselves, so that when it is gone, you will be welcomed into eternal dwellings" (Luke 16:8-9). I can't wait to meet people in heaven who are there because of the affordable investments my family made into missional enterprises.

Heritage Ranch and Affordable Capital

Heritage Ranch received its initial capital for land purchase and start-up costs through investors who want to make sure that capital is affordable for businesses with clear spiritual impact objectives. They consider that concessionary financial returns are acceptable provided that other bottom-line outcomes are achieved. Using low-interest loans (at or below five percent) with long maturities (seven to twenty years), the initial two million dollar capitalization of land and farm equipment has started. The purchase of nearly three hundred acres of land is an amazing accomplishment in and of itself, yet that's not all. Those acres are the location of an underground seminary that functioned during the Soviet communist era. The spiritual implications of redeeming and reusing that holy ground are magnificent. The investors believe that this project is standing on the shoulders and prayers of many Christian teachers and pastors who studied, worshiped, and prayed on those hills decades ago. Low-interest loans, long-term equity, and grant funding will ensure that the land itself is set aside for God's purposes for generations to come.

Patient

Investors in missional businesses in emerging and frontier markets should be patient as these businesses will likely require the building of foundational systems and take more time to grow toward profitability than businesses in locations where supply chains, rules of law, and many other factors are already available and established. As discussed above, capital naturally flows to where business is easy and return of capital is predictable. As God's *oikonomos* we must invest in the places secular investors don't—places where infrastructure is poor, electricity is unreliable, water is dirty, education is low, property ownership rights are lax, exploitation is real, corruption is endemic, and the Gospel is absent. These are precisely the places where Jesus commands us to go. As the incarnation of Christ, Christians can bring justice, mercy, hope, and love through good business development, training and discipling employees, community service, above-reproach ethics, and fair labor practices.

It all takes time, sometimes long periods of time. As one friend who lives in a difficult part of the world puts it, "We want to plant seeds so that the gospel can grow, but first we must start to break the concrete-like ground before it can become fertile soil for planting." Patience is a critical quality for capital deployed by the Lord's *oikonomos*. We do not demand a limited time frame for capital to work. We invest with the eternal time frame of the True Owner.

Chapter six presented the idea of planting trees under whose shade you will never sit. Our authority over the Lord's resources requires that we deploy resources with a longer timeline than the typical venture capitalist or private equity investor, recognizing that there will be unforeseen hurdles that may delay repayments or impact plans for a clean and on-time exit strategy. It won't be easy. Kingdom investments in frontier markets take longer to establish and grow to sustainability than traditional investments in developed economies. Investors must have a patient mindset, allowing capital to work over longer periods of time. Agriculture is often a foundational business in frontier markets because food is a necessity and the production of food builds stability in a brand-new economy.

Heritage Ranch and Patient Capital

Agriculture, farming, livestock, fruit production, and land management take significant capital up front to purchase land, equipment, stock, and other necessary elements. Some agriculture projects may take a decade or more before they are cash-flow positive. Heritage Ranch has been capitalized by like-minded patient investors who invest with an eternal time frame in mind. The hills and trees which once sheltered the underground Church,[94,95] and "seminary in the woods" are now dedicated to the Lord for generations to come.

94. For further reading about the underground Church during the Soviet communist era, see Richard Wurmbrand's book *Tortured for Christ,* Voice of the Martyrs, 1967.

95. Most remarkably, when the ranch manager was walking the property with the previous owner (who is not a Jesus follower) to determine property lines, they came across several dilapidated structures in very remote and odd locations—hidden in the woods, in a ravine, near a cave, etc. When the manager asked why there were

Kingdom investors commit to time horizons ranging from seven to thirty years or longer knowing that capitalization of such visions will not be accomplished quickly. Soil nutrition may take a decade or more to bring depleted soil back to health. Newly planted fruit and nut trees take seven to ten years to be productive. Establishing a healthy and growing herd of Angus cattle will take time, as will implementing organic chicken production. Corrupt government practices, weather-related hindrances, and COVID-19 have derailed many of the strategies in the first few years, but Heritage Ranch investors are patient, knowing they are seeking not just financial gain but also growing God's kingdom on earth. Patience is required to accomplish their long-term goal for the lands of Heritage Ranch. They are investing so Heritage will become a blessing for the Bihor region, Romania, eastern Europe, and to the ends of the earth.

They are investing so Heritage will become a blessing for the Bihor region, Romania, eastern Europe, and to the ends of the earth.

Liberal

A mission-minded investor, acting as the Lord's fiduciary, deploys capital liberally.

Capital is in short supply, especially for enterprise startups in frontier markets and restricted-access countries. It is unlikely that you will find local investors who have the financial resources to capitalize small to medium enterprise (SME) businesses in cultures where there is less than one percent Christian population and the average wage is less than a thousand dollars per year. Capitalization must come from Christians to whom the Lord has already entrusted greater financial resources.

Much of the constraint on capital is a result of risk aversion. I have already written extensively about risk in chapter ten, so I will add only a few additional thoughts here as it pertains to why liberal capital is so necessary and yet so constrained. When a new enterprise

small houses in such strange places, the previous owner answered without hesitation, "Oh, that's where Christians read the Bible in hiding during Soviet times." Furthermore, the second largest cave in Romania is on the ranch property. Although it's not yet been explored, there is likely evidence there that would confirm it was a hiding place for the underground seminary.

starts in a location where religious visas are unavailable, there are both known and unknown risks. Known risks can usually be planned for, but unknown risks can cause considerable delays in financial performance which require increased capital input and an extended time horizon for existing investors.

In a Western context it often makes sense for a SME to start with a minimum initial investment and then fund business growth by reinvesting profits into the business. This strategy limits risk for the investors. We have learned over the years that while missional investment must be affordable and patient, it also needs to be liberal and generous. In hindsight we have seen that too-frugal capital can increase risk and almost always reduces flexibility and choices when problems arise.

It may be less risky to have ample and abundant capital in place prior to implementation and to be ready to mobilize that capital quickly during the early phases of business development in locations where value chains are underdeveloped or nonexistent, infrastructure is weak, and bureaucratic support is nonexistent. This provides sufficient resources to overcome challenges during the initial implementation phase and better ensures that everything is in place for production and moving products to market as quickly as possible.

I have observed that many smart and successful Western business owners who start helping BAM enterprises virtually starve the business for capital. These same business owners think nothing of spending whatever is needed on technology, infrastructure, capital expenditure, or human resources in their businesses at home to secure their market share, stabilize the business, or grow it for the future. Yet, when they put on their "missions hat," they claim to be "good stewards," seeking immediate financial and spiritual outcomes while feeding a missional business as little money as possible. They provide minimal funding, after initial pro forma calculations, to establish cash flow, and they are not liberal in spending or providing liquidity in the same way they are with their own businesses back home. This behavior is inconsistent with the abundance mentality demonstrated by our Lord.

Heritage Ranch and Liberal Capital

Initial funding for Heritage Ranch was based on assumptions investors thought were realistic at the time. Some obstacles were overcome with the addition of extra capital, such as capital expenditure on road construction and maintenance to allow large commercial vehicles access to the ranch. However, corruption at the highest level resulted in unanticipated delays in approvals, certifications, and licenses. This was an unforeseen risk that delayed chicken processing by several months. This delay cost tens of thousands of dollars, putting stress on the anticipated cash flow and budget. A liberal capital mindset supports fledgling businesses through unforeseen issues so that such businesses can survive as beacons of light, bringing blessing to their communities.

De-Risking

The Lord's *oikonomos*, especially those defined as the wealthiest on the planet (see chapter three), should consider de-risking missional investments for future investors who have fewer financial resources to deploy. Every person in the body of Christ is God's fiduciary and should have the opportunity to participate in the kind of investing this book describes. But in some cases, especially for Christians who themselves live in impoverished countries, the risks may indeed be too high. In the kingdom economy, those who have an abundance can de-risk high-risk endeavors so that in time, everyone can participate in businesses that seek kingdom-of-God outcomes, Great Commission results, and Great Commandment influence.

In the kingdom economy, those who have an abundance can de-risk high-risk endeavors so that in time, everyone can participate in businesses that seek kingdom-of-God outcomes, Great Commission results, and Great Commandment influence.

The microfinance movement which began in the 1970s is a good modern-day example of de-risking investment. In its early form, especially in the most impoverished locations with the most broken economic systems, philanthropy plus patient, affordable, de-risking capital was used to get programs up and running. It took too much time for the microcredit loans to be repaid at a high enough ratio for commercial lenders to be willing to assume the risks. Over time, microlending programs that were initially funded through generous de-risking capital became profitable enough to be financed or even purchased by commercial institutions with traditional debt and equity financing.

There are still many microfinance institutions that are backed by philanthropic and de-risking dollars and many large organizations that support these programs. However, the most successful projects reach a point where regular, small investors can participate using online microlending services such as Kiva.

Heritage Ranch and De-Risked Capital

Heritage Ranch is capitalized by a small group of investors who understand that one of the purposes of their investment is to de-risk this company for future investors. They understand that a successful enterprise will need additional capital throughout its life cycle and early investors help to stabilize a project so that it can eventually qualify for commercial funding through more traditional lenders such as banks. The early investors in Heritage are using the Lord's resources to de-risk a large-scale business startup in a difficult place.

Catalytic

In a kingdom economy, capital should be catalytic, facilitating change, transforming lives and communities, and transferring wealth creation mechanisms (businesses) to people and regions where it would not naturally flow. Generally, fair wages alone will be insufficient to change the culture and insufficient for a local employee to build enough wealth to purchase ownership of a successful business from the original financiers. Therefore, proper succession and continuity planning must be adopted at inception. Missional investors need to plan to pass ownership into the hands of like-minded local managers and employees who have been discipled to run businesses that are rooted in Christian principles. If we wait until the business is sustainable or successful, the value will already be too high for most locals to buy into it. Kingdom-minded investors must think about being catalysts, using capital to establish systems that are sustainable and that will multiply in the hands of local followers of Christ. This requires investors to see their role as servants of those they are trying to help.

This requires investors to see their role as servants of those they are trying to help.

One of the greatest criticisms of traditional missions is the proliferation of Western churches all over the world. Sometimes the word *imperialism* is used to describe the results because some missionaries did not contextualize the locations where they served and tried to convert people to Western-style Christianity. Western-style worship, liturgy, and even architecture was maintained for decades or generations rather than the body of Christ exhibiting the natural characteristics of its own culture. Similarly, investors in missional businesses might pat themselves on the back for bringing justice and fair wages to the local people, but without catalytic capital the successful businesses could easily remain under the ownership and control of Westerners (or their foundations) who continue to reap the financial benefits instead of sharing it with those who are part of the local economy.

Heritage Ranch and Catalytic Capital

An objective of the investors in Heritage Ranch is to be catalytic. From the start, majority land ownership has belonged to a Romanian foundation that was established for the express purpose of building long-term, sustainable Christian businesses that will bring blessing to the Roma people. At its inception, shares were set aside so they could be granted or sold at an affordable price to local Christians in the future.

Serving

The best use of capital in the hands of God's fiduciary is to build people and communities. Capital ought to imitate the character of Jesus, who "did not come to be served, but to serve" (Mark 10:45). In chapter six we discussed the idea of the "covenant funnel" and our responsibility to be a blessing. The Lord's *oikonomos* has a serving-capital mindset and uses capital to help others, not to cause them to be subservient to a lender or equity shareholders.

The Church's first martyr, Stephen, just before his death, spoke powerfully of the history of redemption. He began his overview not with Creation but with the calling of Abraham out of Mesopotamia (Acts 7:2-3). When God called Abraham, He said, "I will bless you . . . and you will be a blessing" (Gen. 12:2), and while people frequently measure blessing in economic terms, the blessings from God are much more varied. A close friend who is the CEO of a BAM business that employs more than one hundred workers suggested to me that we have been taught that the goal of safe money management is for "money to make money" rather than for "money to make people." In a kingdom economy, *people* are the object of God's love, and building and restoring *people* is His primary loving activity. Traditional investing and business building requires that *people* are used to get *things* done and to generate revenue. However, in the kingdom economy, *things* (financial resources) are used to get *people* done (to bring them closer to God). For the Lord's *oikonomos*, discovering and employing the Owner's intentions is paramount. Turning blessing into more blessing for all stakeholders is the goal.

Heritage Ranch and Serving Capital

The investors in Heritage Ranch understand that their capital is invested with the underlying focus of turning their blessing into a blessing to others. Their capital facilitates opportunities for other followers of Jesus to be salt and light in their communities through work and products they create as responsible and trustworthy employers. The investors in Heritage desire to use their capital to serve rather than be served.

CONCLUSION

Kingdom capital should be used differently than traditional earthly capital. Paul reminds us that our citizenship is in heaven, not here on earth, and he warns that destruction is the consequence of those who focus on their own desires: "Their destiny is destruction, their god is their stomach, and their glory is in their shame. Their mind is set on earthly things. But our citizenship is in heaven," he says (Phil. 3:19-20).

As God's *oikonomos* we must strategically fight the natural tendency to invest capital in ways that primarily benefit the investor and not all stakeholders. Traditional capital is expensive, impatient, frugal, risk-averse, imperialistic, and selfish. Kingdom capital should be affordable, patient, liberal, de-risking, catalytic, and serving. These character qualities seem better aligned with the character of God who designed and created economic systems in the first place. If Christian investors don't begin thinking and acting differently, kingdom capital will not flow to frontier markets or unreached peoples. We can work together to prioritize a different set of qualities for our capital and make it a priority and move it from where it is piled up in abundance to places where it is scarce, so that lives will change and the name of Jesus will be exalted.

QUESTIONS FOR STUDY

1. Read Matthew 6. Consider the use of the words *heaven, kingdom, treasure, need* (needy); *give* (giving), *reward, bread, debt* (debtors); *thieves, steal, money* (mammon, things); *food* (eat, drink), *clothes* (wear, dressed); and *store away* (barns), *labor* (sow, reap, spin). How clear is Jesus' instruction that His followers' earthly mindset toward mammon must change to a mindset that reflects God's economy? Reflect on contemporary attitudes toward giving, providing for the needy, and saving for and obtaining personal comforts and luxuries. How do Christians' actions specific to these matters compare or contrast with non-Christians?

2. Briefly describe the six characteristics of capital in the kingdom economy.

3. How can affordable capital level the playing field for a missional business in a corrupt market? How does a faithful business practicing integrity and transparency in its operations influence a local community?

4. What is concessionary capital, and how does it correlate to the common practice of subsidizing businesses? Read Luke 16:8-9 and discuss its relevance to the subject of providing concessionary capital for missional businesses. Is concessionary capital an investment or charitable donation?

5. Why is patient capital necessary for missional business investment? What time horizon can the True Owner reap benefits from for an investment made today?

   Consider these questions: What is the hurry? Why is your time horizon so short? Why do you expect investment capital to be returned in a short time frame when you comfortably make grants that will never be returned? The principal that you have accumulated in your foundation or DAF could be invested very strategically for long-term cultural and spiritual transformation in societies where this kind of investment is desperately needed.

6. How does liberal capital reduce risk in missional investments?

7. Are resources abundant or scarce in God's economy? What biblical texts support your conclusion? How might your answer influence an investor who is risk averse to consider an investment in a missional enterprise?

8. What is de-risking capital, and how can it play a role in opening the door for greater deployment of capital in the future?

9. How can making a succession plan during the initial phase of a missional business lay the groundwork for catalytic, transformational change in a community decades later? How does this kingdom mindset differ from an earthly mindset influenced by the spirit of mammon?

10. Reflect on the author's statement regarding serving capital: "Traditional investing and business building requires that *people* are used to get *things* done and to generate revenue. However, in the kingdom economy, *things* (financial resources) are used to get *people* done (to bring them closer to God)." Is using capital to serve rather than be served in keeping with what you know about the True Owner's purposes?

Chapter 14

RETIREMENT PLANNING

For the eyes of the LORD roam to and fro over all the earth, to show Himself strong on behalf of those whose hearts are fully devoted to Him. (2 Chron. 16:9, BSB)

In 1904, William Borden, heir to the Borden Dairy estate, graduated from a Chicago high school a millionaire. As Borden traveled the Middle East, Asia, and Europe on a cruise his parents had provided as a graduation gift, he observed for the first time in his life the deep poverty of body and soul of so many people around the world. He was overcome with a burden for the world's hurting, vulnerable, and lost. Writing home, he indicated a possible call to become a missionary. One friend expressed amazement, believing that Borden was throwing his life away by forsaking his family birthright and submitting to a life of service to others.

Borden continued to passionately pursue God while studying at Yale University. He served the poor on the streets of New Haven, Connecticut, and prepared for a life of service as a missionary. He turned away from his fortune to pursue missions, writing the words, "No Reserves" inside his Bible. In faith, William made a firm decision to trust God for everything in his life.

Upon graduation from Yale, Borden turned down many profitable and prestigious employment opportunities. He also turned down the opportunity to manage the multi-million-dollar family business. Determined to fulfill God's call on his life, he again penned two words into his Bible: "No Retreats."

On December 17, 1912, Borden set sail for China to work with Muslims, stopping first in Egypt for some additional language preparation. While there he was stricken with spinal meningitis and died within a month at the age of twenty-five. Years of training and a promising future and Borden never even made it to China. A waste? No, not in God's plan.

A college friend who received his Bible after his death found that Borden had written two more words in the flyleaf: "No Regrets."[96] Before he was even twenty years old, Borden made decisions about life and finances that contradicted everything our culture teaches about personal and financial success.

F.I.R.E. AND SETTING A FINISH LINE

There is a current movement among young adults in the United States called F.I.R.E. which stands for *financial independence, retire early*. It encourages people to live below their means so they have more money to invest toward early retirement or part-time work. The higher your savings rate and the percentage of income you don't spend, the faster you can become "work optional"—in other words, financially independent. Our entire culture is built on this desire to be "work optional" so we can live a life of leisure and luxury. But this philosophy for life is not biblical.

A similar movement among Christians is setting a financial "finish line," a type of target that is supposed to trigger a behavioral change. For decades I have heard people promise to begin tithing once they've paid off their student loans and saved an emergency reserve. Others anticipate entering full-time ministry, but not until they've become financially independent, probably sometime in their forties. Some admit postponing a call to become a missionary to get some career experience first but find themselves nearing retirement having never made it to the mission field. Another refrain I've often heard is someone setting a lifestyle based on an amount—$150,000,

96. Omar C. Garcia, "William Borden" (July 1, 2009): https://gobeyond.blog/2009/07/01/william-borden.

for example—and declaring that once they achieve that goal, they will release more than their ten percent tithe for God's purposes. Sadly, in most of these cases, people talked about a "finish line" but somehow life happened: marriage, children, houses, and other responsibilities took priority and they either delayed or fully abandoned planned changes in their vocation or money management.

Among the few Christians who even set such finish lines, many frequently move the line as their net worth and income increase. I call this "lifestyle creep" or "keeping up with the Joneses." In practical terms it means that Christians in the United States and other wealthy nations generally follow the patterns of this world, seeking financial independence and a life with increasing leisure and luxury without ever sacrificing or stretching to serve God with their financial resources. They may give numerically more as their wealth increases, but few choose to give a higher percentage as their discretionary income and net worth grow. It is rare to find Christians who deliberately limit consumption, live in sacrificial ways, or reduce their standard of living so that their wealth can be used to serve God. Finish lines seem to be a declaration that I will eat until I am full and then God can have the leftovers.

Finish lines seem to be a declaration that I will eat until I am full and then God can have the leftovers.

The apostle Paul indicates that by the time he finishes the "race," he has exhausted his resources in service to God and does not have anything left over or unspent. He states, "I have fought the good fight, I have finished the race, I have kept the faith" (2 Tim 4:7). In every race, the finish line is set by the race organizer, not the runner. If we dialogue with God before the race begins and at every checkpoint along the way about how He wants us to spend our time, resources, relationships, influence and portfolio, we can more fully glorify Him and build His kingdom. After all, God owns the energy He gave us to run the race in the first place, not just the energy we have left once we cross the finish line.

Applying this thinking to our role as God's *oikonomos,* we should start strategically deploying investments and donation at the beginning of our career, not at the point where we feel we have secured enough for ourselves so that we can then focus our attention on God's priorities without depending on His provision in our lives.

An honest conversation with God might reveal that His plan for us is not financial independence in this world, but ongoing God-dependence until He brings us home.

WHOM DOES THE LORD HELP?

Several years ago, I came across the story of King Asa while reading Chip Ingram's book *Holy Ambition*. His introduction caused me to dig deeper into Asa's story. Even though Asa lived thousands of years ago, there are many parallels to the financial lives of twenty-first century Americans. The story, found in 2 Chronicles, is a reminder that many start the race well, but far fewer finish strong. From the very first sentence introducing Asa as successor to his father, Abijah, we learn that the country was at peace for a decade and that "Asa did what was good and right in the eyes of the LORD his God" (2 Chron. 14:2). Asa's kingdom experienced tremendous blessing, peace, and prosperity because he followed the Lord. He removed idols from the land, repaired the altar, and led his people to earnestly seek God. My guess is that many of us have experienced a similar life of blessing.

> [But in the tenth year] Zerah the Cushite marched out against [Asa] with an army of thousands upon thousands and three hundred chariots, and came as far as Mareshah. Asa went out to meet him, and they took up battle positions in the Valley of Zephathah near Mareshah. Then Asa called to the LORD his God and said, "LORD, there is no one like you to help the powerless against the mighty. Help us, LORD our God, for we rely on you, and in your name we have come against this vast army. LORD, you are our God; do not let mere mortals prevail against you." The LORD struck down the Cushites before Asa and Judah. (2 Chron. 14:9-12)

Think back with me to when you were in your twenties, early in your career—perhaps newly married and just starting out. Maybe you lived in a tiny apartment and ate a lot of chicken, potatoes, or ramen noodles. You needed faith that God would provide, and you prayed for him to meet your most basic needs. Like Asa, you cried out for help, recognizing your own powerlessness, and God answered your prayers. You experienced subsequent years of peace, prosperity, and blessing.

Second Chronicles 15:17 states that "Asa's heart was fully committed to the Lord," and then in verse 19, "There was no more war until the thirty-fifth year of Asa's reign." However, the story of Asa starts to take a turn after these first thirty-five peaceful years. In chapter 16, we learn that "In the thirty-sixth year of Asa's reign Baasha king of Israel went up against Judah [Asa's kingdom] and fortified Ramah to prevent anyone from leaving or entering the territory of Asa king of Judah" (v. 1). Sounds like when the Cushites marched out against Asa twenty-five years earlier.

How did Asa respond this time? Did he stop and pray to the Lord for deliverance? Did he fully rely on God to protect his kingdom and to display His power? No. Instead, he took the silver and gold of his own palace and the treasury of the Lord's temple and used it to make a treaty with Ben-Hadad, the king of Aram. He bought a treaty with this powerful king instead of trusting God to protect his kingdom from an attack.

How many of us begin to think that we are in control when we live through a time of prosperity? We think, "I can handle this" when problems arise. Or we evaluate our resources and make plans to resolve the issue, taking matters into our own hands, never even stopping to think that we should pray to God for deliverance, protection, healing, and resolution.

My years of experience have taught me that Americans become more risk averse as they become more prosperous (chapter ten, Figure 2). When we are young, we take chances and are forced to rely on God. We pray for His leading and guidance. We pray for Him to *come through*. As we get older and more financially independent, we, like Asa, begin to put our hope and trust in something other than God. Asa chose to buy an alliance with a foreign king. We put our confidence in our 401(k), our nest egg, our savings, our home, our insurance policies, maybe even gold or silver. We forget that our only hope is in the living God.

As a result of the treaty with Ben-Hadad, King Baasha abandons the attack and King Asa's kingdom is saved. He did it! But in verses 7-8 we read, "At that time Hanani the seer came to Asa king of Judah and said to him: 'Because you relied on the king of Aram and not on the Lord your God, the army of the king of Aram has escaped from your hand. Were not the Cushites and Libyans a mighty army with great numbers of chariots and horsemen? Yet when you relied on the Lord, he delivered them into your hand.'"

And here is the verse we have been waiting for: "For the eyes of the LORD roam to and fro over all the earth, to show Himself strong on behalf of those whose hearts are fully devoted to Him," says the seer (2 Chron. 16:9, BSB). We often stop and take comfort in that verse without realizing the condemnation that follows in the next sentence. Hanani continues, "You have done a foolish thing, and from now on you will be at war" (v. 9).

IN WHOM DID ASA AND IN WHOM DO WE TRUST?

Asa is condemned because he relied on his own resources rather than trusting God. Asa's story mirrors the professional life of many in our affluent society, even those who set finish lines. Most of us devote thirty-five to forty years to our vocation. Initially we struggle to keep our heads above water when we are in our twenties and thirties. We live in small apartments, and we struggle to make ends meet. We are forced to take risks, praying and trusting God to provide for our needs. Then through our forties and fifties, up until retirement, we experience peace and prosperity, much like Asa experienced for twenty years. We buy homes, cars, "toys," second homes, and many other indulgences to make life comfortable. We save and invest and pay off our debts, building nest eggs and cash reserves and retirement portfolios. We become "financially independent," and we tend to forget about trusting God. We trust in ourselves and our savings, just like Asa.

As we approach retirement, we think that we have worked hard enough, have paid our dues, and have sacrificed for our jobs. We claim success as our own and do not acknowledge that God orchestrates our path. We save up nest eggs and think we are entitled to relax and enjoy life. We brag about our financial independence. But the unspoken presumption is that *we* have done this ourselves, *we* can take care of ourselves. We are done taking risks. We do not even need to depend on God anymore.

However, scripture makes it clear that God wants us to obediently trust Him and use the rich resources He's provided to accomplish life-changing impact in the lives of others, not our own. He wants us to proactively deploy, even forsake and deplete, so that His purposes—caring for the poor, bringing healing to the afflicted, promoting justice for the exploited, and proclaiming salvation for the lost—can be accomplished.

We are extraordinarily wealthy. One day we will be *accountable* to the True Owner of all the resources. God will judge how we live our lives and how we use the resources entrusted to us. The world calls giving all to Jesus *failure*. It fails to grasp the significance of such sacrifice, mistakenly calling it waste. The Bible reveals a different perspective.

The Gospel of Mark records the story of a woman who has an expensive jar of perfume. While Jesus is dining in Bethany at the home of a man named Simon the Leper, she approaches Jesus and does the unexpected. She breaks the jar and pours the perfume on Jesus' head (Mark 14:3). Some ask critically, "Why has this fragrant oil been wasted?" arguing that it could be better used by selling it to benefit the poor. Jesus calls what she does a "beautiful thing" and tells the critics to stop troubling her and leave her alone. Jesus received the extravagant gift that He knew wasn't wasted.

Are we like the critic, looking solely at the financial numbers or projections of profit for a business when we invest? The immense cost of the perfume did not stop this woman from offering such a generous gift (perhaps her most valuable resource) to her Lord. Her offering showed her all-consuming love for Him. Some would say that profit is the most valuable thing in business or investing. However, redirecting profits into better health care for employees or better stewardship of a community isn't a waste of a company's bottom-line profit. Like the valuable jar of perfume poured on a single person, Jesus would call it a "beautiful thing."

RETIREMENT AS WE THINK OF IT ISN'T A BIBLICAL CONCEPT

Retirement does not seem to be a biblical concept, at least not the idea of leisure and self-indulgence that Americans have come to plan for. Instead, those who are older and more mature have greater responsibility in the body of Christ. For example, the Israelite leader Caleb, at the age of eighty-five, said, "I am still as strong today as the day Moses sent me out; I'm just as vigorous to go out to battle now as I was then" (Josh. 14:11). Caleb was forty when he and Joshua helped spy out the Promised Land (Num. 13), and more than forty years later, after wandering in the wilderness, the Canaanite lands were finally divided among the tribes of Israel, and Caleb received a portion as his inheritance. And how did he view himself? He considered himself as strong at age eighty-five as he was at age forty, and he was ready "for battle," for whatever God might call on him to do (Josh. 14:11). I am honored to know several men in their seventies and eighties who, like Caleb, aggressively serve the Lord. These men travel to developing nations to mentor BAM entrepreneurs. Their example challenges me and motivates me to do the same for the next two decades. If you are retired or planning for retirement, have you considered what work the Lord has planned for when you become "work optional"?

Some popular Christian financial advisors suggest that we should live like no one else while we are young, disciplined with spending and saving. Then in retirement we can live and give like no one else, enjoying luxury and giving from our surplus. While disciplined money management is wise, the assumption that we get the credit for any surplus and can manage it as we please reflects an unbiblical arrogance. We must remember that God is the one entrusting us with more resources. He tells the Israelites, "You may say to yourself, 'My power and the strength of my hands have produced this wealth for me.' But remember the Lord your God, for it is he who gives you the ability to produce wealth" (Deut. 8:17-18). We make a grave mistake when we don't seek God's direction but think our abundance is primarily ours to use for our own personal comfort or to deploy for deliverance from troubles. The story of Asa reminds us of these principles and that we should submit to ongoing dependence on God who provides wealth in the first place.

The apostle Luke recalls a parable about and a condemnation of a successful farmer who uses his wealth to create a life of self-indulgence, a parable discussed in greater detail in chapter sixteen. As God's *oikonomos*, rather than pursuing a life of enjoyment and relaxation in retirement, we should deploy ourselves and our resources to do the things that God placed us on earth to do: love and serve Him, love and serve our families, and proactively spend ourselves and our resources for Him. In the words of the apostle Paul, "I will have a reason to boast that I did not run in vain nor labor in vain. But even if I am being poured out like a drink offering on the sacrifice and service of your faith, I am glad and rejoice together with all of you" (Phil. 2:16-17, NET).

Robert Murray M'Cheyne was a Scottish pastor who died in the early part of the nineteenth century. Although he lived nearly two hundred years ago, his words are astoundingly appropriate for today:

> I am concerned for the poor; but more for you. I know not what Christ will say to you in the great day. . . . I fear there are many hearing me who may well know that they are not Christians, because they do not love to give. To give largely and liberally, not grudgingly at all, requires a new heart; an old heart would rather part with its life-blood than its money. Oh, my friends! Enjoy your money; make the most of it; give none away; enjoy it quickly for I can tell you, you will be beggars throughout eternity.[97]

The big question will not be whether we achieved financial independence, becoming "work optional," but whether the resources we had were used for God's purpose or our own. Will you hear "well done" on the final day because your resources were used to build the kingdom of God, to disciple the nations, to feed the hungry, and to heal the sick? Will you defend yourself because you gave ten percent to your church or to missions, ignoring the fact that you spent the other ninety percent on yourself? Do you handle the Master's resources more like the "rich fool" in Luke 12 or more like the farmer in Matthew 13 who found treasure in a field and promptly sold all that he had to purchase the field? God's *oikonomos* will invest *everything* to see God's kingdom come. We should learn from the widow in Mark 12 who proves that in God's economy, the size of our investment is not as important as sacrificial deployment of resources and trust in God for the provision of our needs.

> ***The big question will not be whether we achieved financial independence, becoming "work optional," but whether the resources we had were used for God's purpose or our own.***

"You Should Only Be Opening This In the Event of Death"

"You should only be opening this in the event of death," begins the letter that Valley Baptist Church Pastor Phil Neighbors held. "To obey was my objective, to suffer was expected, His glory my reward," the letter continued. Written just before she left for Iraq in 2003,

97. [A]nd also with you, "Rev. Robert Murray McCheyne" (November 30, 2011): https://aawy.wordpress.com/2011/11/30/rev-robert-murray-mccheyne-2/.

that epistle became Karen Denise Watson's self-penned epitaph after she and three of her missionary colleagues were gunned down by unknown attackers in the northern Iraqi city of Mosul.[98]

It is not uncommon for Christian servants who move to high-risk cultures to scribble their own last letters, just in case they do not return home alive. The tradition began hundreds of years ago with letters penned in Bibles and on weathered parchment in a desperate attempt to explain their divine compulsion to give up everything to serve the lost and the hurting.[99]

Watson, thirty-eight at the time of her death, sold her home and possessions to focus on missionary work. Surrounded by parents and siblings before she left, she handed her father her unopened letter and embarked on a journey from which she knew she might never return. At her funeral, that letter was read in full by her pastor:

> *Dear Pastor Phil and Pastor Roger,*
>
> *You should only be opening this letter in the event of death. When God calls there are no regrets. I tried to share my heart with you as much as possible, my heart for the nations. I wasn't called to a place; I was called to Him. To obey was my objective, to suffer was expected, His glory my reward, His glory my reward....*
>
> *The missionary heart:*
> *Cares more than some think is wise*
> *Risks more than some think is safe*
> *Dreams more than some think is practical*
> *Expects more than some think is possible*
> *I was called not to comfort or to success, but to obedience....*
>
> *There is no Joy outside of knowing Jesus and serving Him. I love you two and my church family.*
>
> *In His care,*
> *Salaam [Peace], Karen*[100]

98. Jean-Paul Renaud and John Johnson, "Missionary Slain in Iraq Mourned" (March 17, 2004): https://www.latimes.com/archives/la-xpm-2004-mar-17-me-karen17-story.html.

99. https://www.sermoncentral.com/sermon-illustrations/79820/missions-by-sermon-central

100. Erich Bridges, *Lives Given, Not Taken: 21st Century Southern Baptist Martyrs* (Richmond, VA: International Mission Board, SBC, 2005), 191. Used with permission.

CONCLUSION

What do you have planned for retirement? Will you seek leisure and relaxation, hobbies and activities which make you feel good? Have you built a retirement nest egg and portfolio to accomplish complete financial independence, with the proper amount saved and the right insurances in place? Are you like Asa, arrogant and self-sufficient because you have accumulated the resources to solve every problem for yourself? Or might your retirement plan include going to battle in service of the Lord as Caleb described? The apostle Paul reminds us that the goal for a well-lived life as the Lord's *oikonomos* is to "run with endurance the race that is set before us" (Heb. 12:1, ESV) and to fight the good fight, to finish the race, and to keep the faith (2 Tim 4:7).

QUESTIONS FOR STUDY

1. What compelled William Borden to decide to choose a path for his life that was the opposite of what our culture teaches about personal and financial success? How is his story relevant for today?

2. Share an example of a time in your life when you knew you didn't have the resources to meet a personal need and you found yourself fully dependent on the Lord. How did you respond to this situation? How did God respond?

3. Briefly recap the story of King Asa from 2 Chronicles 14-16. What happened after the first thirty-five years of Asa's prosperous and peaceful reign? In whom did Asa trust at that time? What did the prophet Hanani say to King Asa in 2 Chronicles 16:9? What danger is there in our accumulation of great reserves?

4. Discuss the concept of the "work optional" F.I.R.E. movement or "retirement" philosophy that prioritizes amassing substantial reserves so that a life of leisure and luxury can be pursued. How does your household budget reveal your prioritization of a "work optional" or "retirement planning" mindset? What has influenced your present course of investing in this matter, the spirit of mammon or the Spirit of God? What do the scriptures teach regarding such a pursuit? Cite a biblical text.

5. Discuss the idea of setting a financial finish line and the pros and cons of this concept. Can you cite any biblical references that support it? Are there any finish lines you have established?

6. How might God's counsel influence the choices of God's fiduciaries who are beginning to invest in their twenties and thirties? How might this differ for those who are in their forties and fifties or for those no longer working? What conscious actions can an investor, or anyone with savings, take to remain obediently trusting God to meet personal needs while remaining God's faithful fiduciary, always prepared to deploy God's resources to accomplish God's purposes in this fallen world?

7. Reflect on the following statement attributed to Rev. Robert Murray M'Cheyne: "To give largely and liberally, not grudgingly at all, requires a new heart." William Borden saw desperate needs with his own eyes, and it transformed his mind. Read Luke 12:34. What can change a heart that is not yet generous?

Personal Reflection

Determine for yourself if resources entrusted to you are being used now for God's purposes or your own. Consider the author's question, *Will you hear "well done" on the final day because your resources were used to build the kingdom of God, to disciple the nations, to feed the hungry, and to heal the sick?*

Chapter 15

GIVE US THIS DAY OUR DAILY BREAD

Our Father, who art in heaven, hallowed be thy name; thy kingdom come; thy will be done; on earth as it is in heaven. Give us this day our daily bread. And forgive us our trespasses, as we forgive those who trespass against us. And lead us not into temptation; but deliver us from evil. (Matt. 6:9-13, KJV)

I have spent a lifetime advising people how to accumulate wealth and how to preserve it for their own benefit. But as I more completely understand the job of an *oikonomos* and our role as God's fiduciaries, I must admit that modern financial planning has led us astray. This book is my attempt to correct our thinking and persuade people of means, both large and small, to reconsider the methods for accumulating wealth and the purpose of it in our lives. After years of study, prayer, and practice to better understand God's nature and the financial principles in His Word, I have concluded that as God's fiduciary, I must be less consumed with accumulation for myself and my family. Instead, I am more deliberately deploying greater percentages of my net worth toward building God's kingdom.

WHY WOULD ANYONE TAKE GREATER RISK AS THEY GET OLDER?

I want to call our attention to two key phrases in the prayer Jesus taught His disciples. The phrases, "thy kingdom come; thy will be done; on earth as it is in heaven," and "our daily bread," lead me to conclude that one hundred percent deployment is God's design and wish for us all. The Lord's Prayer brings together many of the principles discussed in previous chapters such as ownership, stewardship, wealth, blessing, fear, and greed. It challenges us to exercise faith with what we keep for ourselves and what we deploy for God's purposes.

"Thy Kingdom Come; Thy Will Be Done"

The first phrase, "thy kingdom come; thy will be done; on earth as it is in heaven," addresses the goal God has for our time on earth. We are called to be His ambassadors, ushering in more of His kingdom on earth. The apostle Paul affirms our role, saying, "And he gave us this wonderful message of reconciliation. So we are Christ's ambassadors; God is making his appeal through us. We speak for Christ when we plead, 'Come back to God!'" (2 Cor. 5:19-20, NLT). Kingdom building requires capital as we reconcile everything broken in the Fall described in Genesis.

Investors control the flow of capital, and as Christian investors, we must strategically direct investment capital to build the kingdom of God. When we pray, "thy kingdom come," we are not *asking* God to do something, we are *agreeing* to participate in what He is already doing. Therefore, we should aggressively and faithfully invest and deploy resources so we can engage in God's redeeming and reconciling work. Remember, wise stewards make specific types of investments to increase God's kingdom through QBL impact. These may carry higher risk of personal financial loss but have greater potential in achieving "thy kingdom come" outcomes compared to traditional and publicly traded investments.

"Thy kingdom come" living requires that nothing is off-limits.

"Thy kingdom come" living requires that nothing is off-limits. God is calling you to let go of materialism. Randy Alcorn, in his book *Managing God's Money,* makes this provocative statement: "If anything we have is off-limits to God, if it's not subject to prayerful dialogue, then let's be honest about it—we aren't stewards, we're embezzlers. We aren't *serving* God; we're *playing* God."[101] Alcorn believes without equivocation that all of our possessions and assets are not actually ours but God's. Any attempt to box God out of our financial planning or refuse to let Him inform our resource management reveals our belief that we are, in Alcorn's words, "pretending to be owners rather than God's money managers."[102]

This belief stands in sharp contrast with advice of modern financial planners who generally recommend that certain assets are off-limits to risk. They advise that you should never use the corpus of your portfolio but only use a portion of your earnings. They rarely advise you to downsize your home or use home equity for unorthodox investments. The idea of using IRA or retirement resources to invest in start-up companies in developing nations would be anathema. However, this philosophy contradicts Alcorn's view and mine, the view that God's resources are His to direct where He deems best. The corpus of our portfolio, the equity in our home, a retirement nest egg, and the resources of our family-owned business are all subject to His direction and calling. If God is willing to risk His money, we need to let Him risk it through us. Living with this attitude and perspective will help us avoid the pitfalls the apostle James warns against: hoarding wealth and living in luxury and self-indulgence (James 5:5).

Keeping Nothing Back

Most of us know that John Wesley started the Methodist Church in eighteenth-century England and that he was a great preacher and hymn writer, penning such hymns as "And Can It Be That I Should Gain?" and "Christ the Lord Is Risen Today." But few of us are aware that Wesley had an enormous income from teaching at Oxford and from the sale of his writings. He became one of England's wealthiest men with an annual income that reached fourteen hundred pounds in an age when thirty pounds per year could provide a single man with a comfortable living. Wesley's annual income would be similar to a two-million-dollar annual income today.

101. Randy Alcorn, *Managing God's Money: A Biblical Guide* (Carol Stream, IL: Tyndale House Publishers, 2011), 198.

102. Alcorn, *Managing God's Money.*

John Wesley lived in a way that honors James's teaching and illustrates Alcorn's principles. He held thoughtful principles about money, and with such a high income he had the opportunity to put his ideas into practice. He declared, "[When I die,] if I leave behind me ten pounds . . . you and all mankind [may] bear witness against me, that I have lived and died a thief and a robber."[103] Faithful to those words he wrote nearly fifty years before his death in 1791, the only money left when his will was read were the miscellaneous coins in his pockets and dresser drawers. He had given away the thirty thousand pounds he had earned during his lifetime.

"My own hands will be my executors."

Wesley said, "I cannot help leaving my books behind me whenever God calls me hence; but in every other respect, my own hands will be my executors,"[104] indicating his choice to be deliberate in deploying his resources to see God's kingdom come instead of stockpiling them to provide a windfall to his heirs at his death. I can imagine that if there were missional investment opportunities in his day, Wesley would have surely made such investments. Wesley did not consider any part of his net worth off-limits to God and His purposes.

Perhaps you have retained the services of competent and professional legal, tax, and financial advisors to plan your estate, minimize taxes, and create a perpetual legacy. Do these advisors share your Christian worldview and a conviction to manage resources as God's *oikonomos* would? Does their planning consider your responsibility to fulfill God's commands to make disciples to the ends of the earth or be the hands and feet of Jesus, becoming champions for the vulnerable and exploited? Advisors who do not share your Christian perspective do not typically provide advice and guidance on investing to build God's kingdom on earth, which is, in fact, our primary role as God's fiduciaries.

As previously emphasized, we must refrain from the natural tendency of looking at donations as sacred and investments as

103. David Swanson, "John Wesley on Money" (September 10, 2007): https://dwswanson.com/2007/09/10/john-wesley-on-money/.

104. Charles White, "What Wesley Practiced and Preached About Money," from *Money & Missions*, September-October 1994 issue (September 1, 1994): http://www.missionfrontiers.org/issue/article/what-wesley-practiced-and-preached-about-money.

secular. It is all God's from a biblical point of view. Ask yourself if your financial and estate plan maximizes God's objectives during your lifetime like John Wesley's did.

"Thy kingdom come" living informs our response to the human needs that God brings to our attention. Here is a set of questions that might be helpful in evaluating your investment decisions over your lifetime and as part of your estate plan.

- Am I acting as the owner of this money I am investing or as fiduciary for the True Owner?
- Is my investment strategy in line with scripture?
- Should I offer up this investment as a sacrifice to the Lord?
- Does God promise to reward such investments?[105]

"Thy kingdom come" investing requires us to act when we see or hear of a need. Has God called you recently to liquidate something to meet a need? The movie *Schindler's List* tells the true story of Czech-born Oskar Schindler, a businessman who tried to make his fortune during the Second World War by exploiting cheap Jewish labor. In the end, Schindler ended up penniless, having used all his wealth to rescue more than eleven hundred Polish Jews during the Holocaust. In the final scene, Schindler ponders what other luxury items he possesses, such as a watch or gold ring, that might have been sold to save even more lives.

"Thy kingdom come" investing requires us to act when we see or hear of a need.

We should be especially quick to evaluate the luxury items in our lives. What could be accomplished if a highly appreciated asset like stock or real estate, or a luxury investment like an expensive car, was sold to fund Bible translation, church planting, or disciple making, or to free young women from slavery and sex trafficking? When we pray the words, "thy kingdom come; thy will be done, on earth as it is in heaven," we are agreeing to join God in fulfilling this goal. It is quite possible that God has provided you with the financial

105. Here are John Wesley's four questions, found quoted in many sources: (1) *In spending this money, am I acting like I own it, or am I acting like the Lord's trustee?* (2) *What Scripture requires me to spend this money this way?* (3) *Can I offer up this purchase as a sacrifice to the Lord?* (4) *Will God reward me for this expenditure at the resurrection of the just?*

resources you have so you can help accomplish it. Are you investing to build God's kingdom?

Give Us This Day Our Daily Bread

Jesus also instructs us to ask only for what we need for each day as it comes. However, it seems that we are not just praying for today's needs but rather we are pleading for enough bread to last thirty years. We are taught that we must accumulate "bread" to provide enough income to maintain our standard of living until we die. That is financial independence. But the Bible consistently points out that God desires us to be financially dependent *on* Him, not independent *from* Him.

Some scholars believe that when Jesus uses the phrase, "give us this day our daily bread," He is referencing manna, the supernatural food that God gave to the Israelites during their forty-year wandering in the desert. Moses instructed the people to gather an *omer*, or about two quarts' worth of manna, for each person per day. When some of the Israelites tried to gather and store up extra, the manna became wormy and spoiled. The Israelites needed to trust God to supply their physical needs one day at a time. Similarly, the Lord's Prayer indicates that we should be dependent on God for daily provision. Many scriptures point to this truth.

The apostle Paul seems to agree with the principle of financial dependence not financial independence when writing to the Christians in Philippi:

> Not that I am speaking of being in need, for I have learned in whatever situation I am to be content. I know how to be brought low, and I know how to abound. In any and every circumstance, I have learned the secret of facing plenty and hunger, abundance and need. I can do all things through him who strengthens me. (Phil. 4:10-13)

Paul was a wealthy Pharisee and a successful businessman when he became a Christian. Could it be that his real-life boom and bust experience was caused at least in part by a generous deployment of capital to build churches when he had abundance, trusting that the Lord would replenish the resources the next time they were needed? This seems to be the case, since he later writes to the Corinthian Church: "Now he who supplies seed to the sower and bread for food will also supply and increase your store of seed and will enlarge the harvest of your righteousness. You will be enriched in every way so that you can be generous on every occasion" (2 Cor. 9:10-11). Note how Paul prays that we will be enriched *so that* we can bring blessing through our generosity, not so that we can elevate our own standard of living.

Note how Paul prays that we will be enriched so that we can bring blessing through our generosity, not so that we can elevate our own standard of living.

> Jesus sat down opposite the place where the offerings were put and watched the crowd putting their money into the temple treasury. Many rich people threw in large amounts. But a poor widow came and put in two very small copper coins, worth only a few cents. Calling his disciples to him, Jesus said, "Truly I tell you, this poor widow has put more into the treasury than all the others. They all gave out of their wealth; but she, out of her poverty, put in everything—all she had to live on." (Mark 12:41-44)

Jesus illustrates the proper spiritual attitude toward money by lifting up this widow. She deployed her meager resources for God's work and trusted that He would provide what she needed for today and tomorrow. At the same time, He critiques the gifts from the wealthy because the amount they put in the offering was not sacrificial. Although this story is usually used to encourage charitable giving, I believe it also provides guidance for our mindset toward investing. We should invest liberally to achieve godly objectives while depending on God to meet our daily needs.

The writer of Hebrews further encourages a proper view of dependence through this warning: "Keep your life free from love of money and be content with what you have." We fail to recognize greed's insidious hold on us because there is always someone who has more whom we compare ourselves to. The writer continues with this reminder: "I will never leave you nor forsake you." So we can confidently say, "The Lord is my helper; I will not be afraid. What can mere mortals do to me?" (Heb. 13:5-6).

Matthew reminds us of Jesus' advice: "Do not be like them [those who heap up empty phrases], for your Father knows what you need before you ask him" (Matt. 6:8, ESV). Jesus continues, "Do not store up for yourselves treasures on earth, where moths and vermin destroy, and where thieves break in and steal. But store up for yourselves treasures in heaven, where moths and vermin do not destroy, and where thieves do not break in and steal. For where your treasure is, there your heart will be also" (Matt. 6:19-21).

"You shall remember the LORD your God, for it is he who gives you power to get wealth, that he may confirm his covenant that he swore to your fathers, as it is this day" (Deut. 8:18, ESV). This is a warning for us not to think too highly of ourselves or of how we achieved any financial success.

Or most direct of all, "No one can serve two masters. Either you will hate the one and love the other, or you will be devoted to the one and despise the other. You cannot serve both God and money" (Matt. 6:24). Simply put, if money is your master, then God is not.

CONCLUSION

Jesus and other biblical writers condemned hoarding and encouraged using resources to build His kingdom. "Thy kingdom come" investing requires that our portfolios proactively seek to fulfill Great Commission outcomes and Great Commandment objectives. This may mean more financial risk and lower financial returns for ourselves but greater impact for God's kingdom. Let's invest in ways that deliberately seek God's kingdom on earth as it is in heaven, knowing that He will provide our daily bread.

QUESTIONS FOR STUDY

1. (1) Set aside enough resources to maintain your standard of living until you die. (2) Make a plan to remain continually dependent on God financially as you deploy resources He has given you so that you can participate with Him in building the kingdom of God on earth. Which of these financial planning philosophies are you familiar with? Comment on the author's statements, "modern financial planning has led us astray," and, "I am more deliberately deploying greater percentages of my net worth toward building God's kingdom."

2. Discuss this statement from author Randy Alcorn's book *Managing God's Money*: "If anything we have is off-limits to God, if it's not subject to prayerful dialogue, then let's be honest about it—we aren't stewards, we're embezzlers. We aren't *serving* God; we're *playing* God."

3. Read James 5:5. How does James' warning contradict the advice of modern financial planners?

4. Were you familiar with John Wesley's status as one of England's wealthiest men throughout the 1700s, earning the equivalent of two million dollars annually from teaching and sales of his books? How do these statements regarding his own estate plan affect how you are thinking about your own financial plan: "If I leave behind me ten pounds . . . you and all mankind [may] bear witness against me, that I have lived and died a thief and robber," and, "My own hands will be my executors"? If Wesley felt he would be a robber, from whom would he have stolen the ten pounds? What do you think about being the executor of your own estate before you die?

5. Are you persuaded, as John Wesley was, that every penny, every dollar that flows through your hands belongs to God? Whether spending, giving, or investing, do you ask yourself similar questions that Wesley asked himself before transacting an exchange of money? Regarding your investments, can you answer his reframed questions positively: *Am I acting like I own it, or am I acting like the Lord's fiduciary? What Scripture requires me to invest in this way? Can I offer up this investment as a sacrifice to the Lord? Will God reward me for this investment at the resurrection of the just?*

6. Explain the point of God's instruction to Israel to gather a set amount of manna daily and compare that to the Lord's Prayer teaching His followers to ask God the Father for our daily bread.

7. Read and reflect on Paul's teaching in 2 Corinthians 9:10-11, the words of Jesus in the account of the poor widow in Mark 12:41-44, and Hebrews 13:5-6. What affirmations and promises are found in these passages for those who will give generously and trust God for their own needs?

Chapter 16

DIE BROKE: RICH FOOLS, FAITH, AND POOR HEROES

The parable of the rich fool in Luke 12 gives our final insights about wealth accumulation, hoarding, and financial independence. Jesus begins by telling His hearers, "Watch out! Be on your guard against all kinds of greed; life does not consist in an abundance of possessions" (Luke 12:15). Then He launches into a story about a farmer whose land produces an abundant crop. As God continues to bless the man and his land, he becomes focused on accumulating and growing his own wealth. He decides to tear down his barns and build bigger ones to store the fruit of his labor. He says to himself, "You have plenty of grain laid up for many years. Take life easy; eat, drink and be merry" (12:18). Don't his words sound like the person planning for an early retirement filled with luxury, leisure, and self-indulgence? James warns, "You have lived on earth in luxury and self-indulgence. . . . [and] have fattened yourselves in the day of slaughter" (James 5:5).

Instead of self-focus and leisure indulgence, the parable in Luke teaches that the farmer should have used his increase to further the will of God. "But God said to him, 'You fool! This very night your life will be demanded from you. Then who will get what you have prepared for yourself?' This is how it will be with whoever stores up things for themselves but is not rich toward God" (Luke 12:20-21). Remember the covenant funnel described in chapter six? We are "blessed to bring blessing." God trusts us with resources to manage so we can be a blessing to others and build His kingdom. The Bible says we are not to set our hearts upon our riches (Ps. 62:10). God's *oikonomos* is rich for heavenly purposes, not to hoard for ourselves or our posterity. Jesus could hardly be clearer about how foolish we are when we hoard resources for ourselves.

MODERN RETIREMENT PLANNING: CREATING RICH FOOLS

It is impossible to be the Lord's fiduciary if you have not mastered basic financial competence (chapter one). But not everything that Christians have been taught about financial competence applies to Christians managing God's resources as His *oikonomos*.

The 4% Rule

Modern financial planning teaches us to build nest eggs and portfolios that will last until we die. This principle by itself does not seem to align with scripture. But, taking it a step further, the broadly accepted 4% Rule also implies that our primary goal and top priority is protecting our savings. The 4% Rule is the most frequently used guide regarding a safe withdrawal rate during retirement which is the maximum rate at which you can spend your retirement savings such that you don't run out of money during your lifetime. Since the sequencing of booms and crashes in the economy is the major factor in determining whether your nest egg will last, most financial advisors err on the side of caution when suggesting a withdrawal rate. Four percent is generally accepted as reasonable to prevent corpus depletion. The underlying goal is that by using a 4% withdrawal rate, retirees will never need to pray for their "daily bread."

Capital Retention or Capital Depletion

In addition to using the 4% Rule, most advisors suggest that a retiree calculate their nest egg withdrawals based on a *capital retention* methodology and not a *capital depletion* methodology. Capital retention means that you only withdraw an amount equal to your average annual earnings each year and never from the principal. As a result, a retiree should have the same amount in their nest egg at death as they started with the day they retired since they are only spending the earnings. Using a capital retention calculation results in a larger nest egg than actually needed to provide a lifetime income and, in the end, leaves a large windfall for their heirs.

In contrast, the capital depletion method calculates withdrawals using both earnings and principal. For example, actuaries use the capital depletion method to calculate pensions. A pension must be funded with sufficient capital so that a combination of principal and earnings can be withdrawn each year, resulting in a balance of zero at the pensioner's life expectancy. This method, implemented by an individual, can result in greater risk of running out of money if the retiree lives longer than life expectancy or the rate of return is lower than anticipated. These risks can be managed with ongoing portfolio monitoring or lifestyle adjustments or through various insurance products.

As God's fiduciary, it is important to consider which method best optimizes the multiple goals of providing income for a retiree and simultaneously deploying resources to build the kingdom of God. Capital retention may be "safer" because it requires the retiree to retain a larger nest egg, draws only earnings, and inherently passes wealth to the next generation. On the other hand, capital depletion methodology may facilitate the deployment of greater resources for kingdom building.

Depleting Capital for the Kingdom

Most missionaries must pray constantly for their daily bread. They depend on others to provide for their financial needs and typically live with just enough and just in time. Individuals and organizations are under-resourced, with insufficient funding to provide anything above basic needs, while at the same time, trillions of dollars in the portfolios of Christian investors remain undeployed to achieve spiritual goals. In fact, these under-resourced people are often the most generous toward kingdom priorities. They frequently donate to or invest in local families or projects because they see the world's grief far more clearly than we who have not traveled to frontier markets where poverty is endemic. As a result, many missionaries do not have nest eggs that could provide for a comfortable retirement through either a capital retention or capital depletion method. It's a sad fact, but millions of Christians are oblivious to the desperate, daily needs of their brothers and sisters while they themselves live in comfort and hoard wealth in the name of security and financial independence.

Many years ago, my wife and I agreed to live differently. We supported many families in ministry who struggled to make ends meet and were keenly aware they lived with faith that the Lord would provide through others. We began to consider what it would take to live with a similar level of faith as those we supported. I knew that for us to live in faith like theirs and honestly pray, "give us this day our daily bread," we would need to do something radical.

We began to consider what it would take to live with a similar level of faith as those we supported.

By nature, I am a calculating person. I love Microsoft Excel and use it daily to develop business plans, budgets, and profit and loss and cash flow statements for my clients. It became clear that my family's faith decisions would not fit on a spreadsheet. Even our consistent tithing required little faith—certainly not at the level of the friends we supported. So we began making faith pledges at the beginning of the year which reached beyond our budget—giving and missional investing goals that would only be met if God "came through." We willingly committed our existing savings and investments in the event the Lord did not provide added income to meet our faith pledges. From a financial competence point of view, this seemed foolish, but in obedience, as God's fiduciaries, we took the step of faith. I cannot list all the projects that the Lord miraculously funded.

We live a life of faith, financially, because we are committed to deploying more for God's purposes than we consume ourselves. Although this exercise of faithful living began with radical generosity, it carried over into our investing and all other money management matters. At age fifty-one, nineteen years before my planned retirement, I felt called to serve on the management team of a Christian economic development fund that provides funding to missional businesses in frontier markets. We were not close to having the family resources necessary for me to serve as a full-time volunteer with the organization. We had not accumulated enough to "retire," especially from a capital retention standpoint. The Lord challenged me by asking, *Do you trust me? Are you dependent on me? Are you willing to do the opposite of what you have been taught in the financial services industry for thirty years? Are you ready to start a capital depletion method at age fifty-one?*

The decision to follow God's call would require not only a premature disruption in our financial plans but also a change in our business structure that colleagues said was impossible. That it would require surrendering about five hundred thousand dollars of deferred compensation, an important part of our retirement nest egg, was icing on the cake. For a financial planner, this was the perfect financial storm which would truly require us to mean it when we prayed for our daily bread.

We continue to voluntarily serve missional businesses, deploy more than fits on a spreadsheet, and invest our assets in businesses that proactively seek to build the kingdom of God and prioritize stakeholders other than ourselves or our children. Our children understand that we intend to be one hundred percent deployed for God, leaving no inheritance behind except the custodianship of missional investments.

THE BASIS FOR YOUR FINANCIAL BEHAVIOR: FACTS OR FAITH?

Is your financial behavior based on facts or faith? Most Christians, I imagine, would like to answer that they live with a strong level of faith. But a hard look at financial strategies would probably indicate a fact-based, independence-not-dependence strategy. In my three decades of working with Christians and seeing how they handle money, I have observed that they are usually quite measured in their approach to being generous. The motivation appears to be both preservation of wealth for themselves and a fear that they may be taken advantage of in their generosity. We have all wrestled with this issue when a person who is poorly clothed and unkempt approaches us on the street asking for help. Our mind quickly scrolls through questions like, *Is this person really homeless? Is this a scam or a real need? How much should I give to alleviate the guilt I am currently feeling? How much cash do I have in my pocket, and will I have enough to do the things I want to do today if I give some to meet the needs of this beggar?* The questions reflect both our fear of being taken advantage of and our desire to minimize any personal loss through our generosity.

Most of us consider ourselves generous, and we think an important part of being a good Christian steward is to qualify our giving and limit our donations. We mistakenly reason that prudently limiting the scope of our generosity is necessary so that we don't become squanderers or fools by contributing to someone's misuse of donated dollars. I believe that this mindset is a fundamental misunderstanding of the generous nature of God and our responsibility as His stewards. I have observed this behavior in the ways Christians approach both donations and investing.

Matt Perman, director of career development at The King's College in New York City, discusses Jonathan Edwards' provocative sermon, "The Duty of Christian Charity: Explained and Defended." Perman emphasizes Edwards' argument that,

> [H]elping the poor is one of the *highest duties* of the Christian. It is not just a small duty, but a great duty—and even heaven and hell lie in the balance with how we respond to the poor (Matthew 25:41-46). Christians are not just to help the poor from a little bit of their surplus, but are to be *abundant, liberal, and utterly generous in giving to the poor.*[106]

Edwards concludes his sermon with the chief objections that Christians use to defend their unwillingness to help the poor: they maintain an overprotective eye towards limits, prudence, and those who might benefit unscrupulously. Edwards' comments penetrate because we can see ourselves making these kinds of objections. Edwards goes on to explain how bad theology or poor excuses lead us to making decisions which are contrary to God's directives. His examples include,

1. I don't have anything to spare; I have only enough for myself.

2. I don't know whether a person or program should receive charity—are they deserving? I do not fully know their circumstances. What kind of person or program is it? What if their need is a result of idleness or mismanagement? I can't give in good conscience until I know these things.

106. Matt Perman, "11 Objections on Giving to the Poor Answered by Jonathan Edwards" (August 11, 2014): https://mattperman.com/2014/08/11-objections-on-giving-to-the-poor-answered-by-jonathan-edwards/.

3. I have given to the poor in the past but have not experienced the expected blessing because I did it; I've even experienced great difficulty and loss.
4. I am not obliged to give because their need isn't great enough yet.
5. Since I am a sinner, if I give to the poor, it won't be out of good motives, and so I wouldn't gain anything by doing it.
6. If I give generously, it would be like showing off my righteousness, and that's not a good look for a humble Christian.
7. I am not inclined to give because the recipient doesn't deserve it—they are mean, ungrateful, and have treated me and others poorly.
8. I am not obliged to give to the poor until they ask. If someone has a need, that person should come and let me know.
9. Other people have not done their duty in giving; if they did, the poor would have enough. Why should I help when others won't?
10. The law and government offer help to the poor; they don't need my help, too.[107]

Although Jonathan Edwards' sermon specifically focuses on generosity through donations, the same attitude and excuses apply to our financial and investment decisions. God's people must abandon the fallacy that charity is sacred and investment is secular; in the hands of God's *oikonomos* all assets can be deployed to achieve God's divine purposes. God is generous all the time. Generosity should infuse every facet of our lives as His image bearers. He calls us to build His kingdom. We can't achieve this by investing in publicly

God's people must abandon the fallacy that charity is sacred and investment is secular; in the hands of God's oikonomos all assets can be deployed to achieve God's divine purposes.

107. Paraphrase from Jonathan Edwards, "The Duty of Christian Charity: Explained and Defended" (January 1732): https://www.biblebb.com/files/edwards/charity.htm.

traded companies with little to zero commitment for God's kingdom or by focusing on increasing personal wealth while giving only a small portion of the gains to fund the Lord's work. I am not arguing for a lack of accountability in how we invest—we must hold recipients to high moral standards and repayment terms (see Appendix B: The Entrepreneur's Pledge)—but these conditions sound like the behavior that James warns against. For most people, the nest egg they save is much larger than the portion they deploy for kingdom building. Investing a portion of your large portfolio, including your nest egg principal, home equity, and retirement through missional investments is the most effective way to build God's kingdom.

I have heard many investors and investment advisors state that charity and investment are two entirely different things and that investments by nature cannot achieve charitable goals. They use the illustration of a houseboat, making the argument that a houseboat is neither a good boat nor a good house. Perhaps that's true, but a houseboat optimizes and accomplishes two purposes simultaneously. It is a place to live, and it floats. God's *oikonomos* is generous because generosity reflects one of God's primary attributes. Missional investments can also achieve multiple objectives at the same time. They can stave off immediate needs and accomplish QBL outcomes through long-term investment in frontier enterprises.

Let me challenge you with a few last questions regarding making investment decisions by fact or faith. Are your assets primarily focused on temporal gain for yourself or for accomplishing eternal impact for God? Are most of your investment decisions based on modern financial planning principles or on accomplishing God's goals? Are they primarily measured, calculated, prudent, and without risk? Or could they be considered self-sacrificial and generous toward the less fortunate? Are you deploying extravagantly to build God's kingdom in difficult and risky places and circumstances? Does your advisor understand your role as God's *oikonomos*, and have they demonstrated by example their own commitment to deploy resources to build God's kingdom?

Hebrews 11:4 has been a core life verse of mine as far back as I can remember: "By faith Abel brought God a better offering than Cain did. By faith he was commended as righteous, when God spoke well of his offerings. And by faith Abel still speaks, even though he is dead." I don't think the point is whether their gifts were vegetable or meat. The difference was Abel's dependence on God versus Cain's independent self-reliance. Maybe the problem with Cain's gift was that it was measured, calculated, prudent, and affordable—no blood shed, and no faith required. In contrast, Abel's gift was sacrificial and extravagant. Blood must be shed for the forgiveness of sins. But we must realize that there are also real business and investment implications to Abel's action. The shedding of blood meant the end of the animal's line of descent and the gain that could be achieved through that line. This kind of sacrifice carried great risk and great faith, forcing Abel to depend on God's future provision. Have you ever sacrificed your best investment opportunity, the one with the greatest growth potential, as an offering to the Lord?

Have you ever sacrificed your best investment opportunity, the one with the greatest growth potential, as an offering to the Lord?

A MAN WHO INTENDS TO DIE BROKE

It is not unusual to read stories about athletes, Hollywood superstars, or lottery winners who die broke because they squandered the tens or hundreds of millions that they had amassed. But Charles "Chuck" Feeney lives in a rented two-bedroom apartment in California not because he squandered his fortune but because he went "broke" intentionally after donating all his wealth to charities. Feeney questioned the value of holding onto his own accumulated wealth when people around the world had such great needs.[108]

Feeney, who amassed billions as the co-founder of Duty Free Shoppers, made a pledge at age fifty-one to donate every penny of his wealth before he died. By age eighty-nine he had successfully deployed over eight billion dollars to charitable causes around the globe while living on the two million dollars he had set aside for retirement.

In 1984, Feeney secretly transferred all his assets, including his 38.75 percent ownership of the duty-free business, to the charitable foundation he had established called Atlantic Philanthropies. This charity became a large operation with more than three hundred employees and ten global offices making high-risk and high-impact

108. "Chuck Feeney – The Broke Billionaire Who Gave It All Away" (Feb 28, 2021): https://karmatheories.com/chuck-feeney/.

deployments around the world. Feeney designed the organization to give away billions of dollars and established a hard deadline by which it would have given everything away and closed its doors. He accomplished his goal on September 19, 2020, when Atlantic Philanthropies closed after nearly four decades of charitable work. In a report published about Atlantic Philanthropies in 2019 called *Zero is the Hero*, Feeney reveals his pleasure in helping worthy causes acknowledging he'll have more fun giving while he's living than after he's dead.[109]

For God's oikonomos, the idea of dying broke should be normal because an oikonomos recognizes that they are already broke. I am not managing financial resources for my own benefit, but everything I possess is, in fact, owned by God.

I don't know what inspired Chuck Feeney to donate his fortune in favor of helping a hurting world. But as a Jesus follower, I know that I should have a similar outlook. For Wesley and Feeney, divesting of their material wealth and dying broke was consistent with their calling. For God's *oikonomos,* the idea of dying broke should be normal because an *oikonomos* recognizes that they are already broke. I am not managing financial resources for my own benefit, but everything I possess is, in fact, owned by God. As I understand my role as God's *oikonomos* more completely, I must make sure that I engage all resources in serving the Master and accomplishing His goals.

I am a small business owner, so I recognize that in most cases it is not practical or realistic to divest a small, privately held company or its assets. But if I recognize that my business is actually the Lord's business, intentional focus on building God's kingdom is non-negotiable. It may mean asking hard questions like how I can leverage my business to create sustainable employment and incarnational witness among an unreached people group or make sure that adequate accountability and monitoring are in place to continue beyond my lifetime.

109. Steven Bertoni, "Exclusive: The Billionaire Who Wanted to Die Broke . . . Is Now Officially Broke" (September 15, 2020): https://www.forbes.com/sites/stevenbertoni/2020/09/15/exclusive-the-billionaire-who-wanted-to-die-brokeis-now-officially-broke/?sh=15095a8c3a2a.

I intend to deploy virtually all our financial resources into missional businesses and missional projects before I die. This does not mean that I must follow exactly the same path as Feeney or Wesley. But when I deliberately invest the corpus of our portfolio in ways that achieve kingdom of heaven outcomes, I show that I recognize that I am already broke. I am simply willing to be an obedient *oikonomos* of God's resources. I may not actually die broke because it is possible that some of the enterprises we invest in will succeed. Many will fail because the locations and projects carry extreme risk. These will become donations because the investment is completely lost. Others may succeed and build God's kingdom for decades or generations or until the Lord returns. One thing is sure, I do not intend to squander God's resources or hoard them for myself or invest them in ways that contradict Christian principles and values. I am committed, as God's *oikonomos*, to see one hundred percent proactively deployed to build the kingdom of God on earth!

CONCLUSION

In conclusion, I'd like to reflect briefly on Demas. The apostle Paul mentions Demas three times, including two references that indicate his partnership as a "fellow worker" spreading the Gospel: "Our dear friend Luke, the doctor, *and Demas* send greetings" (Col. 4:14) "[and] Epaphras, my fellow prisoner in Christ Jesus, sends you greetings. And so do Mark, Aristarchus, *Demas* . . ., my fellow workers" (Philem. 23-24, emphasis mine).

However, while Paul awaited execution in Rome, his reference to Demas reveals a sad turn: "Demas . . . because he loved this world, has deserted me and has gone to Thessalonica" (2 Tim. 4:10). Sadly, Demas left Paul, abandoning his devotion to the Lord, and set his course for Thessalonica, a prominent port city of culture, glamor, and wealth. It was a thriving cosmopolitan destination. His desire to enjoy the pleasures of this world caused him to turn his back on kingdom priorities. Paul warned his young friend Timothy that "the love of money is a root of all kinds of evil. Some people, eager for money, have wandered from the faith and pierced themselves with many griefs" (1 Tim. 6:10). James warned his readers that "friendship with the world is hostility toward God" (James 4:4, NASB). Have you, like Demas, been enticed by the worldly call of culture, glamor, and wealth, and turned your back on the greater call of serving Jesus as His *oikonomos*?

Demas' behavior reminds me of a prayer that is attributed to Sir Francis Drake. This prayer is a constant reminder to me that it is easy to be enticed by the pleasures and riches of this world:

Disturb us, Lord, when we are too well pleased with ourselves,
When our dreams have come true because we have dreamed too little,
When we arrived safely because we sailed too close to the shore.

Disturb us, Lord, when with the abundance of things we possess
We have lost our thirst for the waters of life;
Having fallen in love with life, we have ceased to dream of eternity
And in our efforts to build a new earth, we have allowed our vision of the new Heaven to dim.

Disturb us, Lord, to dare more boldly, to venture on wider seas
Where storms will show your mastery; where losing sight of land, we shall find the stars.
We ask You to push back the horizons of our hopes;
And to push into the future in strength, courage, hope, and love.

Attributed—Sir Francis Drake—1577

This world is not my home. Many years ago I prayed a dangerous prayer which caused my heart to break for the things that break God's heart. This launched me, with my family, on a journey to manage investments differently than if I simply listened to my own advice as a financial advisor. I was moved to deploy, in faith, myself and the resources entrusted to me. I learned to stretch beyond what is comfortable and be more heavenly minded than earthly content. I pray that you will be moved to do the same with the investments God has entrusted to you as His *oikonomos*.

QUESTIONS FOR STUDY

1. Explain the 4% Rule for financial planning and compare or contrast with what you understand regarding the priorities for the Lord's *oikonomos.*

2. What is capital retention? What is capital depletion?

3. Discuss the author's statement, "As God's fiduciary, it is important to consider which method best optimizes the multiple goals of providing income for a retiree and simultaneously deploying resources to build the kingdom of God."

4. Read James 2:14-26. Share an example of a faith commitment that you made in the past or one that is presenting itself to you now. How often in your life are you in a situation to hear these kinds of faith stories? How does hearing others share their experiences impact your own faith?

5. What is the basis for your financial behavior? Is it based on facts (driven by earnings and accumulation, by hoarding for yourself and your posterity? Based on modern financial planning principles, measured, calculated, prudent, and without risk)? Or are your financial decisions based on faith? Are your decisions sacrificial toward yourself but generous toward the less fortunate? Are they extravagantly deployed to build God's kingdom even in risky places or situations?

6. Read Romans 12:1. Consider and discuss the idea of dying broke . . . doing your giving while you are living. Compare how you think God will reward His oikonomos who make decisions to use God's resources for His purposes while living versus a bequeathment at death. Would there be any difference? Cite a biblical text to support your conclusion.

7. Imagine if all of God's fiduciaries based their financial decisions on faith in God who has promised to supply all their needs, to multiply seed for the sower, and to reward them for their acts of righteousness with a rich welcome into their heavenly inheritance. Would extravagant faith giving and investing open flood gates of resources to answer our personal and corporate oft repeated prayer, "thy kingdom come, thy will be done on earth as it is in Heaven"? What might that look like for this world?

8. What will you do next to show your faith by your deeds with respect to your role as God's *oikonomos* handling the investments of the King of Kings?

NEXT STEPS

If you have finished this book all the way through to this section, you are already demonstrating your readiness to take the next steps on the road to becoming God's *oikonomos*. Before we get started with some practical steps, however, I want to reiterate a few key points that undergird any moves we make to deploy our investment funds into opportunities seeking multiple bottom-line outcomes.

1. Jesus reminded His disciples that "where your treasure is, there your heart will be also." When we accept a worldly view of wealth, riches, and money, our heart is stained with impure motives, attitudes, and desires. Soon our entire lives are misdirected toward selfish ambition and vain conceit rather than humility which values others above ourselves. Our hearts and actions cause us to look toward our own interests rather than the interests of others. *Our portfolio is a barometer that indicates the condition of our heart. It will reveal whether we value money over mission.* The lure of mammon is powerful, and I have found that in the absence of wise counsel it not only corrupts our financial behaviors but our very hearts as well. We succumb to treasuring the accumulation of wealth over serving God.

2. We must cast off the false distinction between what is sacred and what is secular. We have inherited a view of money that separates donations from investments. This common but incorrect view considers donations sacred as they appear to directly accomplish "God's work," while investments seem disconnected from direct influence on the kingdom of God. As God's *oikonomos*, however, *we accept the truth that every dollar He's given us belongs to Him, and we are to steward it according to His principles and values.*

3. We must learn how to construct a portfolio that looks different from that of a good, honest, competent, even compassionate investor who does not follow Jesus as their Lord and Savior. *Our relationship with Jesus and our understanding of our role as His steward investor will influence how we manage the*

portfolio of investments He entrusts to us. Investors are owners of the companies they invest in and are responsible for the companies' practices and whether they bring blessing or pain to workers and communities. Obedience in matters of saving, spending, investing, and generosity are intrinsic to our calling as disciples of Christ. We must not "conform to the patterns of this world, but be transformed by the renewing of [our] mind" (Rom. 12:2). Creating a portfolio that matches our values may require us to take actions that are different from generic investment advice offered by those who do not embrace our Christian worldview.

4. We will need to align ourselves with like-minded professionals who can give the necessary guidance to accomplish our goals. The process of building a portfolio that is fully integrated, *blending our personal temporal needs with God's eternal objectives using traditional investments and private placement missional investments, is complex.* There are portfolio allocation considerations, risk management, values alignment, time, and tax considerations that need to be addressed and coordinated with the uniqueness of each investor's situation. The following questions illustrate some of these concerns:

    a. Where can I find missional investment opportunities?

    b. How do I balance my family's financial needs with purposeful investing to achieve *Great Commission and righteous* outcomes?

    c. What investment allocation is needed for my entire portfolio to balance the risks associated with impact investing in *frontier markets for redemptive purposes?*

    d. How should I attend to *core financial factors* such as time horizon, return, and loss, as I serve as God's steward investor?

    e. Who will vet the possible *investee companies* and their owners to confirm that they "are who they say they are"?

    f. Who will monitor the *business's performance* and hold them accountable as they work to achieve the spiritual impact, as well as the set financial, social, and environmental targets?

g. Who will give me guidance on the tax implications caused by investing retirement funds such as IRAs into *impactful private placement investments?*

h. How do I strategically and methodically move from a traditional portfolio to a *kingdom impact portfolio* and allocate more to God's purposes over time?

FOUR STEPS TO STEWARD-INVESTING SUCCESS

While the questions above may seem daunting, your missional investing journey can be successfully completed by following four steps. Although these steps are easy to understand, they are not necessarily simple to accomplish, and you should not plan to take them alone. As scripture teaches us, there is wisdom in many counselors. The body of Christ must work together with each member leaning on the experience and expertise of people and organizations who are already walking this path. Here are your four steps to steward-investing success:

Step 1: Select a Knowledgeable Guide

To act effectively as God's *oikonomos*, you should partner with a like-minded financial advisor who has the knowledge, ability, tools, and personal experience necessary to successfully guide you. This advisor needs access to your entire financial picture because investing for kingdom impact is not a stand-alone activity. It is part of your overall investment and financial plan.

If you currently have a financial advisor, you will need to discern their ability to guide you in the direction you've chosen to go. Having an honest conversation with your advisor will be the necessary first step. You can use these seven questions below as a guide to assess the degree to which your current financial advisor is equipped to guide you on your journey toward becoming a steward investor. Each question reflects a necessary component of kingdom investing. Visit ***StewardAdvisorsGroup.com*** for examples of how an experienced missional investment advisor would answer these questions.

1. Have you considered whether a portfolio for a Christian client should be different from your standard portfolio? How would you advise them to invest based on their goal to honor God and to serve Him through their portfolio?
2. Do you have a methodology to help me invest in ways that advance the kingdom of heaven on earth? Can you explain your methods? How might this affect my financial returns?
3. It is important to me that my portfolio reflects God's purposes such as making disciples, loving my neighbors, and bringing shalom to vulnerable members of society. Can you give an example of how you have helped others to fulfill their role as God's steward by investing into Great Commission businesses with quadruple bottom line impact in the least reached countries of the world?
4. My largest liquid asset is my retirement savings, but before now, I have not considered using it to achieve God's purposes. How might you help me use my IRA to bring salt and light in unreached places by investing in private missional businesses?
5. I have used mutual funds and other traditional investments to populate my portfolio in the past because I was unaware that my investments could be used to bring justice and mercy to broken spheres of society, alleviate poverty, and draw people closer to God. How can you help me harmonize my traditional investments and new missional investments into a single portfolio that, as a whole, is aligned with God's call to invest for His outcomes as well as my own needs?
6. My faith influences how I think about wealth accumulation and financial planning for my own needs. How can you help me utilize portfolio building techniques and estate planning strategies to provide for my family's needs, minimize taxes, and provide for heirs, while balancing my responsibility to deploy God's resources for building the kingdom of heaven on earth?
7. Have you invested in any missional businesses yourself? Or do you have clients whom you have helped to become steward investors who could be a reference for your work? If so, could you give an example of an investment that you or they made?

In reading through these questions, you may realize that your advisor is not sufficiently equipped to guide you. This may be the first "crisis" on your road to becoming a steward investor. Should you continue with your current advisor, or should you seek a guide with the relevant experience and resources? Like many crises, this could open an opportunity to have an honest conversation about matters of faith with someone who already knows you well (because they know about your financial situation). You may choose to speak clearly and directly about your vision of the kingdom of God and your desire to be part of bringing righteousness, peace, justice, mercy, and prosperity to people around the world. As part of your relationship with this trusted professional, you can explain your personal relationship with Jesus and His authority on your life. You can speak the truth about God's presence, goodness, and generosity. This conversation could be a bold step for someone like you who is ready to make a radical change in the way they view and deploy their money.

If you do not currently have an advisor who can answer these questions to your satisfaction, you can visit *StewardAdvisorsGroup.com* to connect with an experienced, knowledgeable advisor to help you build your portfolio of missional and traditional investments. Among other services, these advisors can work beside you to evaluate your traditional investments along moral and ethical guidelines to ensure that they are aligned with your core values as you seek to manage God's resources. They can help you determine the portion of your portfolio that could be allocated toward missional enterprises and can guide you in evaluating whether the investments should be done via pre-tax, after-tax, or donated funds. Additionally, these advisors can help you understand how a portfolio is performing overall despite the potential under-performance of any single investment. They understand the need for a fully integrated portfolio that achieves the mutually important goals of your own financial objectives and God's kingdom objectives.

Perhaps a hiking analogy would be helpful to explain the importance of an appropriate guide. Imagine you'd like to hike in the Himalayas. They are mountain ranges filled with unique terrain, weather patterns, seasonal challenges, and hidden dangers. It would not be wise to hire a sherpa who is experienced—but only on the Appalachian Trail in the eastern United States with mountain peaks below five thousand feet. While an experienced Himalayan guide could easily lead you on the Appalachian Trail, it is unlikely that an Appalachian Trail guide could lead you to the top of Mt. Everest or K2. You need a guide with the appropriate experience and expertise for the most difficult destinations that you wish to explore. In the same way, investing for God's kingdom is like hiking in the Himalayas. You need a guide that has deep experience in traditional financial planning who also possesses the advanced knowledge and experience in building portfolios that achieve kingdom objectives. This guide will capably integrate missional investments with traditional investments and portfolio strategies. Your guide will help you lay out a successful and comprehensive path, balancing risks and rewards, returns, and impactful outcomes as well as meeting the needs of your family, because all of these are important duties for God's *oikonomos*. Sometimes we stumble when we hike, or we may even get lost. A strong and experienced guide can give a helping hand and provide direction to your destination. Similarly, a financial guide who has wrestled with balancing the principles of how money behaves in the world economic system with our call to steward resources for the True Owner, God, will be able to guide you when colliding worldviews cause confusion or anguish.

Step 2: Create a Plan to Integrate Your Traditional and Steward Investing

Once you have partnered with a well-equipped financial guide, collaborate to create a life plan that seamlessly integrates your traditional financial plan with your call to be a steward investor. Traditional financial planning principles are good and necessary, and meeting the needs of your family is part of your role as God's *oikonomos*. Everything you do must be synthesized into a life plan where you can simultaneously meet your family responsibilities and fulfill your duty to participate in building God's kingdom on earth as it is in heaven. A life plan will help you set strategic goals not only for your personal financial needs but also for achieving quadruple bottom line impact as a steward investor.

"Suppose one of you wants to build a tower. Won't you first sit down and estimate the cost to see if you have enough money to complete it? For if you lay the foundation and are not able to finish it, everyone who sees it will ridicule you" (Luke 14:28-30). It is easy to connect the relevance of these verses to our traditional financial planning such as saving for college or retirement. But the planning becomes much more complicated when we include God as the True Owner of the resources, requiring our plan to include achieving

His purposes as well as our own. Your life plan should address non-traditional financial planning questions such as the following:

- *How much is too much* to save for retirement, not *how much do I need* for retirement.
- How can I integrate my *vocational training, relational influence, spiritual gifts, financial resources, core passions,* and *discretionary time* into a meaningful calling during my retirement years?
- *Are my children equipped* to be the best managers of God's resources when I die, rather than *how can I maximize benefit for my heirs* through my estate plan?
- How should Jesus' words, "store up for yourself treasures in heaven" influence my saving, spending, and investing behavior? We might ask *should* I buy the expensive car, rather than *can I afford* to buy the expensive car?
- How can I optimize outcomes for *all* stakeholders, as opposed to how can I maximize financial return for *myself*?

God's financial plan for your life may be more profound than you have ever considered. He may accomplish amazing things through you as you harmonize your finances with His call on your life.

Visit ***StewardAdvisorsGroup.com*** to find a worksheet to help you and your advisor create a holistic life plan. After completing the worksheet, you can schedule a free consultation with an advisor to help you create your life plan, analyze your current situation, and guide you in its implementation.

Step 3: Begin Implementing Your Steward-Investor Life Plan

With a well-equipped financial advisor as a guide and with a thoughtful life plan in place, continue your journey as a steward investor by making your first missional investment with the goal of building a missional portfolio over the rest of your life.

It takes faith to begin implementing your plan. And we know that we can't please God without faith. So once you have your life plan in place, don't delay. After you have dedicated your life plan to the Lord, take that step of faith and make your first missional investment. This will most likely require transferring investment accounts to a custodian who is capable of processing both publicly traded and private placement investments.

To see examples of individual companies and various funds that are seeking quadruple bottom line outcomes for their stakeholders, including investors, visit *StewardAdvisorsGroup.com.*

Step 4: Connect with a Like-Minded Companion

Finding a financial peer (one of similar income or net worth), either a single person or a couple, who is willing to be engaged in mutual transparency and accountability in finance and investing will be indispensable for keeping you on the path as God's *oikonomos.* "Two people are better off than one, for they can help each other succeed. If one person falls, the other can reach out and help. But someone who falls alone is in real trouble" (Eccles. 4:9-10, NLT).

As you know, transparent financial discussion is generally taboo in our culture. However, without this kind of deep, trusting, and mutually sharpening relationship, staying the course may be impossible. Our culture will subtly but forcefully influence you away from the path of being God's steward investor. You will be hard pressed to maintain a proper perspective and take consistent actions that align with the truth that "God owns it all" when inundated with the *me first/this is mine/I deserve this/I need to look out for number one/make as much as you can as fast as you can* mentality abundant in advertisements and magazine and online articles and among friends, relatives, coworkers, social media, financial commentators, and advice givers. If you underestimate the magnitude and the power of this influence, your spending and savings behaviors will mirror our culture rather than follow biblical precepts. A like-minded companion who has chosen to walk the same path of obedient and sacrificial investing is invaluable as you walk this journey for the rest of your life.

A WORD OF ENCOURAGEMENT

Amy and I have been walking the journey of becoming steward investors for more than thirty years. Initially we did not fully understand and could not articulate all the concepts presented in this book. We started learning financial competence in our early twenties and practiced the disciplines necessary to manage money well and give generously. Over time our competence grew to include impactful investing which aligned with our values to "do no harm" to the environment or vulnerable members of society. Eventually our understanding of wealth matured into a call to be God's *oikonomos*—not only as generous givers but also as proactive stewards of investments that glorify God by achieving quadruple bottom line outcomes. The more we invest in missional enterprises in difficult places, the more God changes our hearts to align with His eternal purposes. We do not do it alone. We communicate transparently with each other and with trusted friends who share the spiritual, emotional, and financial loads and who hold us accountable on our chosen road.

We hope this book accelerates your journey and makes the path visible. We look forward to walking beside you as you become steward investors.

To contact the author and share how this book has impacted your life, email: info@thestewardinvestor.com.

or visit TheStewardInvestor.com

To learn more about steward investing, visit StewardAvisorsGroup.com.

APPENDIX A:
Investor Attestation Regarding Missional Investments

In order to address values alignment and transparency to potential investors, we ask investors to sign a pledge similar to this one:

None of the information contained herein has been filed with the securities and exchange commission, any securities administrator under any state securities laws, or any other governmental or self-regulatory authority. No governmental authority has passed on the merits of this offering or the adequacy of the information contained herein. Any representation to the contrary is unlawful.

THE VALUE OF INDIVIDUAL INVESTMENT MAY GO DOWN AS WELL AS UP, AND INVESTORS MAY NOT RECEIVE BACK THE AMOUNT INVESTED BY THEM INTO THE INVESTMENT. THERE IS THE POSSIBILITY THAT INVESTORS COULD LOSE UP TO 100% OF ANY INVESTMENT THEY MAKE.

As transformational impact investors, we recognize that success is measured by multiple bottom lines and not only the financial bottom line. As a result, we are willing to assume higher financial risk as we seek outcomes that are consistent with God's purposes. We understand that long-term, patient, generous, serving capital is often needed to capitalize redemptive businesses in frontier markets.

The investee businesses will seek to achieve financial stability, profitability, and sustainability so that they can meet their obligations to employees and investors while simultaneously pursuing social, spiritual, and environmental outcomes.

However, there can be no assurance that the investment will achieve any or all of its objectives. The value of individual investments may decrease, and investors may not receive back the amount invested.

There is no guarantee that borrowers or investee companies will be able or willing to pay interest or make principal repayments when due.

The financial risks of missional investments, including possible loss of the entire investment, are due to some of the following factors:

a. Loans to borrowers are unsecured and are not guaranteed by investee company owners and/or managers or other collateral.
b. Borrowers are relatively young companies with limited operating history.
c. The countries where the businesses operate often present substantial political, currency, legal and regulatory, economic, social, religious, and physical risks.
d. Agriculture projects carry climate risks such as drought, flood, abnormal heat or cold, pestilence, or virus which can wipe out an entire harvest or animal population and a year's worth of revenue, for example.

BEFORE DECIDING TO INVEST

Prospective investors should,

a. Pay attention to the myriad of risk factors related to investing in emerging and frontier markets.
b. Have the financial ability and willingness to accept these risks.
c. Have a vision to see God's purposes accomplished via business.
d. Demonstrate financial competence.
e. Consult an attorney and tax advisor.

Additionally, because the possibility exists that investors could lose up to one hundred percent of their investment, they should be prepared to absorb the loss. They should not consider such an investment if this would jeopardize necessary cash flow or other obligations that they may have.

+++

I hereby attest to having read this Investor Attestation, and I agree with purposeful investing to achieve God's purposes. I attest that I can withstand the ramifications if the entire investment is lost and that my objectives in making this investment are to accomplish multiple bottom-line outcomes and not only financial returns. I hereby willingly enter into this investment fully aware of the risks.

____________________________________ __________

SIGNATURE **DATE**

APPENDIX B: *The Entrepreneur's Pledge*

As an example of the due diligence we perform on every missional investment, we ask the business owner to sign the following pledge:

By investing in businesses that further God's purposes in the world, Christians answer the call to be generous, impactful stewards. As an entrepreneur leading a kingdom business who receives such an investment, you also have a responsibility to prioritize kingdom values and outcomes through your business and do everything within your power to repay your loans. Relying on biblical principles as the foundation for conducting business and furthering God's kingdom, we ask you to pledge to conduct yourself in a manner consistent with the following values:

1. **Focused Business Practices:** I will uphold all laws, making ethical and moral decisions, supporting the needs of our employees, customers, and community, and appropriately handling money and wealth in ways that reflect biblical principles. I will treat employees and customers with integrity by paying wages on time and debts promptly when they are due. I will be honest, accurate, and forthright in our communications. I will honor our commitments as though they are to the Lord Himself. I will lead with humility, integrity, and compassion.

2. **Intentional Relationships:** I will treat our employees, customers, and vendors with respect while modeling the life of Jesus and displaying the Gospel. I will provide fair compensation, practice fair trade terms, and provide a safe work environment. I will deal honestly with other businesses and agencies and strive to meet all appropriate regulatory requirements with a desire to improve business conduct in our region. I will honor those who have invested in our business, including both donors and investors, by reporting performance and risks accurately, honestly, and in a timely manner. I will never deceive, misrepresent, or omit material

facts, and I will never participate in corruption, unfair competition, or business practices that are harmful to the community. Managers, board members, and investors will always be aware of problems at the earliest possible time.

3. **Purposeful Giving:** I will use our financial resources to build the business and improve the community around us. I will direct a portion of resources to meet critical needs around us even as we build the business brand, because our desire is to see the betterment of the community and the expansion of the kingdom of God through our internal and external kingdom initiatives.

4. **Stewardship:** I will recognize the importance of every stakeholder in each business and missional endeavor. This includes our employees, vendors, customers, government authorities, the community, the environment, and investors. I will seek to manage business risks and rewards responsibly. I will take advantage of every opportunity to help my employees and community flourish while repaying my financial stakeholders on time and in full. In the event of business stress, I will not prioritize any stakeholder over another, nor will I unduly place burden on certain stakeholders. I desire to optimize outcomes so that all stakeholders share benefits or losses. For example, when cash flow is short of meeting all that is required, I will not place this entire burden on employees by not paying their wages, nor will I place the entire burden on investors by not making any payments to them. We will share the burden among those who can bear it. I will operate with transparency and financial integrity. I recognize that since the environment is also a stakeholder, I will minimize my business's negative impact on the environment and seek ways to help the environment flourish.

++

I, the undersigned, pledge to use my God-given talents consistent with the statements above and will remain accountable to my peers, my employees, my financial partners, and the community to uphold these standards.

__________________________________ __________

SIGNATURE DATE

____

TITLE

____

COMPANY

APPENDIX C:
Sample Kingdom Impact Plan

SUPERGREEN SOLUTIONS

COMPANY OVERVIEW

Legacy Environmental Solutions, Incorporated (LES), operates a successful renewable energy brand SuperGreen Solutions. SuperGreen Solutions has a mission to deliver excellent commercial and residential renewable energy solutions coupled with superior customer satisfaction, all while empowering its employees to focus on their quadruple bottom line Kingdom Impact Plan. *The foundation for everything the SuperGreen brand does, from how we conduct business to the way we further God's kingdom, is based on biblical principles.* Three principal ways SuperGreen focuses on its mission are as follows:

1. **Focused Business Practices:** SuperGreen Solutions is built on biblical principles which include upholding all laws, making ethical and moral decisions, supporting the needs of our clients, and appropriately handling money and wealth to ensure we build a profitable and sustainable business that allows us to impact lives for Jesus.

2. **Intentional Relationships**: SuperGreen Solutions views its employees, franchisees, and vendors as its greatest resource and treats them accordingly by actively sharing and displaying the Gospel, providing excellent compensation, practicing fair trade terms, and providing a safe and flexible work environment.

3. **Purposeful Giving:** SuperGreen Solutions seeks to use the financial resources entrusted to it by God for furthering the kingdom of heaven by catalyzing internal and external impact initiatives primarily envisioned by its kingdom-led employees, franchisees, and vendors.

"For even the Son of Man did not come to be served, but to serve, and to give his life as a ransom for many" (Mark 10:45). We strive to have Jesus' voice heard by demonstrating a Christ-like attitude in our everyday interactions with our staff, franchisees, vendors, and communities and the social and governmental organizations within our sphere of influence.

Focused Business Practices

> Whatever you do, work at it with all your heart, as working for the Lord, not for human masters, since you know that you will receive an inheritance from the Lord as a reward. It is the Lord Christ you are serving. (Col. 3:23-24)

Through SuperGreen Solutions, Legacy Environmental Solutions, Inc., upholds all laws throughout their focused business practices and seeks to be above reproach in all moral and ethical decisions. We believe that to maximize our impact for God's kingdom, we must maintain and grow a sustainable for-profit business. The company does not seek profitability for the sake of excessive personal wealth building but instead desires to use money to glorify God in a holistic manner with the end purpose being intentional kingdom impact.

SuperGreen Solutions has the potential to be an extremely profitable company. All levels of management focus on stewarding the corporate financial resources competently and effectively. This means all budget makers focus on the realization of top line results and maintenance of lean expenditure practices leading to the achievement of budgeted profitability targets. The company understands, however, that extreme profitability can potentially influence decision making in a selfish direction. Therefore, to ensure that all financial decisions are made with the glory of God as the top priority, we believe it is important to consider appropriate salaries for key executives that are fair and reasonable but may, in some circumstances, be below the industry standard. The reason for doing this is so that capital can be apportioned to all stakeholders without bias. Our goal is to lead by example in our attitude toward money and not assume a personal wealth building priority but rather a posture of sacrifice.

In Matthew 6:19-20, Jesus tells us to store up treasure in heaven instead of earth. The Bible also says that "A good name is more desirable than great riches; to be esteemed is better than silver or gold" (Prov. 22:1).

Therefore, the SuperGreen Solutions executive management team will work towards becoming a workplace of choice that honors God through biblical excellence. This will start by creating and maintaining a "God and people first" mentality. The company will integrate its professional development program (PDP) immediately with all staff personnel. This PDP is designed to support staff growth in their current roles and develop skills that will serve the company in future roles as designated in the company organizational chart.

Intentional Relationships

> "And you shall love the Lord your God with all your heart and with all your soul and with all your mind and with all your strength." The second is this: "You shall love your neighbor as yourself." There is no other commandment greater than these. (Mark 12:30-31, ESV)

At SuperGreen Solutions, we intentionally invest in relationships with our employees, vendors, and customers to expand the kingdom of God. The Gospel is actively shared within the organization, and glory is clearly given to God for all levels of success of the company. This is demonstrated through management's daily actions and decisions. We also seek to empower employees by providing a well-compensated, safe, and flexible work environment. Family and work/life balance is highly valued and is embodied in the company culture and vacation policies. Fair and ethical trade practices remain core values, and they serve to illustrate a strong message of biblical integrity to the broader business community. SuperGreen Solutions will focus its efforts to incorporate opportunities to be an overt Christian witness and take advantage of all discipleship opportunities presented to its Christian employee base. Where possible, the company will form franchise partner relationships with kingdom-oriented businessmen and women. These partnerships will focus on developing a quadruple (economic, social, environmental, and spiritual) bottom line focus to their business activities. Senior management will envision and support their entire upline team to maximize intentional kingdom outcomes where possible.

Purposeful Giving

> Honor the LORD with your wealth, with the firstfruits of all your crops; then your barns will be filled to overflowing, and your vats will brim over with new wine. (Prov. 3:9-10)

From the outset, even while repaying the initial loan used for the business startup, the company will use God's financial blessings for the furtherance of His kingdom. We will support mission- focused, Christ-honoring ministries by granting a minimum of twenty percent of all after-tax profits. A percentage of these profits will be reinvested into company personnel to help the company achieve its internal development *key performance indicators* (KPIs). Our giving strategy is four-fold in execution. First, the company will designate from among its executive team a chief responsibility specialist (CRS) whose primary function will be to oversee the development and execution of our holistic ministry strategy. Second, the corporate social responsibility team will identify and partner with bi-vocational ministries working among unengaged and unreached people groups globally. Third, an internally managed Kingdom Impact fund will be established and seed funded through the dedication of a portion of the company's net profits. This fund will be used to support the global quadruple bottom line (economic, social, environmental, and spiritual) ministry initiatives of the company. This fund also functions as part of our commitment to support community-based projects near our franchisees to socially integrate into every community where we serve as witnesses for Christ. Finally, we will partner with other like-minded organizations that share our vision through God-honoring missional business entrepreneurship.

DAY-TO-DAY ACTION PLAN

In support of the macro vision of Legacy Environmental Solutions, Inc., and through the franchise brand SuperGreen Solutions, a daily kingdom plan will be initiated by the senior leadership. SuperGreen's chief responsibility specialist will be charged with maintaining a primary focus on the quadruple bottom line Gospel witness of the company. The CRS role will be co-occupied by the CEO and COO until such a time that it makes sense fiscally and strategically to have this role filled. At a minimum, within the first two years, a community engagement strategist (CES) will be employed to support the daily out working of all ministry initiatives.

Daily Kingdom Impact Ministry Will Focus On…

1. Hiring, training, and equipping believers on staff to be overt in their witness, purposeful in their discipleship, and competent in their job function as a testimony to Christ working through them.
2. The company will establish strict day-to-day financial compliance as it relates to the franchisees, vendors, and governing tax authorities.
3. All employees who are followers of Christ will participate in an intentional discipleship training program intended to support them in their ability to bear witness for Christ through their individual work functions.
4. Believers at all levels will be held accountable to build trusting relationships with non-believing staff members and franchisees, for the purpose of being an incarnational witness of Christ in the workplace. Our culture will reflect the glory of the True Owner, God, in everything we do.
5. The company will intentionally partner with global bi-vocational church planters that have a focus on unreached groups by,
    a. Supporting the training and development of indigenous leaders in QBL-focused discipleship multiplication and church planting strategies.
    b. Expanding its ministry impact to reach to minority villages through the utilization of its Kingdom Impact fund to launch or partner in QBL initiatives.

GLOBAL IMPACT

As stated in the purposeful giving statement, the company will allocate a percentage of the company net profit to an intentionally organized Kingdom Impact fund controlled by an appointed group of board-mandated advisors. This net profit will provide the necessary seed funding to support the eternal transformational purposes of the fund. The stated vision and purpose of this fund is to help indigenous Christian business leaders and church planting partners globally have the necessary financial means to launch their kingdom impact efforts.

Our financial projections show the company turning a significant profit within three years and a positive trend every year after. These projections will be achieved by opening more domestic franchises and expanding the network of global master franchisees. SuperGreen management will work hands on with all franchise partners to ensure operational and financial success through the employment of a group of traveling franchisee business and development coaches (FBDC).

PERSONNEL IMPACT PLAN

Implementation of a growth-oriented organizational management structure will support the company's aim to recruit and develop the necessary personnel for business and ministry expansion. A budgeted portion of the corporate profits will be used for staff career development. Staff will also be trained to work in such a way to proclaim Christ through their work ethic, service ethic, quality product delivery goals, and financial integrity. This same core group of employees will be offered additional spiritual disciplines training above and beyond what they may already know as an aspect of their overall holistic professional and personal development.

SuperGreen Solutions plans to increase its domestic franchise group to sixty and its international master franchise community to sixteen by the end of their fourth fiscal year. This business growth will provide the economic engine to fuel the Kingdom Impact Plan.

APPENDIX D: *Additional Resources*

BAM RESOURCES

BAM Global Reports & Manifestos: *BamGlobal.org*

The World's Most Extensive BAM Resource Library: *BusinessAsMission.com*

BAM Material in 22 Languages: *MatsTunehag.com*

Wealth Creation Manifesto in 18 languages: *MatsTunehag.com/Wealth-Creation*

Educational video series based on the Manifesto: Lausanne Global Classroom: Wealth Creation (*YouTube.com/playlist?list=PLYGxDL2dvuo5k-Uk8FGxZj1QYcBe70_Vx*)

Deeply Rooted:

Read more at *MatsTunehag.com/2020/12/23/deeply-rooted-for-the-future/*

Also available at *LinkedIn.com/pulse/deeply-rooted-future-mats-tunehag*

BAM Global Movement: Business as Mission Concepts & Stories by Gea Gort & Mats Tunehag

Mats Tunehag writes here (*MatsTunehag.com/2012/09/29/business-as-mission-is-bigger-than-you-think/*) about doing business as justice, true religion, stewardship, *shalom*, servant leadership, human dignity, reconciliation, creation care, loving your neighbor, the Great Commission, the body of Christ, and glorifying God. Also available as a PDF (*MatsTunehag.com/wp-content/uploads/2011/04/Business-as-Mission-is-bigger-than-you-think.pdf*).

The *BAM A – Z* booklet communicates the concepts of BAM with graphics, single words, and short texts. Using the twenty-six letters of the English alphabet, Tunehag has identified twenty-six key words and concepts related to BAM. They are accompanied by a brief explanation and a graphic. Download it free at *MatsTunehag.com/wp-content/uploads/2021/05/BAM-A-Z-Booklet-25-April-2021.pdf.*

WATER4

Water4 CEO Matt Hangen on putting charity out of business: *https://www.youtube.com/watch?v=YBsEVMv7K-E*

Printed in Great Britain
by Amazon

85409611R00153